Guiding Principles and Strategies

Grades
1–2

Printed in the U.S.A.

ISBN   978-1-328-58167-9

2 3 4 5 6 7 8 9 10   0868   27 26 25 24 23 22 21 20 19

4500762083   ^ B C D E F G

D1404447

Table of Contents

TEACHING AND LEARNING

¡VIVA EL ESPAÑOL!

Dear Teacher:

Welcome to HMH *Into Reading*™ and HMH *¡Arriba la Lectura!*™ for first and second grade! Thank you for your dedication to the children in these very important grades and for your commitment to teaching them.

In your culturally and developmentally responsive classroom, you are guiding children who represent a range of backgrounds, communities, and languages. Literacy may be the most essential tool that you can offer them. How you help them use this tool will be grounded in your understanding of how literacy develops in young learners. That developmental progression forms the bedrock of instruction in the program: the what, when, and how of the things you will be teaching, using this incredible tool.

Importantly, your instruction will occur in a classroom rich with meaningful and purposeful discussions in which children truly communicate—listen, contribute, and appreciate unique and shared perspectives. As you engage children in reading, you will also be guiding their understanding of "how words work"—the foundational knowledge of how sounds are represented by letters and letter patterns and carry meaning. Your instruction will ensure that children's word knowledge will expand through developmentally appropriate, motivating, and integrated lessons and activities.

With *Into Reading* and *¡Arriba la Lectura!,* our goal is to provide a comprehensive set of research-based activities for teaching primary language arts that help you meet the high expectations reflected in your English Language Arts standards. You won't need to spend valuable time searching for the "just right" text, writing lessons and designing literacy centers, or creating practice pages. The program provides all of that for you, allowing you to focus on the important work of meeting the diverse needs of all the children in your class.

As a former first- and second-grade teacher, it is truly an honor to introduce you to Guiding Principles and Strategies, your professional companion and navigation tool for *Into Reading* and *¡Arriba la Lectura!*

Your colleague,

Shane Templeton

Shane Templeton
Into Reading and *¡Arriba la Lectura!* Author

A comprehensive literacy solution based on science and informed by teachers

Student-Centered Instructional Design

A flexible, balanced approach with a focus on small-group instruction designed to develop collaborative, self-directed learners

Data-Driven Differentiation

Planning, grouping, and assessment tools that allow teachers to focus on delivering individualized instruction

Equity for Dual Language Instruction

A research-based and fully equitable Spanish solution for developing biliteracy in dual language classrooms

A Robust Library

Captivating content and high-quality texts that strengthen students' skills and ignite a lifelong love of learning

Social-Emotional Development

Embedded support for development of the whole child with a focus on social-emotional learning and growth mindset

Family and Community Partnerships

Resources that honor families as an integral part of the learning process and extend learning beyond the classroom

Get into Reading!

Grades 1 and 2 of *Into Reading* and *¡Arriba la Lectura!* are each organized into 12 modules. Children build knowledge as they discuss, read, and write about each module topic.

¡Arriba la Lectura! cuenta con todo esto y más. En la sección ¡Viva el español! verá lo que distingue a este programa.

GRADE 1 Overview

	① Nice to Meet You!	② My Family, My Community	③ Amazing Animals
❓ ESSENTIAL QUESTION	How can making new friends and learning new things help us?	How does everyone in my family and community make them special?	How do animals' bodies help them?
MODULE FOCUS	🌐 SOCIAL STUDIES: New Friends and Experiences	🌐 SOCIAL STUDIES: Communities	🌱 SCIENCE: How Animals Live
⚙ LEARNING MINDSET	Seeking Challenges	Belonging	Curiosity
TEXT SETS	**WEEK 1** • *My First Day* • *Pete the Cat: Rocking in My School Shoes* • *Try This!* **WEEK 2** • *You Will Be My Friend!* • *My School Trip* • *A Kids' Guide to Friends* **WEEK 3** • *Suki's Kimono* • *Big Dilly's Tale* • *I'm Me* ◉ *Nuevos amigos*	**WEEK 1** • *Kids Speak Up!* • *Whose Hands Are These?* • *Dan Had a Plan* **WEEK 2** • *Maybe Something Beautiful* • *On the Map!* • *Places in My Neighborhood* **WEEK 3** • *Abuela* • *Who Put the Cookies in the Cookie Jar?* • *Curious About Jobs*	**WEEK 1** • *Animal Q & A* • *Best Foot Forward* ◉ *Aunque viva en el agua* • *The Nest* **WEEK 2** • *Whose Eye Am I?* • *Bluebird and Coyote* • *Have You Heard the Nesting Bird?* **WEEK 3** • *Ol' Mama Squirrel* • *Step-by-Step Advice from the Animal Kingdom* • *Beaver Family* ◉ *El clamidosaurio*
⬇ WRITING TYPE	Oral Story	Descriptive Essay	Research Essay

4	**5**	**6**
Better Together	**Now You See It, Now You Don't**	**Celebrate America**
Why is it important to do my best and get along with others?	Why do light and dark come and go?	What do holidays and symbols tell about our country?
SOCIAL STUDIES: Being Good Citizens	**SCIENCE: Light and Dark**	**SOCIAL STUDIES: Holidays and Symbols**
Asking for Help	**Problem Solving**	**Purpose**
WEEK 1 • *Good Sports* • *Baseball Hour* • *Goal!*	**WEEK 1** • *Super Shadows!* • *On Earth* • *Blackout*	**WEEK 1** • *State the Facts!* • *You're a Grand Old Flag* • *Monument City*
WEEK 2 • *Pelé, King of Soccer* • *Get Up and Go!* • *A Big Guy Took My Ball!*	**WEEK 2** • *How Do You Know It's Winter?* • *Day and Night* • *The Best Season*	**WEEK 2** • *Presidents' Day* • *The Contest* • *The Statue of Liberty*
WEEK 3 • *The Great Ball Game* • *If You Plant a Seed* • *Color Your World with Kindness*	**WEEK 3** • *Oscar and the Moth* • *Waiting Is Not Easy!* • *I'm So Hot*	**WEEK 3** • *Can We Ring the Liberty Bell?* • *Hooray for Holidays!* • *Patriotic Poems*
Procedural Text	**Imaginative Story**	**Personal Narrative**

WELCOME TO *INTO READING*

GRADE 1 Overview (cont.)	**7** The Big Outdoors	**8** Tell Me a Story	**9** Grow, Plants, Grow!
? ESSENTIAL QUESTION	How do things in nature change?	What can we learn from stories?	What do plants need to live and grow?
MODULE FOCUS	🌱 SCIENCE: The Natural World	🌐 SOCIAL STUDIES: What Stories Teach Us	🌱 SCIENCE: Plants and Gardens
⚙ LEARNING MINDSET	Noticing	Resilience	Setting Goals
TEXT SETS	**WEEK 1** • *Storm Report* • *Rainy, Sunny, Blowy, Snowy* • *La asombrosa vida de las mariposas monarca* • *Sam & Dave Dig a Hole* **WEEK 2** • *On Meadowview Street* • *Deserts* • *Handmade* **WEEK 3** • *Do You Really Want to Visit a Wetland?* • *Grand Canyon* • *Water Cycle* • *¿Sabes qué es un volcán?*	**WEEK 1** • *Follow the Story Path* • *Chicken Little* • *Cómo nació el arcoíris* • *Interrupting Chicken* **WEEK 2** • *Red Knit Cap Girl and the Reading Tree* • *Little Red Riding Hood* • *The Grasshopper & the Ants* **WEEK 3** • *My Name is Gabriela* • *Thank You, Mr. Aesop* • *Historias que viajan en el tiempo* • *The Tortoise and the Hare*	**WEEK 1** • *Plant Pairs* • *If I Were A Tree* • *So You Want to Grow a Taco?* **WEEK 2** • *The Curious Garden* • *Which Part Do We Eat?* • *¿Qué comemos hoy?* • *The Talking Vegetables* **WEEK 3** • *Amazing Plant Bodies* • *Yum! ¡MmMm! ¡Qué rico!* • *¡Qué Delicia!* • *A Year in the Garden*
⬇ WRITING TYPE	Poem	Personal Narrative	Descriptive Essay

10	11	12
Dare to Dream	**Genre Study: Nonfiction**	**Genre Study: Literary Texts**

How can thinking in new ways help solve problems?	What are the characteristics of narrative nonfiction, informational texts, and biography?	What are the characteristics of realistic fiction, folktales, and fantasy?
🌐 **SOCIAL STUDIES: Thinking in New Ways**	WEEK 1 Narrative Nonfiction WEEK 2 Informational Text WEEK 3 Biography	WEEK 1 Realistic Fiction WEEK 2 Folktale WEEK 3 Fantasy
Problem Solving	**Self-Reflection**	**Planning Ahead**

WEEK 1 • *Kids Are Inventors, Too!* • *What Can You Do?* • *Young Frank Architect*	**WEEK 1** • *Try This!* • *Have You Heard the Nesting Bird?* • *Oscar and the Moth* • *Can We Ring the Liberty Bell?* • *Do You Really Want to Visit a Wetland?*	**WEEK 1** • *The Nest* • *Blackout* • *Sky Color* • *Maybe Something Beautiful* • *Suki's Kimono*
WEEK 2 • *Charlotte the Scientist Is Squished* • ⊛ *Pájaro amarillo* • *Sky Color* • *We Are the Future* • ⊛ *Somos el futuro*	**WEEK 2** • *Animal Q & A* • *Goal!* • *Grand Canyon* • *Whose Eye Am I?* • *Amazing Plant Bodies*	**WEEK 2** • *Blue Bird and Coyote* • *The Talking Vegetables* • *The Great Ball Game* • *Chicken Little*
WEEK 3 • *I am Amelia Earhart* • *Joaquín's Zoo* • *Marconi and the Radio*	**WEEK 3** • *Pelé, King of Soccer* • *My Name Is Gabriela* • *I am Amelia Earhart*	**WEEK 3** • *A Big Guy Took My Ball!* • *Sam & Dave Dig a Hole* • *Interrupting Chicken* • *Ol' Mama Squirrel* • *Red Knit Cap Girl and the Reading Tree*
Biographical Essay	**Opinion Letter**	**Opinion Essay**

Get into Reading!

Grades 1 and 2 of *Into Reading* and *¡Arriba la Lectura!* are each organized into 12 modules. Children build knowledge as they discuss, read, and write about each module topic.

¡Arriba la Lectura! cuenta con todo esto y más. En la sección ¡Viva el español! verá lo que distingue a este programa.

GRADE 2 **Overview**	① **Be a Super Citizen**	② **Look Around and Explore!**	③ **Meet in the Middle**
? ESSENTIAL QUESTION	How can being a good citizen make a difference to others?	How does exploring help us understand the world around us?	How can people work out disagreements?
MODULE FOCUS	🌐 **SOCIAL STUDIES:** Citizenship	🌿 **SCIENCE:** Discovering Our World	🌐 **SOCIAL STUDIES:** Solving Problems
⚙ LEARNING MINDSET	**Belonging**	**Curiosity**	**Trying Again**
TEXT SETS	**WEEK 1** • *We Are Super Citizens* • *Meet the Dogs of Bedlam Farm* • *Clark the Shark* **WEEK 2** • *The William Hoy Story* • *Spoon* • *El desfile de las nubes* • *Being a Good Citizen* **WEEK 3** • *Violet the Pilot* • *Picture Day Perfection* • *Get Involved: Be Awesome!*	**WEEK 1** • *What's the Matter?* • *The Important Book* • *Many Kinds of Matter* **WEEK 2** • *It's Only Stanley* • *The Great Fuzz Frenzy* • *Water Rolls, Water Rises* **WEEK 3** • *If You Find a Rock* • *The Puddle Puzzle* • *Looking at Art*	**WEEK 1** • *Meet Me Halfway* • *Mango, Abuela, and Me* • *Big Red Lollipop* **WEEK 2** • *Three Hens and a Peacock* • *Working with Others* • *Gingerbread for Liberty!* **WEEK 3** • *Serious Farm* • *Ramiro el cuentista* • *Pepita and the Bully* • *Be a Hero! Work It Out!*
⬇ WRITING TYPE	**Personal Narrative**	**Descriptive Essay**	**Persuasive Text**

4	**5**	**6**
Once Upon a Time	**Lead the Way**	**Weather Wise**
What lessons can we learn from the characters in stories?	What are the qualities of a good leader?	How does the weather affect us?
SOCIAL STUDIES: **Storytelling**	SOCIAL STUDIES: **Leadership**	SCIENCE: **Weather**
Growth Mindset	**Seeking Challenges**	**Noticing**
WEEK 1 • *Recipe for a Fairy Tale* • *Goldilocks and the Three Dinosaurs* • *How to Read a Story* **WEEK 2** • *Rabbit's Snow Dance* • *A Crow, a Lion, and a Mouse! Oh, My!* • *Amiga hormiga* • *Hollywood Chicken* **WEEK 3** • *A Perfect Season for Dreaming* • *If the Shoe Fits* • *Those Clever Crows* • *¡Laboriosas hormigas!*	**WEEK 1** • *What's Good to Read?* • *Seed by Seed* • *Going Places* **WEEK 2** • *My Dream Playground* • *Wilma Rudolph* • *Frida Kahlo* • *Great Leaders* **WEEK 3** • *Whoosh!* • *Who Are Government's Leaders?* • *Thomas Edison and the Light Bulb*	**WEEK 1** • *Weather Through the Seasons* • *Freddy the Frogcaster* • *Wild Weather* **WEEK 2** • *The Story of Snow* • *Cloudette* • *Get Ready for Weather* **WEEK 3** • *Fall Leaves* • *Whatever the Weather* • *Tiempo al tiempo* • *Rain Cloud in a Jar* • *Las estaciones*
Imaginative Story	**Personal Essay**	**Poem**

GRADE 2 Overview (cont.)	⑦ Everyone Has a Story	⑧ Time to Grow!	⑨ Home Sweet Habitat
❓ ESSENTIAL QUESTION	How do our experiences shape our lives?	What do plants need to live and grow?	How do living things in a habitat depend on each other?
MODULE FOCUS	🌐 SOCIAL STUDIES: Important People	🌱 SCIENCE: Weather	🌱 SCIENCE: Animal Habitats
⚙️ LEARNING MINDSET	Resilience	Setting Goals	Asking for Help
TEXT SETS	**WEEK 1** • *Get to Know Biographies* • *Miss Moore Thought Otherwise* • *Juana Inéz* • *I Am Helen Keller* **WEEK 2** • *The Camping Trip That Changed America* • *How to Make a Timeline* • *The Stories He Tells: The Story of Joseph Bruchac* **WEEK 3** • *Molly, by Golly!* • *Drum Dream Girl* • *Roberto Clemente*	**WEEK 1** • *The Growth of a Sunflower* • *From Seed to Pine Tree* • *Experiment with What a Plant Needs to Grow* **WEEK 2** • *The Legend of the Indian Paintbrush* • *Jack and the Beanstalk* • *Jackie and the Beanstalk* **WEEK 3** • *The Patchwork Garden* • *Don't Touch Me!* • *George Washington Carver*	**WEEK 1** • *The Best Habitat for Me* • *Nature's Patchwork Quilt* • *The Long, Long Journey* **WEEK 2** • *Kali's Story* • *Sea Otter Pups* • *At Home in the Wild* **WEEK 3** • *Out of the Woods* • *Abuelo and the Three Bears* • *Ducklings Jump from Nest*
⬇️ WRITING TYPE	Imaginative Story	Procedural Text	Research Report

⑩	**⑪**	**⑫**
Many Cultures, One World	**Genre Study: Nonfiction**	**Genre Study: Literary Texts**
What can we learn from different people and cultures?	**What are the characteristics of biography, opinion writing, and informational texts?**	**What are the characteristics of realistic fiction, fantasy, and poetry?**
🌐 SOCIAL STUDIES: World Cultures	WEEK 1 Biography WEEK 2 Opinion WEEK 3 Informational Text	WEEK 1 Realistic Fiction WEEK 2 Fantasy WEEK 3 Poetry
Problem Solving	**Grit**	**Self-Reflection**

⑩ Problem Solving

WEEK 1
- *Hello, World!*
- *Trombone Shorty*
- *Where on Earth Is My Bagel?*

WEEK 2
- *Time for Cranberries*
- *May Day Around the World*
- *Goal!*

WEEK 3
- *Dreams Around the World*
- *Poems in the Attic*
- *What's for Lunch Around the World?*

⑪ Grit

WEEK 1
- *Gingerbread for Liberty!*
- *Wilma Rudolph*
- *I Am Helen Keller*
- *The Stories He Tells: The Story of Joseph Bruchac*
- *Trombone Shorty*

WEEK 2
- *What's Good to Read?*
- *Great Leaders*
- *Get to Know Biographies*
- *The Best Habitat for Me*

WEEK 3
- *Many Kinds of Matter*
- *How to Read a Story*
- *Get Ready for Weather*
- *Experiment with What a Plant Needs to Grow*
- *Sea Otter Pups*

⑫ Self-Reflection

WEEK 1
- *Picture Day Perfection*
- *Big Red Lollipop*
- *Pepita and the Bully*
- *Where on Earth Is My Bagel?*
- *My Dream Playground*

WEEK 2
- *Clark the Shark*
- *Spoon*
- *El desfile de las nubes*
- *The Great Fuzz Frenzy*
- *Hollywood Chicken*
- *Three Hens and a Peacock*

WEEK 3
- *Water Rolls, Water Rises*
- *Whatever the Weather*
- *Tiempo al tiempo*
- *Drum Dream Girl*
- *At Home in the Wild*
- *Poems in the Attic*

| **Thank-You Letter** | **Personal Narrative** | **Opinion Essay** |

Instructional Model:
A Day of *Into Reading*

Target children's diverse needs using whole-class instruction, teacher-led small groups, and options for collaborative work and independent practice.

¡Arriba la Lectura!
cuenta con todo esto y más.
En la sección ¡Viva el español!
verá lo que distingue a
este programa.

WHOLE-CLASS INSTRUCTION

BUILD KNOWLEDGE AND LANGUAGE/ VOCABULARY	10–15 minutes/day
FOUNDATIONAL SKILLS	15–30 minutes/day
READING WORKSHOP	20–30 minutes/day
WRITING WORKSHOP	20–30 minutes/day

WHOLE-CLASS WRAP-UP AND SHARE

5 minutes/day

INDEPENDENT PRACTICE

COLLABORATIVE WORK

45–60 minutes

TEACHER-LED SMALL GROUPS

OPTIONS FOR SMALL GROUPS

TEACHER-LED SMALL GROUPS

GUIDED READING GROUPS

FOUNDATIONAL SKILLS DEVELOPMENT

SKILL AND STRATEGY INSTRUCTION

ENGLISH LEARNER SUPPORT

OPTIONS FOR INDEPENDENT AND COLLABORATIVE WORK

LITERACY CENTERS

 WORD WORK

 CREATIVITY CORNER

 DIGITAL STATION

 READING CORNER

 TEAMWORK TIME

*my*BOOK

Individuals and partners can read and respond to texts.

GENRE STUDY BOOK CLUBS

Children can have meaningful conversations about texts.

STUDENT CHOICE LIBRARY BOOKS

Selecting books for independent reading increases engagement and provides opportunities for children to practice skills and strategies.

INQUIRY AND RESEARCH PROJECTS

Children work on the week's focus for the module project.

Planning for the Year

Follow this suggested timeline to plan instruction and administer assessments throughout the course of the school year.

BEGINNING OF YEAR				MIDYEAR	
Module 1	Module 2	Module 3	Module 4	Module 5	Module 6

Module 6

	WEEK 1					WEEK 2	
	Lesson 1	Lesson 2	Lesson 3	Lesson 4	Lesson 5	Lesson 6	Lesson 7
Selection Quizzes			✓				✓
Weekly Assessments					✓		
Module Assessment							

Foundational Skills

LESSON SEQUENCE

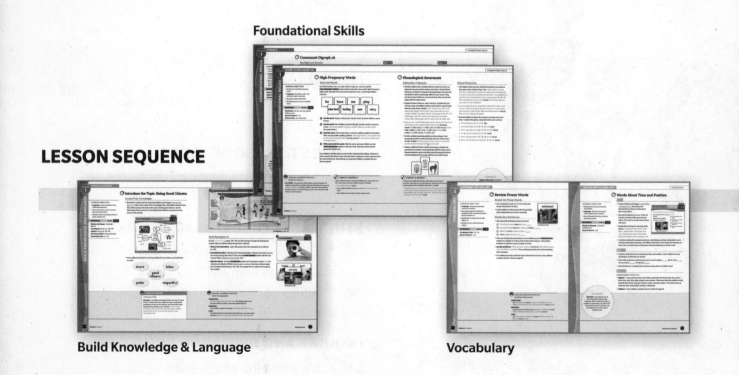

Build Knowledge & Language

Vocabulary

END OF YEAR

| Module 7 | Module 8 | Module 9 | Module 10 | Module 11 | Module 12 |

			WEEK 3				
Lesson **8**	Lesson **9**	Lesson **10**	Lesson **11**	Lesson **12**	Lesson **13**	Lesson **14**	Lesson **15**
	✓			✓			
		✓					✓
							✓

Small-Group Instruction

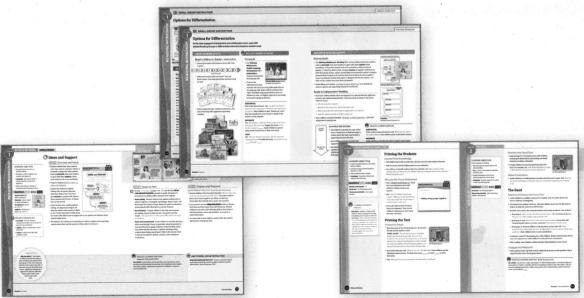

Reading Workshop

Writing Workshop

Materials for Building Knowledge and Language

Guide children to engage in active viewing and listening, vocabulary exploration, and collaborative discussions to build background knowledge and language for literacy success.

¡Arriba la Lectura! cuenta con todo esto y más. En la sección ¡Viva el español! verá lo que distingue a este programa.

Teacher's Guide, Volumes 1–5

Build Knowledge and Language instruction includes:

- **Introduce the Topic** lessons to build knowledge networks around engaging content-area and social-emotional topics.

- **Big Idea Word** lessons with opportunities for children to use newly acquired words in speaking and writing.

- **Wrap Up the Topic** lessons to encourage children to build, synthesize, and extend topic knowledge while using active viewing and discussion skills.

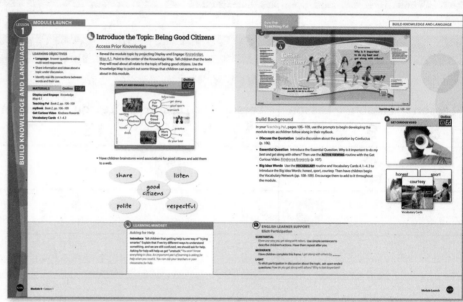

Teaching Pal, Books 1–5

At the beginning of each module, using the **Teaching Pal**, introduce children to the module topic, the module's Essential Question, and a thought-provoking quotation that helps build background about the topic. Also introduce each module's Big Idea Words.

At the end of each module, have children revisit the Essential Question and reflect on and synthesize their learning by choosing one of the culminating activities in their **myBook**.

🖥️ Display and Engage: Knowledge Maps

As children view and interact with module texts and activities, they build new knowledge networks. Use the **Knowledge Map** to preview what children can expect to learn at the beginning of each module, revisit and add to it each week, and use it to synthesize the information children have learned as they wrap up the topic.

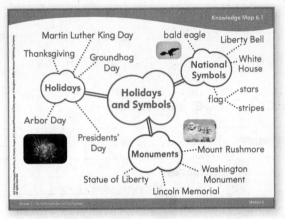

🖥️ Get Curious Videos

Children watch a **Get Curious Video** at the beginning of each module to build background knowledge about the topic and provide exposure to vocabulary related to the topic, allowing children to hear new words in context and build active viewing and responding skills.

Vocabulary Cards

Use the **Vocabulary Cards** to introduce the Big Idea Words, help children connect the words to the topic, and guide them to understand and use the words.

Materials for Foundational Skills

Support children in building a strong foundation for literacy as they engage in activities that develop phonological awareness, phonics skills, spelling, handwriting, recognition of high-frequency sight words, and fluency.

¡Arriba la Lectura! cuenta con todo esto y más. En la sección ¡Viva el español! verá lo que distingue a este programa.

Teacher's Guide, Volumes 1–6

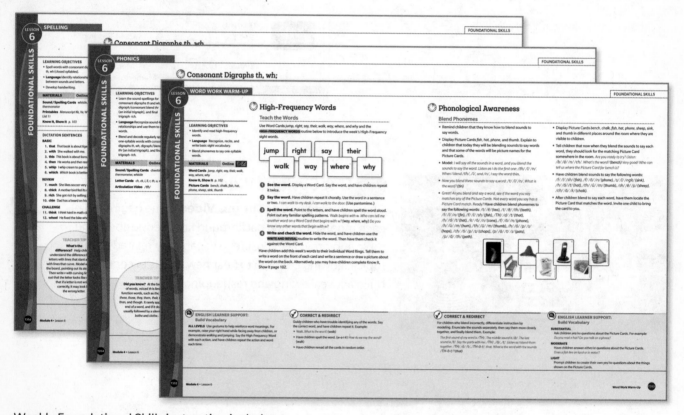

Weekly Foundational Skills instruction includes:

- **High-Frequency Words** lessons to teach and practice reading, spelling, and using high-frequency sight words.

- **Phonological Awareness** lessons to have children identify, produce, and manipulate the sounds in spoken words and syllables.

- **Phonics** lessons to introduce sound-spellings that help children associate consonants, consonant blends, digraphs and trigraphs, short and long vowels, vowel digraphs and diphthongs, and other common vowel spellings with the sounds they represent and to read words with these sound-spellings.

- **Make Minutes Count** options to support children in targeted small-group instruction, based on need.

- **Fluency** lessons to practice reading fluently with appropriate rate, intonation, phrasing, and expression and to practice self-correcting using context and decoding skills.

- **Spelling** lessons to help children make decoding-encoding connections and practice handwriting skills.

- **Read Decodable Text** lessons for practice decoding words and recognizing high-frequency words in context and to reinforce fluency skills.

- **Differentiated Spelling** support for children who are below- or above-level, located in the online Teacher's Guide Additional Resources.

Start Right Readers

The **Start Right Readers** provide opportunities for children to practice reading texts containing words with new and previously taught phonic elements and high-frequency words. Each week's Start Right Reader texts have a connected storyline or topic across texts for the week to build interest and anticipation. Activity pages for each text review decoding skills and high-frequency words, and they also gauge comprehension. Start Right Reader texts are also used for fluency practice.

 Black-and-white printable versions of the Start Right Reader texts are available online.

GRADE 1 • 6 Books

- Four connected texts per week
- Activity pages:
  - » Phonics skill review
  - » Blending practice
  - » High-frequency words review
  - » Comprehension
  - » Reread and Response

GRADE 2 • 6 Books

- Two connected texts per week
- Activity pages:
  - » Blending practice
  - » High-frequency words review
  - » Reread and Comprehension/Response

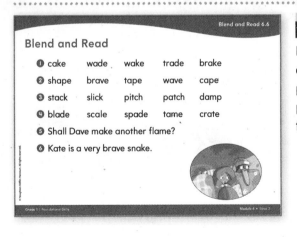

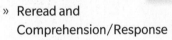

Blend and Read 6.6

Blend and Read

1. cake   wade   wake   trade   brake
2. shape   brave   tape   wave   cape
3. stack   slick   pitch   patch   damp
4. blade   scale   spade   tame   crate
5. Shall Dave make another flame?
6. Kate is a very brave snake.

Display and Engage

Project **Display and Engage** resources for the whole class to practice blending and reading words with new phonic elements, decoding words with previously taught phonic elements, and decoding more challenging words for children who are ready.

Materials for Foundational Skills

Sound/Spelling Cards

Use **Sound/Spelling Cards** to introduce common spellings for the sounds in English words. Includes cards for:

- consonants
- consonant digraphs
- short vowels
- long vowels
- vowel variants and diphthongs
- consonant plus -*le*

Grade 1

Grade 2

Letter, Word, and Picture Cards

Letter Cards

Use **Letter Cards** to build words for children to read in phonics lessons. The set includes cards for capital and lowercase letters, vowel teams and diphthongs, consonant digraphs, and punctuation marks.

Word Cards

Use **Word Cards** to introduce and help children practice reading and spelling each week's high-frequency words with automaticity.

Picture Cards

Use **Picture Cards** in phonological awareness and phonics lessons. Pictures on the cards support instruction for consonants and their sounds, consonant blends and digraphs, short and long vowels, *r*-controlled vowels, other vowel sounds and diphthongs, as well as work with multisyllabic words.

Online Ed | Articulation Videos

Use **Articulation Videos** to support children to articulate sounds by modeling the mouth positions needed to pronounce each sound.

Printables for **Articulation Support** include step-by-step instuctions and photos of mouth positions to accompany each video.

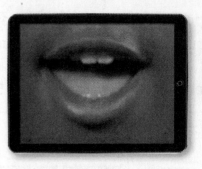

Online Ed | iRead

Have children use **iRead** during Literacy Centers or designated technology time for personalized instruction and in-depth practice with alphabet, phonological awareness, phonics, high-frequency words, and word analysis.

Online Ed | Know It, Show It

In **Know It, Show It,** children independently practice and apply what they have learned from high-frequency words, phonics, and spelling lessons. The online **Know It, Show It Teacher's Guide** includes teacher annotations.

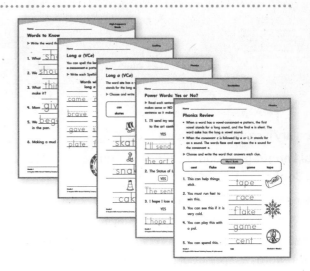

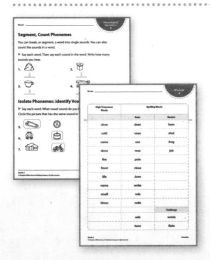

Online Ed | Printable Resources

Access **Printable Resources** online to differentiate instruction, provide additional practice, or supplement the Foundational Skills lessons in the Teacher's Guides.

- Word Lists contain word cards for each week's High-Frequency Words and Spelling Words for children to use in practice activities.
- Provide additional practice for phonological awareness skills.
- Use Handwriting printable resources for handwriting practice— models available for manuscript and continuous stroke in both grades and cursive in Grade 2.

Materials for Vocabulary

Support children as they acquire academic vocabulary and encourage curiosity about language.

Teacher's Guide, Volumes 1–5

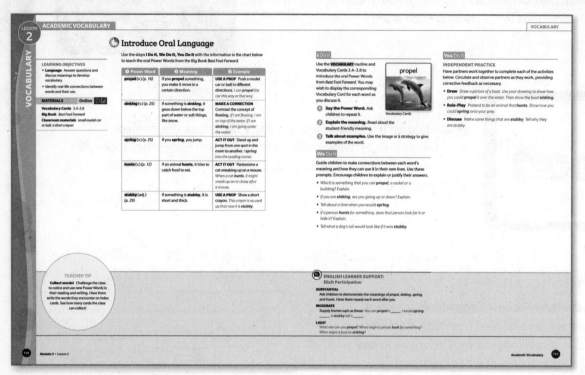

Vocabulary instruction includes:

- **Oral Language** lessons to introduce and have children use oral Power Words from **Big Books** and **Read Aloud Books.**

- **Power Words** lessons to introduce and review high-utility academic and content vocabulary from children's ***myBook*** texts.

- **Generative Vocabulary** lessons, which provide weekly opportunities to use known words as springboards to new, unknown words with morphological or semantic relationships.

- **Vocabulary Strategy** lessons that equip children with tools to uncover the meanings of unknown words when they read.

- **Cumulative Vocabulary** lessons at the end of each module, which offer a variety of engaging activity options to review the module's Power Words and use them in different contexts.

Vocabulary Cards

Use the **Vocabulary Cards** to introduce the module's Power Words from Grade 1 **Big Books, Read Aloud Books,** and *myBook* texts.

The front of each card includes the vocabulary word and an image that illustrates it. The back of each card guides teachers through the **VOCABULARY** routine for introducing the word, explaining its meaning, and providing examples to make personal connections.

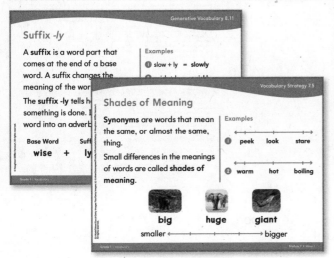

Online Ed. Display and Engage

Project **Display and Engage** resources for the whole class during Generative Vocabulary and Vocabulary Strategy lessons. These digital resources support the introduction of each lesson's skill in a visual way and provide some exercises for guided practice.

Online Ed. Know It, Show It

Children independently practice using Power Words and applying vocabulary skills they have learned each week in **Know It, Show It**. The online **Know It, Show It Teacher's Guide** includes teacher annotations.

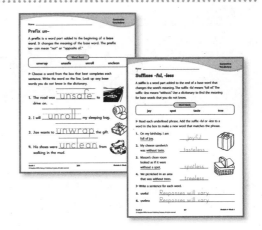

Materials for Reading Workshop

Support children's reading comprehension development through meaningful experiences with texts and opportunities to practice and apply new skills.

¡Arriba la Lectura! cuenta con todo esto y más. En la sección ¡Viva el español! verá lo que distingue a este programa.

Teacher's Guide, Volumes 1–5

Weekly Reading Workshop instruction includes:

- **Read Aloud** and **Shared Reading** minilessons to introduce and discuss each **Read Aloud Book** or Grade 1 **Big Book** and related skills.

- **Shared Reading** minilessons to teach and apply comprehension skills and strategies for the student *myBook* texts and to develop close reading skills.

- **Reader's Vocabulary** notes to help develop children's use of academic vocabulary to understand and discuss their reading.

- **Response to Text** activities to connect reading and writing and to support children's abilities to cite text evidence in writing.

Teaching Pal, Books 1–5

Refer to color-coded, point-of-use instructional notes in the **Teaching Pal** to use *myBook* texts across multiple readings for different purposes.

Online 😊Ed Know It, Show It

Children apply comprehension skills to *myBook* texts in **Know It, Show It**. The online **Know It, Show It Teacher's Guide** includes teacher annotations.

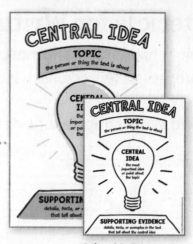

Printable Resource

◎ Ed Anchor Charts

Online

Display Reading **Anchor Charts** to support instruction and "anchor" children's learning about genres, story elements, text structures, and comprehension skills.

Text Sets

Ten collections of high-interest and diverse texts arranged in topically related **text sets** deepen comprehension and allow children to explore text characteristics and structures across a range of genres, while also developing topic knowledge.

Read Aloud Books are complex and sophisticated texts that build children's topic knowledge, academic vocabulary, and comprehension skills and strategies through interactive read alouds and comprehension lessons.

Grade 1 Big Books build children's topic knowledge, academic vocabulary, and comprehension, as well as support print concepts instruction.

Online
◎ Ed *myBook* texts

myBook texts for shared or independent reading include a wide variety of texts and media in a consumable format, allowing children to annotate the text and make notes right in their books.

Genre Study Teacher's Guide

The instruction in the **Genre Study Teacher's Guide** focuses on literary and informational genres and author's craft. Comprehension skills are viewed through the lens of each week's focus genre and will help children recognize why an author made certain choices to deliver a text's message and how those choices affect the reader.

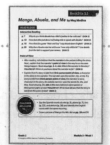

BookStix

Attach **BookStix** sticky notes to the back of **Read Aloud Books** and Grade 1 **Big Books** and refer to them while reading aloud to guide discussion. Use the "Children Will Love to..." ideas to focus on the unique features of each book.

Materials for Writing Workshop

Advance children's writing independence with interactive writing and process-based lessons that build on their developing skills.

¡Arriba la Lectura!
cuenta con todo esto y más.
En la sección ¡Viva el español!
verá lo que distingue a
este programa.

Writing Workshop Teacher's Guide

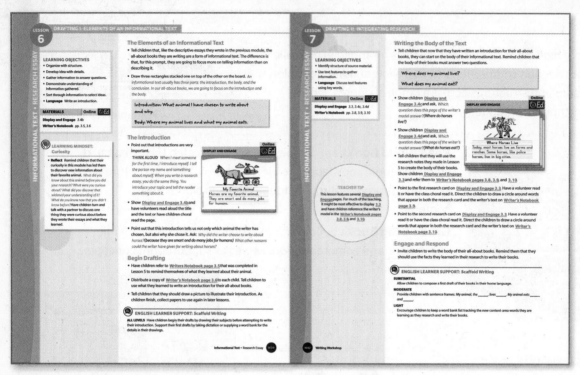

Writing Workshop instruction includes:

- Modules that explore **genre characteristics** of narrative, informational, opinion, correspondence, and poetry writing.
- Authentic **connections between reading and writing** using mentor texts.
- Daily opportunities for **independent writing**.
- **Process-based writing** to generate ideas, organize drafts, revise and edit, and share multiple texts.

- Minilessons for ideas, organization, word choice, conventions, and presentation that follow a **gradual-release model**.
- Support for **peer feedback and conferences** to provide guidance with revising and editing writing.
- **Embedded grammar lessons** to teach sentence construction as part of writing, along with a bank of **grammar minilessons** for further direct instruction on specific grammar topics.

Writer's Notebook

Children use the **Writer's Notebook** to directly support their writing as they plan, organize, and revise their writing. They record interesting words and phrases to incorporate into their writing, set goals, choose and narrow topics, interact with a student model, and plan their writing with graphic organizers.

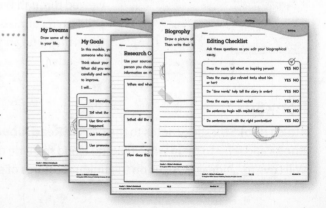

Online Ed Anchor Charts

Display the Writing **Anchor Charts** or use them as models to create your own charts to "anchor" children's learning about features of writing types, craft and structure, and grammar and conventions.

Anchor charts are also available online as printable resources for children to keep and reference in their writing folders.

Writing Anchor Charts:

- Steps for Writing
- Find a Word's Meaning
- Good Sources
- Elements of a Narrative
- Elements of Informational Text

- Elements of Opinion
- Elements of Poetry
- Parts of a Letter
- Revise Your Work!
- Check Your Writing!
- Linking Words
- Subject-Verb Agreement

- Capitalize
- Apostrophes
- Clocking
- Be Great When You Participate
- Publish Your Work
- Sharing Your Writing Orally

Additional Writing Anchor Charts, Grade 2:

- Types of Questions
- Presenting Work

- Steps for Research
- Research and Sources

Printable Resource

Online Ed Display and Engage

Access the projectable **Display and Engage** resources for Writing Workshop lessons, including writing prompts, student models, grammar support, and revising and editing checklists.

Online Ed Printable Resources

Access **Writing Graphic Organizers** online to provide independent practice with planning, organizing, and drafting a variety of writing types.

- Story Map
- Two-Column Chart
- Three-Column Chart
- Four-Column Chart
- Idea-Support Map
- Web
- Time-Order Chart

- Story Structure
- Problem-Resolution Chart
- Inference Map
- Central Idea Map
- Four-Square Map
- Character Description
- Star Organizer

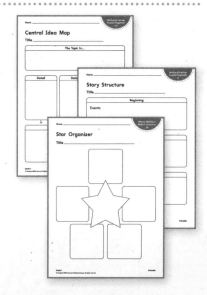

Use **Reproducible Rubrics** to record notes while reviewing children's writing in conferences and throughout the writing process to note and foster improvement.

Materials for Guided Reading

Support children to build knowledge and reading independence using leveled texts during small-group guided reading.

Rigby Leveled Reader Library

Use **Rigby Leveled Readers** to match children to books based on guided reading level, Lexile, skill, or genre. Each grade offers a continuum of 90 fiction and informational texts.

GRADE 1

Levels C through K, 10 titles per level

GRADE 2

Levels I through N, 15 titles per level

Online *Ed* *Locate the complete collection of Leveled Readers online. Filter by level, skill, or genre.*

Take and Teach Lessons

Each Rigby Leveled Reader has a corresponding **Take and Teach Lesson** that includes:

- Text X-Ray and text complexity measures.
- Flexible use sessions that allow teachers to select text and instruction based on genre, target skill, or topic.
- Coordinated instructional segments with stopping points to ask guided questions.
- Scaffolding for English learners.
- Bank of student response activity options that support and reinforce comprehension.

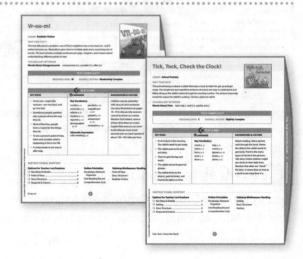

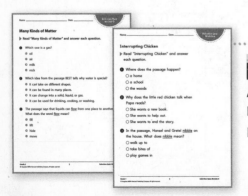

Online *Ed* ## Leveled Reader Quizzes

Assess children's comprehension of each **Leveled Reader** with a **Leveled Reader Quiz**, available as a printable resource for a pencil-and-paper test or used as digital auto-scanned assessments.

Materials to Support English Learners

Meet with English learners to target their language development and provide support at various proficiency levels.

Teacher's Guide, Volumes 1–5

Daily small-group lessons in the Teacher's Guide provide additional support for English learners and focus on a particular language function for the week. Use the text-based prompts in the lessons to guide children's application of the language function.

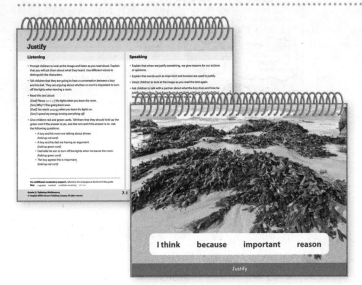

Tabletop Minilessons: English Language Development

The **Tabletop Minilessons: English Language Development** provide instruction for each week's language function, with a different daily focus on one of these domains:

- Listening
- Speaking
- Reading
- Writing
- Collaborative problem-solving

Online Ed Printable Resources

Children can use the **Language Graphic Organizers** to guide their interactions with texts they read independently and apply the weekly language function.

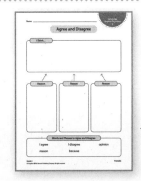

Materials to Reinforce Skills and Strategies

Provide targeted support for skills and strategies introduced during whole-group minilessons.

Teacher's Guide, Volumes 1–5

Daily small-group lessons in the Teacher's Guide reinforce and extend comprehension skill and strategy instruction from the lesson.

- Review the whole-group minilesson skill with children in small groups, based on need.

- Guide children to apply the skill to self-selected independent reading books.

- Use the Scaffold and Extend notes and the English Learner Support to tailor instruction based the needs of the children in each group.

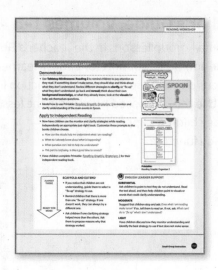

Tabletop Minilessons: Reading

Use **Tabletop Minilessons: Reading** with small groups to support children with applying reading skills from whole-group instruction to any text. The stand-up charts feature student-facing **Anchor Charts** on one side and teacher support on the back.

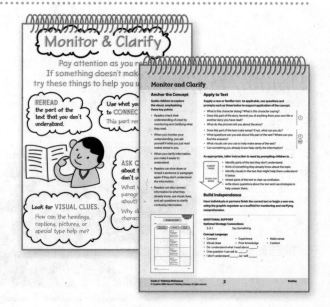

Online Ed 📺 Printable Resources

Children can use the **Reading Graphic Organizer** printables to guide their interactions with the texts.

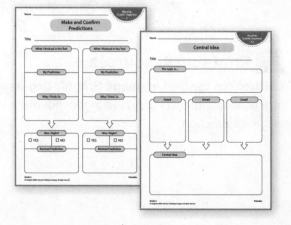

Materials to Reinforce Foundational Skills

Meet with small groups to build children's foundational reading skills.

Teacher's Guide, Volumes 1–6

Daily small-group lessons in the Teacher's Guide provide support for using the **Start Right Readers** to reinforce and apply phonics, high-frequency word, and fluency instruction. These lessons include:

- Instruction and scaffolding for the decodable **Start Right Reader** texts, including prompts to check children's comprehension and fluency support.

- Suggestions for short Make Minutes Count activities— additional support for the week's phonics, spelling, handwriting, and high-frequency word instruction for children who need it.

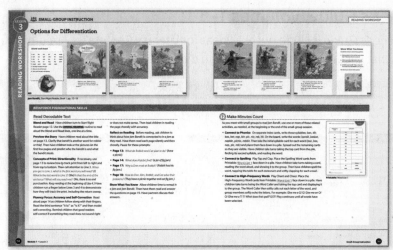

Start Right Readers

Children use **Start Right Reader** texts to practice and apply new phonics skills and each week's target high-frequency words.

Grade 1

Grade 2

Online Ⓔd Foundational Skills and Word Study Studio

Use this bank of lessons to teach prerequisite foundational skills or reinforce daily foundational skills lessons. Assess children's needs and then select lessons to provide strategic intervention in small groups for up to 30 minutes per day.

WELCOME TO *INTO READING*

Materials for Literacy Centers

Introduce Literacy Centers where children can work independently and with partners while you meet with small groups.

¡Arriba la Lectura! cuenta con todo esto y más. En la sección ¡Viva el español! verá lo que distingue a este programa.

Teacher's Guide, Volumes 1–5

The Teacher's Guide includes weekly ideas for Literacy Centers that reinforce and extend what children are learning through direct instruction.

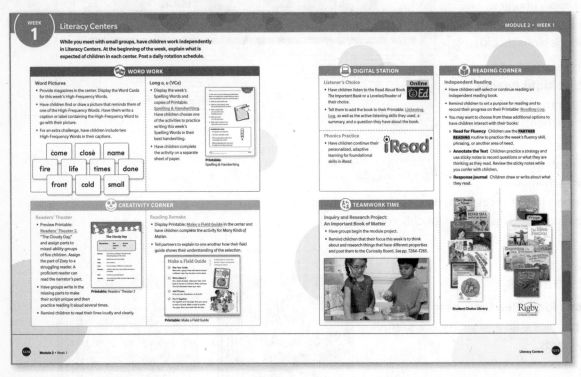

Creativity Corner

Online Ed **Reading Remake** printables develop children's reading response skills through a variety of engaging formats.

- Make a Mural
- Make a Trading Card
- Make a Field Guide
- Make a Map
- Make an Ad
- Write a News Story
- Make a Movie
- Make an Invention
- Make a Post Card
- Write a Poem

Online Ed **Readers' Theater** scripts, which include leveled parts, engage children in reading collaboratively and with expression.

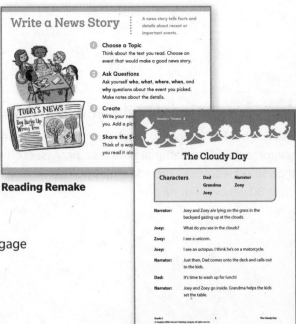

Reading Remake

Readers' Theater

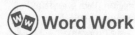 Word Work

Online **Word Cards** are used to reinforce the week's High-Frequency Words through a variety of rotating activities.

Online The **Spelling & Handwriting** printable offers children a choice for how to practice the week's Spelling Words and includes handwriting reinforcement.

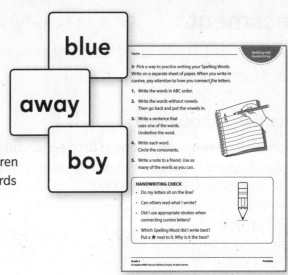

Printable Resource

💻 Digital Station

Online The **Listening Log** printable provides a place for children to demonstrate their active listening skills and listening comprehension.

Online Use *iRead* to have children learn and practice foundational skills through a personalized program that adapts instruction and activities based on student performance.

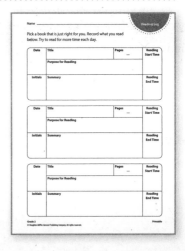

📖 Reading Corner

Online The **Reading Log** printable offers a consistent place for children to track their independent reading progress and reflect on it throughout the year.

Assessments

Use assessments to track children's progress and determine when they need extra support or practice.

¡Arriba la Lectura! cuenta con todo esto y más. En la sección ¡Viva el español! verá lo que distingue a este programa.

Intervention Assessments

Administer the **Screening Assessment** to screen and diagnose children for intervention instruction, determine flexible groups for foundational skills instruction, and monitor progress as needed.

ASSESSMENT TYPE	FREQUENCY	ASSESSED IN GRADE 1	ASSESSED IN GRADE 2
Screening	• Beginning of year • Midyear (Grade 1)	• Letter Identification • Phoneme Segmentation • Nonsense Word Reading • Word Identification • Oral Reading Fluency	• Word Identification • Oral Reading Fluency
Diagnostic	• Follow-up, as needed	• Print Concepts Inventory • Phonological Awareness Inventory • Letter-Sound Correspondence	• Print Concepts Inventory • Phonological Awareness Inventory • Letter-Sound Correspondence
Progress Monitoring	• Every two weeks, as needed	• High-Frequency Words • Decoding • Sentence Reading • Oral Reading	• Oral Reading Fluency

Online Ed Weekly and Module Assessments

- Weekly Assessments: 1 per week; 36 total
- Module Assessments: 1 per module; 12 total

Administer the paper-and-pencil or online **weekly and module assessments** to assess:

- reading comprehension
- vocabulary strategies
- generative vocabulary
- phonics (Grade 1)
- high-frequency words (Grade 1)
- grammar
- writing (module)

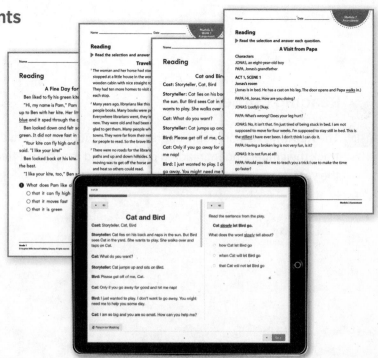

Selection Quizzes

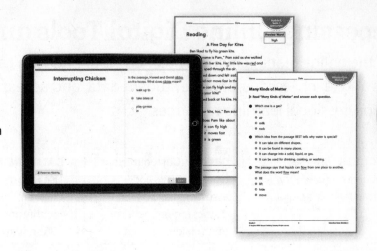

- 1 per main *myBook* text; 40 total

Administer the paper-and-pencil or online **Selection Quizzes** to assess comprehension of the main texts.

Data Reports

View **data reports** online to analyze children's gaps and gains, group children for differentiated instruction, and locate resources to target children's learning needs.

- Assessment Report
- Single Assessment Drilldown
- Standards Report

Module Inventories (Grade 1)

Administer the one-on-one **Module Inventory** to assess foundational skills in more depth as needed. Use some or all parts of the inventory depending on children's needs:

- Part 1: Phonological Awareness
- Part 2: High-Frequency Words
- Part 3: Decoding
- Part 4: Print Concepts

Rubrics

Use the following rubrics available to assess children's writing and projects:

In your Writing Workshop Teacher's Guide:

- Opinion Writing Rubric
- Narrative Writing Rubric
- Informational Text Writing Rubric
- Research Writing Rubric
- Inquiry and Research Project Rubric

In your Teacher's Guide:

- Inquiry and Research Project Rubric
- Analytic Writing
- Multipurpose Writing

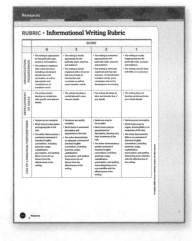

See pages 80–87 for more information about Grades 1 and 2 assessments, data, and reporting.

Accessing Online Digital Tools and Resources

Use the online management center "Ed: Your Friend in Learning" to plan and teach lessons, analyze student data, and access teaching and professional learning resources.

DISCOVER Browse Resources by category, such as Teacher's Guide.

CREATE Customize your teaching plans and assessments to match district requirements or meet children's needs.

DATA & REPORTS Use reports to track children's progress and identify areas for differentiated instruction.

WELCOME Select **Roster** to set up your class and add children.

MODULES Click a module to access teacher and student materials for each lesson.

RESOURCES View resources for teaching lessons, assessing children, differentiating instruction, communicating with families, and professional learning.

STANDARDS Locate resources correlated to your standards or use the search tool to search by keyword.

GROUPS Create and manage groups based on your own classroom observation or assessment results.

Modules

Access a digital version of the Teaching Pal.

View resources available for an entire module.

Find the *my*Book, Read Aloud, and Grade 1 Big Book titles for a week.

View digital resources available for each lesson, including Teacher's Guide lessons.

Teacher's Guide and Teaching Pal

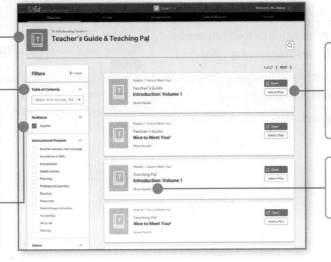

Choose a resource category to **browse**, such as Teacher's Guide.

Use the **Table of Contents** filter to choose a specific module, week, or lesson.

Filter resources by **Instructional Purpose, Audience, Purpose, Lexile,** or **Guided Reading Level**.

Open the resource, assign it to students, or select **Add to Plan** to customize your teaching plans.

Choose **Show Details** to read a description of the resource.

Data and Assessments

Find the percentage of children at different levels of proficiency using the **Assessment Proficiency** graph.

Track children's **Assessment Performance** to more effectively differentiate instruction.

Use the **Standards Report** to follow children's progress in standards proficiency and to access resources that support learning those skills.

Evaluate the average class score for each assessment with the **Assessment Average** graph.

Building Expertise with Embedded Professional Learning

Engage in ongoing professional learning through embedded teacher support, facilitated sessions, and coaching.

Embedded Support

Into Reading and *¡Arriba la Lectura!* Teacher's Guides include embedded support for building professional knowledge and enhancing your instruction with high-impact strategies.

On the Spot Professional Learning

Look for the blue boxes in Teacher's Guide Volume 1 for research-based support at the beginning of the year. Support is offered for these categories:

- **Getting Started** notes provide implementation support for introducing classroom and engagement routines.
- **Research Foundations** convey research-based rationales for teaching a skill or a particular instructional approach.
- **Teaching Terms** notes define technical literacy terms and clarify commonly confused terms, using examples.
- **Best Practices** notes offer research-based suggestions for effective teaching.

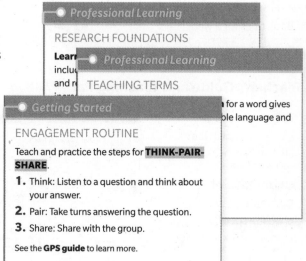

⦿ *Professional Learning*

RESEARCH FOUNDATIONS

Lear
includ
and r

⦿ *Professional Learning*

TEACHING TERMS

for a word gives
ble language and

⦿ *Getting Started*

ENGAGEMENT ROUTINE

Teach and practice the steps for **THINK-PAIR-SHARE**.

1. Think: Listen to a question and think about your answer.
2. Pair: Take turns answering the question.
3. Share: Share with the group.

See the **GPS guide** to learn more.

TEACHER TIP

Use it or lose it! Reinforce Power Words by using them frequently in classroom situations. For example: *You look **serious** today, _____. Why is that? Who can **guide** us through the next page? What do the **images** tell us about the setting of the story?* Encourage children to repeat the words as they respond to your questions or comments.

Teacher Tips

Use the orange Teacher Tip feature in the Teacher's Guide for all modules to see suggestions for:

- adapting or extending instruction to practice and apply skills.
- incorporating movement, music, and play into lessons.
- reinforcing word relationships and foundational skills throughout the day.

Online ⊙Ed **Classroom Videos**

View videos online that feature teachers in classrooms modeling a range of instructional routines and lessons from the program.

Personalized Blended Professional Learning

Explore ongoing, comprehensive support for implementing *Into Reading* and *¡Arriba la Lectura!* and further developing effective teaching practices.

Getting Started with *Into Reading*

Attend professional learning sessions in-person, online, or both. Topics include:

- experiencing *Into Reading*.
- using resources for planning and teaching.
- accessing student and teacher technology.
- administering assessments and using data.

The interactive **Professional Learning Guide** supports the Getting Started sessions and provides practical information for implementation.

Online Ed Getting Started Professional Learning Modules

Explore a series of on-demand, interactive digital topics designed to provide immediate support for getting started. You can view these topics sequentially when you begin teaching the program and then pick and choose which ones to revisit later for a refresher.

Follow-Up Support

Choose from a variety of topics, such as whole-class and small-group instruction, data and reports, or assessment and differentiation to design an in-person or live online experience to meet your goals.

Ongoing Support

Work with HMH consultants to develop instructional practices that cultivate strong readers, writers and critical thinkers.

Learn more at <https://professionalservices.hmhco.com/>.

Coaching

Grow your understanding of using *Into Reading* and *¡Arriba la Lectura!* to support student achievement through coaching by an HMH consultant on topics such as instruction, lesson design, data-driven decision-making, and more.

askHMH

Get on-demand access to program experts who will answer questions and provide personalized conferences to support implementation.

Arranging the Classroom

Organize your classroom environment with areas for whole-class instruction, small-group time, and Literacy Centers.

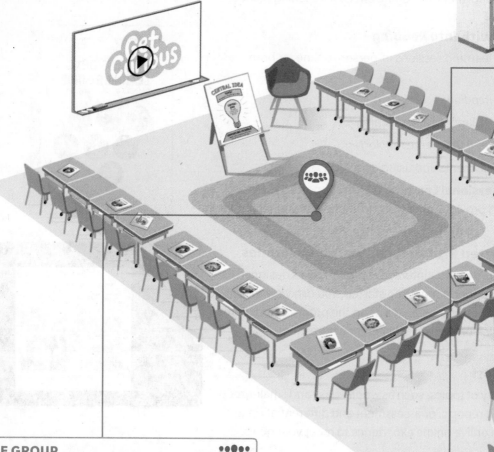

WHOLE GROUP

- Place a large rug where the whole class can gather comfortably for community building, shared reading, and other work.
- Select an area facing the screen or whiteboard to project videos and other digital resources.
- Use wall space around the community area to display the calendar, messages, and other important content.
- Arrange individual desks in groups where children can work in teams or pairs. Allow children to sit on the rug or at their seats during whole-group work.

SMALL GROUPS

- Designate a classroom table or area to meet with flexible groups for small-group instruction. If you have a smaller classroom, consider using a table that shifts purposes throughout the day.
- Choose a place away from areas where more collaborative Literacy Center activities take place, so children in the group can focus.
- Store materials such as Leveled Readers, Tabletop Minilessons, Start Right Readers, and instructional cards nearby for easy access.

LITERACY CENTERS

Provide multiple places in the classroom where children can engage in Literacy Center work, such as for Word Work, Creativity Corner, and Teamwork Time.

- Prepare designated areas with materials and resources children need to complete tasks independently and in pairs or groups.

- Designate a comfortable space in the classroom for a Reading Corner for children to enjoy quiet independent reading.

Classroom Considerations

Consider these suggestions for setting up a child-friendly learning environment:

- Anticipate the flow of traffic during different times of day as you decide where to place furniture.

- Set up systems of expectations and routines to maintain an organized classroom and limit clutter.

- Resist overcrowding the room at the beginning of the year, and allow children to co-create the space during the year.

- Provide multiple areas in the classroom for children to collaborate or work independently.

- Make flexible seating available, such as sensory seats, stools, or bean bag chairs.

- Decorate with soft colors (blues, greens, browns) and use brighter, stimulating colors (red, orange) only as accents. Create a warm environment, using natural light and lamps when possible.

- Designate a quiet space in the classroom where children can go when they need to regulate and manage strong emotions.

Creating a Literacy-Rich Environment

Build a literacy-rich environment and a community of learners in which every child is a reader and a writer.

¡Arriba la Lectura! cuenta con todo esto y más. En la sección ¡Viva el español! verá lo que distingue a este programa.

Use Your Words

Since words are the basis of listening, speaking, reading, and writing, children who enter school with more words are at an advantage. In order to close this gap and to provide a literacy-rich environment, there need to be numerous opportunities—both formal and informal—for children to grow their vocabularies in service of learning and building social skills. Teachers cannot directly teach the estimated thousands of words necessary to "do school," so the classroom environment needs to be rich in print and send the message that words matter.

We're in This Together

Work together to create a classroom that reflects the children in your class and conveys the message that everyone has a space.

- Keep the walls relatively bare and avoid overdecorating at the start of the year.

- Tell children you value their input and let them know you will co-create the classroom environment.

- Involve children in designing print for the classroom, such as creating procedures, anchor charts, labels, and messages together.

- Consider the instructional purpose of print you post in the classroom and make adjustments throughout the year, removing charts or hangings that no longer serve as references.

- Model how to "read the room" and encourage children to read and reference classroom print.

Make It Personal

Personalize the classroom using children's names, photos, and interests.

- Create name labels using children's photos to label their personal spaces in the classroom, or use them to post class helper charts and Literacy Center rotations.

- Designate a wall space or hanging area to post children's writing— make sure each child has a labeled place to showcase work.

- Survey children and make an effort to display books that match their reading interests.

Label It!

Use labels to engage children with print around the classroom.

- Involve children in making labels for parts of the classroom, class schedule, calendar, supplies and materials, and book baskets or bins.

- Label supplies and the areas where they belong to support reading skills and help make children responsible for taking and putting away supplies.

- Ask for children's input on how to organize and label new supplies when you introduce them.

- Keep large sticky notes or index cards handy, and encourage children to add labels in the classroom throughout the year.

Literacy Tools

Promote reading and writing independence by posting literacy tools so they are easily visible and accessible.

- Display **Sound/Spelling Cards** and **Word Cards** in a central area so you can refer to them when teaching and children can reference them when reading and writing independently.

- Hang **Anchor Charts** on an easel in the whole-group area to develop or build on with children during lessons.

- Hang a pocket chart in the whole-group area for working with instructional cards during lessons, such as the **Sound/Spelling Cards, Word Cards, Letter Cards,** and **Picture Cards.**

For more information about setting up a literacy-rich classroom, see pages 46–49 and 162–163.

Professional Learning

RESEARCH FOUNDATIONS

❝*Children in highly decorated classrooms were more distracted, spent more time off-task and demonstrated smaller learning gains than when the decorations were removed.*❞

—Association of Psychological Science (2014)

Getting Started with Literacy Centers

Well-defined and organized Literacy Centers provide children with opportunities to practice skills, make decisions, and work cooperatively.

Introducing Centers

Use these suggestions to introduce Literacy Centers to your class:

- **Start slow.** Introduce one or two Literacy Centers at a time, making sure to model the procedures and give time for children to practice.

- **Discuss expectations.** Lead a discussion with children to co-create a list of expectations for working independently and with others during Literacy Center activities. Discuss appropriate voice levels. Consider using the **SILENT SIGNALS** and **ASK THREE, THEN ME** Classroom Management Routines to teach and reinforce expectations. *See the routines on pages 55–57.*

- **Practice procedures.** Begin with three or four centers during the first few weeks of school before introducing more. Circulate around the classroom, give targeted feedback, and reinforce procedures during center time before starting small-group instruction. Review and revise procedures as necessary throughout the year.

- **Hold children accountable.** Provide a bin for children to turn in center work at the end of each session. Scan children's work each day and make note of children who may be off task or may benefit from a brief check-in.

- **Meet to solve problems.** During whole-group wrap-up, ask children to talk about how things went, share your observations, and work together to solve problems.

- **Update activities.** Refresh centers periodically, adapting them according to children's developing skills. Refer to Teacher's Guides, Volumes 1–5, for Literacy Center ideas that reinforce the skills children are learning each week (e.g., pp. T26–T27).

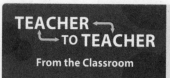

TEACHER ↹ TO TEACHER

From the Classroom

❝ *We talk about and practice the expectations for working in centers a lot during the first few weeks of school. It makes all the difference when I start meeting with my small groups.* ❞

Reading Corner

In the Reading Corner, children practice their reading skills and build motivation and enjoyment of reading by exploring self-selected books, rereading and responding to familiar texts, and reading with peers.

How to Prepare

- Designate a quiet, cozy area of the classroom that has low open shelves with books that are easy to browse.

- Include a rug and comfortable seating, such as bean bag chairs, a small couch, or floor pillows.

- Offer a variety of books of different genres, topics, levels, and formats, including books based on children's interests and some student-made books.

- Provide a book bag or book bin for each child to store **Leveled Readers** or other books they have already read with teacher guidance. You might use a plastic zipper bag or magazine file folder labeled with each child's name, which children can also use to store their Reading Log and a pencil.

- Include pencils, crayons, markers, and copies of printables children will need, such as Printable: **Reading Log**.

See pages 162–163 for more information about selecting and organizing books for independent reading.

Creativity Corner

During Creativity Corner activities, children build communication, collaboration, and social-emotional skills by working together on reading response activities, participating in Readers' Theater, writing, and creating artwork.

How to Prepare

- Set up an accessible area with a variety of materials for children to use, such as lined and unlined paper, colored paper, sticky notes, index cards, envelopes, crayons, markers, colored pencils, and oil pastels.

- Stock the center with recyclable building materials such as paper cups, paper towel rolls, and shoeboxes.

- Laminate all the **Reading Remake** printables to keep them in good condition, and display the one children will be using each week. Be sure to include all the necessary materials.

- Designate a low, visible place for posting and celebrating children's work, and update it frequently with child-selected pieces. Display children's creations or take photos of them to place in their portfolios or send to their families.

Word Work

In Word Work activities, children review and practice high-frequency words, spelling, and handwriting.

How to Prepare

- Consider keeping materials for Word Work in a storage box or file folder box that children can use on any classroom table.

- Clearly label containers and the materials that go in them. Include all materials children need for each activity. For example, include scissors and kid-friendly magazines so children can identify high-frequency words in print materials.

- Store Word Work materials, such as **Word Cards,** in plastic zipper bags and hang the bags on a bulletin board to conserve space. Another option would be to store materials in file folders and place the folders in plastic storage bins.

- Choose a child to demonstrate how to complete an activity with you. Model for the whole class, thinking aloud as you role-play how to take turns and be a good partner. Be sure to model non-examples, such as speaking too loudly, and then discuss more considerate ways to respond.

 **Teamwork Time**

During Teamwork Time activities, children work on an aspect of a module's Inquiry and Research Project. Over the course of a module, children collaborate to generate ideas, research, complete, and present an inquiry-based project.

How to Prepare

• Gather and set out the materials needed for each stage of the project. Check that children understand the overall project goals as well as the steps that make up the weekly focus of the project.

• Display a Curiosity Board near the area where children will meet to work on the project.

• Keep children's research questions and their work from each stage of the project to refer to when they make presentations and reflect on their learning.

Digital Station

At the Digital Station, children practice foundational reading skills by interacting with **iRead** and reading along with eBooks.

How to Prepare

• Set up a designated table or area near electrical outlets with several computers or tablets and headphones so children can use devices without disturbing others.

• Post a list of the programs or apps that children can use while they are at the center.

• Teach children how to log in, and keep any necessary login information easily accessible.

• Remind children to wash their hands before and after using the computers or devices.

• Model how to carefully handle and charge the computers or tablets, and tell children what to do if a technical issue arises.

• Keep copies of Printable: **Listening Log** in the center for children to use with eBooks. Model how to use the Listening Log.

Scheduling for Success

Use these suggestions to help you plan a schedule that suits your needs.

¡Arriba la Lectura! cuenta con todo esto y más. En la sección ¡Viva el español! verá lo que distingue a este programa.

Sample Schedules

Following a consistent schedule helps children know what to expect and helps you make the most of instructional time. Consider these recommendations for how much time to spend on each *Into Reading* section, and use the sample schedule as a jumping-off point for creating your own plan.

FOUNDATIONAL SKILLS.............................15–30 minutes
READING WORKSHOP ....60–75 minutes
VOCABULARY ....10–15 minutes
WRITING WORKSHOP...............................20–30 minutes

SAMPLE SCHEDULE

Meet and Greet	10 minutes
Foundational Skills	20 minutes
Vocabulary	15 minutes
Reading Workshop	35 minutes
Small-Group Instruction/Literacy Centers	40 minutes
Lunch	20 minutes
Recess	30 minutes
Writing Workshop	25 minutes
Math	45 minutes
P.E./Art/Music/Media Center	30 minutes
Science/Social Studies	30 minutes
Wrap Up	10 minutes

Best Practices for Scheduling

No two classrooms are the same, so it's crucial to consider children's needs, your own preferences, and school requirements when scheduling. Here are some tips for planning the day that works for you.

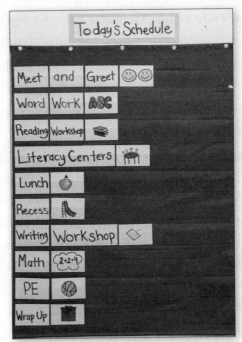

- Incorporate choice into the day where possible. Allowing children some freedom to choose how to spend certain periods of time gives them a sense of agency and instills decision-making skills.

- Be realistic about how long children are able to sit and listen, write, or do any other activity. Divide activities into 15–20 minute chunks. This is especially important at the beginning of the year.

- Include "body breaks" and "brain breaks" throughout the day. Getting children moving and giving them time to blow off steam helps them get the most out of instructional time. For example, following Foundational Skills instruction and activities, allow some time for children to choose between quick break activities such as reading alone or with a partner, playing a game, or catching up on work. Mixing it up keeps children engaged.

TEACHER ↰↱ TO TEACHER
From the Classroom

❝ *Scheduling is everything. Kids thrive on a regular schedule, but the day also needs to be dynamic, to keep them engaged. Once I figured out how to tailor my schedule to the needs of the classroom, my instruction really took off.* ❞

Welcoming Children to School

Set the tone for the year with carefully planned opportunities for children to meet others and explore the school environment during the first days of school.

Meeting and Greeting

Use the first few days of school to help children become comfortable in their school surroundings and build a sense of community.

- **Post names.** Hang children's names on a bulletin board outside the classroom to help them feel a sense of ownership over their classroom upon arrival.

- **Greet each child.** Introduce yourself to each child. Offer a handshake or high five at the door each day.

- **Get to know each other.** Use a morning meeting time to introduce children to their peers. Model formal language for introductions: *Hello, my name is* _____. and have the class greet each child chorally: *Hello,* _____!

- **Build community.** Engage children in activities that reinforce their important role in the classroom community. For example, have children decorate a name tag, work together to organize community supplies, or draw self-portraits.

Exploring the School Environment

Guided discoveries of the classroom and school campus give children a sense of ownership over their space and provide opportunities to model expectations.

- **Explore the classroom.** During the first days of school, allow children to explore the classroom. Encourage children's questions about what they see in the room.

- **Introduce flexible work areas.** Explain to children that they can use these areas to work in groups of different sizes and for different purposes. Create a system of expectations and routines for work in small groups and Literacy Center work.

- **Introduce materials.** Show children where to find basic materials, such as pencils, Literacy Center and writing materials, books, shelves, and bins. Introduce the materials gradually in the first few days.

- **Build social skills.** Tell children they will be responsible for caring for shared spaces and supplies as well as helping out when they see a need.

- **Tour the school campus.** Point out people and places of interest throughout the school, and ask adults who work in the school about their jobs.

TEACHER ⟶ TO TEACHER
From the Classroom

❝ *I take individual photos of all the children the first week of school. Then I use them throughout the year for classroom labels and different community-building activities.* ❞

Setting Goals with Children

Set goals with children to give them a sense of purpose and motivate them to take on challenges.

Establishing Goals

As children become more comfortable and gain experience in school, lead them to articulate specific and achievable learning goals for the year.

- **Define goals.** Explain that a goal is something to work toward over a period of time.

- **Set goals.** Each time the class begins a module, review suggestions in the Teacher's Guide for setting personal goals for the module, using sentence frames like the ones above to support children as they set learning goals. Encourage them to reflect on prior learning as well.

- **Brainstorm steps.** Guide children to break down goals into achievable steps. Then support them to track their progress and ultimately reach their goals.

- **Revisit goals often.** Have children keep their goals in a folder where you can easily revisit them and make adjustments. Encourage children to set new goals as they meet existing goals and develop new interests.

> I want to read stories about _____.
>
> I want to learn about _____.
>
> I will _____ so I can _____.

Tracking Progress

Once children have established goals, help them work toward meeting them. Check in on children's reading and writing goals periodically to discuss and track their progress.

Celebrating Success

When children reach a goal, celebrate it! You may wish to create certificates to acknowledge and celebrate success. Possibilities include:

- Remarkable Reader
- Word Wizard
- Wonderful Wordsmith
- Handwriting Hero
- Special Speller

Establishing Classroom Routines

Clear and consistent classroom routines help all children follow expectations, focus on productive learning, and build confidence and independence.

Classroom Management Routines at a Glance

You may want to consider establishing some or all of the classroom management routines at the beginning of the year.

CLASSROOM MANAGEMENT ROUTINES	OTHER ROUTINES
• Quiet Cue • Silent Signals • Give Me Five! • Ask Three, Then Me • Partner Up	• Entering the classroom • Walking in line • Handling books • Using supplies • Packing up

It's All Routine!

The time and effort you spend introducing and practicing routines during the first weeks of school will set the tone for the whole school year.

• **Ask for input.** Involve children in creating classroom routines, and they will be more likely to feel invested in following them.

• **Use positive language.** As you record steps for routines, avoid words such as *don't* or *no* and reframe negative language. For example, use "Walk slowly" instead of "No running" or "Listen carefully" instead of "Don't talk."

• **Make it visual.** Post the steps for routines with images in the area where children will reference them. For example, display the routine for entering the room near or on the door.

• **Be explicit.** Teach children the steps and model expectations, sharing clear examples and non-examples. Then provide opportunities for practice.

• **Problem-solve as a class.** If you notice a breakdown, bring children together to share your observations, review the routine, and talk through solutions.

● *Professional Learning*

RESEARCH FOUNDATIONS

“ *By explicitly teaching routines to students, teachers can (a) set students up for success, (b) decrease the possibility of behavior errors, and (c) reduce the amount of time spent reminding students about the routines on a daily basis.* ”

—Myers et al. (2017)

QUIET CUE

QUIET CUE is a clear, consistent, and quick routine to cue children to stop what they are doing and listen for directions.

Use this routine:

- while children are working in small groups or independently.
- at the start of a transition from one activity to another.

IMPLEMENTATION SUPPORT

- Choose an audible signal, such as chimes or a rain stick, a clapping pattern, or a verbal cue.
- Demonstrate the quiet cue and model expectations for children to stop, look, and listen.
- Have the class practice from different areas of the room. Ask children what went well and what they can improve.
- Wait until all children are looking and listening before giving directions. Review and practice expectations until the class responds quickly and consistently.

SILENT SIGNALS

SILENT SIGNALS are a set of nonverbal hand signs that children can use to get your attention without interrupting a lesson.

Use this routine:

- during whole-class lessons.
- when you are working with small groups or individuals.
- during classroom transition times.

IMPLEMENTATION SUPPORT

- Identify the most frequent reasons children may need to get your attention. Assign a simple hand sign for each, or work with the class to decide what the signals should be.
- Explain the purpose of using silent signals and introduce signals like the following: crossed fingers for using the restroom, three fingers in a "w" shape for a drink of water, pointing to nose for tissues, raising a hand for help. Work with the group to add signals as different needs arise.
- Practice as a class. For example, say "bathroom" and have children use the signal. Model how you will respond to each signal.
- When children ask verbally, show them the signal and have them use it silently.

GIVE ME FIVE!

GIVE ME FIVE! is a routine to teach the elements of active and respectful listening.

Use this routine:

• before beginning a whole-class lesson or activity.

• when children are sharing ideas or making presentations to the class.

• to get children ready for a classroom visitor.

IMPLEMENTATION SUPPORT

• Explicitly teach, model, and practice the elements of active listening at the beginning of the school year.

• Use cues to remind children to "Give Me Five!" For example, tell children to "listen with their whole bodies" or hold up one finger at a time while naming the element until you have all five fingers up.

> **1:** *Eyes are looking.*
>
> **2:** *Ears are listening.*
>
> **3:** *Mouths are closed.*
>
> **4:** *Bodies are still.*
>
> **5:** *Hearts are open.*

• Maintain reasonable expectations for still bodies and be aware of children who may be better listeners while moving or fidgeting. In these cases, consider using flexible seating, such as cushion seats, or focus tools, such as stress balls.

• Provide visible boundaries, such as individual carpet squares, for children who need extra support to stay in their personal space.

• Give children language to talk about their personal space. For example, have children imagine that each person has an invisible bubble around them. Talk about how it feels when someone "pops your bubble" and remind children to give others enough space so they don't "pop someone's bubble."

Professional Learning

RESEARCH FOUNDATIONS

" *One key to success with routines is helping students understand that by following routines, they make their classroom and school a better place to be. When students understand this, they're more likely to feel invested and to take more responsibility for their behavior.* "

—Wilson (2010)

ASK THREE, THEN ME

ASK THREE, THEN ME is a strategy to minimize interruptions by encouraging children to ask three classmates a question before coming to you with the question.

Use this routine:

- when you are working with a small group.
- during Writing Workshop when children are writing independently and you are conferring.

IMPLEMENTATION SUPPORT

- Ensure children working independently have clear procedures for their tasks and easy access to the materials they need.
- Teach and practice language to ask classmates for help. For example:

    Excuse me.

    Could you please help me _____?

    Do you know where I can find _____?

- If a child comes to you before asking three classmates for help, hold up three fingers to remind the child of the routine.
- During the whole-group wrap-up, ask children to reflect on how they did using the Ask Three, Then Me routine, and work together to solve any problems.

PARTNER UP

PARTNER UP is a strategy to pair children to collaborate as partners.

Use this routine:

- before partner discussions.
- to kick off partner reading.
- when children are writing or doing other work with partners.

IMPLEMENTATION SUPPORT

- Pair children with special attention to children's English proficiency and ability to stay on task.
- Assign numbers (1, 2) by having children count off or using reference points in the classroom. *Number 1 partners are closest to the windows. Number 2 partners are closest to the door.*
- If you have an odd number of children, assign one pair to have an additional Partner 2. When it's time for number 2 partners to share, both number 2 partners share.
- Ask children to confirm their number by holding up the number of fingers, raising a hand, or standing up when you call their number.
- Tell children which partner goes first. *Number 1 partners share first this time. Number 2 partners listen. Then switch.*
- Have children keep partners for set time periods and change partners every few weeks.

Supporting Effective Transitions

Make the most of valuable class time by setting up clear procedures for transition times and using the time between scheduled tasks efficiently.

Options for Literacy Centers

Establish procedures for transitions during small-group time and select an approach for choosing Literacy Centers and meeting with small groups.

Children's Choice

Each child selects a center and moves to the next one at his or her own pace.

Benefits

- Providing choice promotes independence and decision-making.
- Moving on after completing a center activity helps keep children on task.
- Small groups can change from day to day and children can be part of multiple small groups.

How It Works

1. Post a pocket chart or a sign-up sheet at each center with the name of the center and the number of children who can use it at one time.

2. Pass out name cards that children can use to choose a center. If a center is full, children choose a different center.

3. Call children from centers for small-group instruction. When they finish working in a teacher-led small group, they return to the center where they were working, and you call the next group.

Timed Rotations

Small groups move from center to center together after a set interval of time.

Benefits

- Assigning centers ensures children practice skills in activities they may not select on their own.
- Keeping groups together for a period of time encourages collaboration and community building.

How It Works

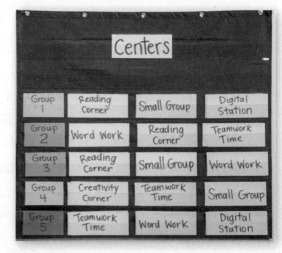

1. Assign children to groups. Hang a pocket chart with index cards for each group and center.

2. Use a signal, such as a timer or chimes, to let children know it's time to transition to the next center.

3. Change small groups often based on children's changing needs.

Reinforcing Skills During Transitions

Use transition times, such as going to lunch or packing up at the end of the day, to reinforce skills.

TRANSITION TIME	MODEL LANGUAGE
Phonological Awareness • Ask children to provide a rhyming word. • Play onset-rime "Simon Says." • Have children say words with a specific number of syllables. • Use alliteration when giving directions.	*Think of a word that rhymes with* lend. *Simon says touch your /h/ /ĕd/. Touch your /l/ /ĕg/.* *Tell me a word that has three syllables.* *Tiptoe to the table.*
Phonics and Spelling • Ask children to line up in alphabetical order. • Have children say words with target vowel sounds or that begin or end a certain way. • Have children call out Spelling Words for the group to spell.	*Line up in ABC order by first/last name.* *Say a word that begins with s-h like* shark. *Say a word with the same vowel sound as* hawk. *Let's all spell* blue.
High-Frequency Words • Play guessing games using the week's words. • Have children use the week's words in sentences.	*Which word rhymes with _____? Ends in ch? Which word means the same as "chilly"?* *Say a sentence that uses one/two of the words.*
Vocabulary • Ask children to categorize the week's Power Words and then work with one of the categories. • Ask children to share synonyms or antonyms. • Have children find occasions to use Power Words in classroom conversations.	*Which words name people, places, or things? Which are action words? Act out the words for actions.* *What are some other words for* quiet? *Name some words that mean the opposite of* quiet. *Did you hear Tamika say she was* serious?
Comprehension Skills/Strategies • Ask children to tell about parts of stories that surprised them. • Have children name effects and others name possible causes.	*What part surprised you? What did you think would happen instead?* *Here's an effect: broken glass and a puddle of water on the floor. How might that have happened?*

TEACHER ⤷ TO TEACHER

From the Classroom

❝ *Sometimes, I use transitions to give children 'body breaks' or 'brain breaks.' I play calming music and we stretch or do a few simple yoga poses. It helps get the wiggles out so children are better able to focus on the next activity.* ❞

Creating a Culturally Responsive Environment

Work to promote inclusivity, resist bias, and cultivate a classroom where every child feels welcomed, appreciated, and encouraged.

¡Arriba la Lectura! cuenta con todo esto y más. En la sección ¡Viva el español! verá lo que distingue a este programa.

Don't Avoid Differences—Embrace Them

It's wonderful to teach children the ways in which we're all the same. In fact, to some teachers it may seem misguided to talk about differences at all. But pointing out how we're unique (judiciously and respectfully) demonstrates to children that our differences are to be celebrated, not glossed over. In your classroom, strive for a balance between pointing out ways we're alike and ways we're unique.

Honor Home Languages

It's increasingly common for children to speak a language other than English outside of school. Creating links between children's home languages and the school environment is key to fostering a sense of belonging.

A simple way to do this is to ask children to share a few words or phrases in their home languages, and have the class learn them. As a teacher, you can take it upon yourself to learn a few more words, and share those. You'll be showing kids that you respect their home languages and that you too are a language learner!

Learn About Cultural Differences

As a teacher, stay mindful of the fact that certain ways of behaving can have different meanings in different cultures. For example, making eye contact with authority figures, patting children on the head, or showing your feet may be considered offensive in some cultures. This applies not only to interactions with children, but to those with their families, too. For example, in some cultures, the classroom is considered the teacher's domain. Teachers may misinterpret parents' refusal to come inside as a sign of disinterest or a lack of involvement. In fact, it may be the opposite—perhaps in their culture, parents show their respect by staying out of the classroom!

Show a Variety of Representations—*Good* Ones

An essential part of making children feel validated and affirmed is exposing them to books and other learning materials that reflect who they are, be it in terms of ethnicity, culture, family structure, or socioeconomic status.

While having a good *quantity* of these varied representations is important, it's not the same as *quality*. Some "diverse" books actually reinforce stereotypes and bias. It's important to show children that people in all professions come from a wide range of backgrounds. Seek out materials that reject stereotypes and reflect the limitless possibilities of all children.

The books featured in *Into Reading* were carefully chosen with this philosophy in mind. Extend this approach to other materials you bring into the classroom, ensuring that all children see themselves reflected and are shown possibilities for lives that move beyond the ones they know best.

Be Mindful of Gender

As children grow, they're exposed to the messages that the subtleties of language can send. Make a point of using gender-neutral language, representations, and practices. Include images of female scientists, use "businessperson" and "firefighter" instead of "businessman" or "fireman," and so on. Pay attention to how often you call on girls versus boys and how you respond to and praise them.

Point Out Bias

When an instance of bias *does* arise—say, in an older book, or between children on the playground—seize the opportunity for a teachable moment. Teach children to recognize bias and talk about why it's wrong and hurtful, and you'll be helping children learn to reject bias themselves.

Whether you're just beginning to unpack these complex issues or if you've already devoted your career to doing so, working toward an environment that honors all children may be one of the most lasting and meaningful aspects of the critical work you do each day.

● *Professional Learning*

RESEARCH FOUNDATIONS

66 *When children see themselves and their families reflected in their early childhood setting, they feel affirmed and that they belong. When children's identities and families are invisible, the opposite happens. Children feel that they are unimportant and do not belong.* 99

—Derman-Sparks & Edwards (2009)

Social-Emotional Learning

Focusing on building a strong social-emotional foundation for children can lead to school success and a lifetime of benefits.

Lead with a Learning Mindset

A **learning mindset** is a set of beliefs that drive children to seek challenges, feel that school is a safe place to make mistakes, and know that there is value in working hard. Set children up for success by introducing and reinforcing each of these beliefs throughout the year.

Growth Mindset: *the belief that people can increase their ability*

Individuals with a growth mindset believe that intelligence and ability can be developed through hard work, while those with a fixed mindset believe that they are born with a set amount of effort and learning. Children with a growth mindset are more likely to pursue challenges and persist through them because they believe they are capable of improving.

Help children establish a growth mindset by explicitly teaching these key ideas:

- Focused effort is more important than talent when working to master a new skill.

- Mistakes, challenges, and setbacks are an essential part of the learning process.

- The connections in your brain grow and change with effort and practice—the more you use your brain, the stronger it becomes.

Purpose and Relevance: *the belief that work has value*

Children are more likely to value their daily work when they understand its purpose and relevance to their own goals or interests.

Help children see the value of their daily work by guiding them to answer questions like these:

- *Why am I doing this?*

- *How will this task help me in the future?*

See page 53 to learn more about setting goals with children.

Belonging: *the belief that one is part of an academic community*

When children feel a sense of belonging, they are more likely to take academic risks, ask for help, and try new things.

See page 65 for strategies for creating a sense of belonging in your class.

See page 53 to learn more about setting goals with children.

◉ Professional Learning

RESEARCH FOUNDATIONS

❝ *Mindset is not a fixed attribute. Like other beliefs, it is learned from experience and instruction. Intervention studies show that students' motivation, perseverance, and achievement can be increased by teaching a growth mindset.* ❞

—Dockterman & Blackwell (2014)

Learning Mindset: Grades 1–2

Into Reading and *¡Arriba la Lectura!* incorporate the latest research from Mindset Works® and Dr. David Dockterman of Harvard's Graduate School of Education. Children focus on one learning mindset behavior or strategy per module that is closely connected to the module topic and reinforces a specific learning mindset belief.

BEHAVIOR/STRATEGY (Grade 1 Modules) (Grade 2 Modules)	LEARNING MINDSET BELIEF			KEY MESSAGES
	Growth Mindset	Belonging	Relevance/ Purpose	
seeking challenges (1) Nice to Meet You! (5) Lead the Way	⚙			*Seeking challenges without fear of failing is important to learning!*
belonging (2) My Family, My Community (1) Be a Super Citizen		⚙	⚙	*You are valuable members of our community—we are all here to help each other learn and grow.*
curiosity (3) Amazing Animals (2) Look Around and Explore!	⚙		⚙	*Curiosity leads to learning; asking questions helps your brain grow.*
asking for help (4) Better Together (9) Home Sweet Habitat	⚙	⚙		*Asking for help is a way of "trying smarter" and helps you progress.*
problem solving (5) Now You See It . . . (10) Many Cultures, One World	⚙			*There are many different ways to solve a problem: look for clues, ask for help, try a different way.*
purpose/grit (6) Celebrate America (11) Genre Study: Nonfiction	⚙		⚙	*The work you do in school has a purpose. As you persist, you find ways to apply what you learned.*
noticing (7) The Big Outdoors (6) Weather Wise	⚙		⚙	*Paying attention to details helps you learn things and improve your work.*
resilience (8) Tell Me a Story (7) Everyone Has a Story	⚙		⚙	*Focused effort and our response to failure along the way lead to growth.*
setting goals (9) Grow, Plants, Grow! (8) Time to Grow!	⚙		⚙	*You can achieve your goals by making a plan and persisting through challenges.*
perseverance/trying again (10) Dare to Dream (3) Meet in the Middle	⚙			*When you persevere, your brain forms new connections that make it even stronger!*
self-reflection (11) Genre Study: Nonfiction (12) Genre Study: Literary Texts	⚙		⚙	*Good learners reflect on their work and ask themselves, "How can I make this better?"*
planning ahead/growth mindset (12) Genre Study: Literary Texts (4) Tell Me a Story	⚙		⚙	*Planning steps to meet our goals helps us reach them step by step.*

Social-Emotional Learning

Teaching Learning Mindset Skills

As children move through a module, use the learning mindset resources to introduce, apply, and reflect on the learning mindset focus.

- **Introduce** and define the learning focus using Anchor Chart: <u>My Learning Mindset</u> and the model language in the Teacher's Guide.

- **Apply** the learning mindset focus in the context of daily lessons using the strategies provided in the Teacher's Guide.

- **Reflect** on the learning mindset focus at the end of each module and reinforce key concepts. For example, recognize examples of when children use the mindset focus and acknowledge their learning.

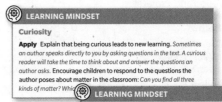

Grade 1 Anchor Chart

Grade 2 Anchor Chart

Reinforce Learning Mindset

Work to develop an awareness of your own mindsets, and infuse learning mindset behaviors into teaching and learning throughout the year.

- **Be mindful.** Consider how your own mindsets crop up in your language and teaching practices.

- **Praise effort instead of intelligence.** Instead of saying *"You're so smart,"* try *"I noticed you were frustrated when you didn't get the answer the first time, but you tried again and you figured it out. Good job!"*

- **Normalize frustration.** Help children understand that struggling with a challenging task is common and productive. *"No one does everything right the first time. What's important is that you keep trying."*

- **Communicate with families.** Send home the Printable: <u>Family Letter</u> for each module to help families understand the learning mindset focus children are working to develop and to encourage them to reinforce it at home.

- **Celebrate learning mindset.** Acknowledge children for their hard work in developing learning mindset behaviors using the Printable: <u>Learning Mindset Certificate</u>.

LEARNING MINDSET

Curiosity

Apply Explain that being curious leads to new learning. *Sometimes an author speaks directly to you by asking questions in the text. A curious reader will take the time to think about and answer the questions an author asks.* Encourage children to respond to the questions the author poses about matter in the classroom: *Can you find all three kinds of matter? Whic...*

LEARNING MINDSET

Curiosity

Reflect Review why it is important to be curious, particularly when learning new words. *When you are curious about new words you see while reading, you grow your vocabulary. Being curious causes you to ask questions and learn more about the world around you!* Encourage children to share Power Words or other words from *The Great Fuzz Frenzy* that they were curious about. Prompt them to explain why they were curious and what they did to understand the meaning of the word.

Building Children's Sense of Belonging

Establishing a sense of belonging—the belief that everyone is respected and valued—is central to creating a learning environment where all children can thrive.

Create Community

Use these strategies in your classroom to establish a sense of community early in the year.

- **Make children feel welcome.** Help children get to know one another and celebrate the individual experiences each child brings to the classroom.

- **Co-create expectations.** Work with children to create expectations, routines, and procedures to give them a sense of control, making them feel valued.

- **Consider the physical environment.** Allow children to feel a part of the classroom community by keeping the walls empty at the beginning of the year and having the class work together to create and decorate the space.

- **Connect with families.** Send home a welcome letter to introduce yourself to families, share information about ways to be involved at the school, and encourage them to connect with one another to build a support system for children that extends beyond school.

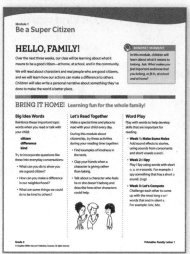

Strengthen Connections

Reinforce children's sense of belonging throughout the year.

- **Use images and texts.** Thoughtfully choose images that represent the diversity of your class, select books and media that are relevant to children, and display photos of children's communities and families.

- **Connect daily.** Greet each child and acknowledge children by making eye contact. Use children's names when you address them.

- **Build in collaboration time.** Establish routines that encourage peers to share equally, such as THINK-PAIR-SHARE and TURN AND TALK.

- **Teach social skills.** Hold regular class meetings to model social skills, including how to handle conflicts when they arise.

- **Involve families.** Encourage family participation in school events and activities whenever possible.

Classroom Community

Professional Learning

RESEARCH FOUNDATIONS

> **❝** An important predictor of academic tenacity is students' feelings of social belonging in school as well as their relationships with other students, and with teachers. **❞**

—Dweck, Walton & Cohen (2014)

Social-Emotional Learning

Promoting Positive Behavior

Set positive behavior goals that require children to meet the expectations in different classroom contexts and school settings.

Establish Expectations

Use the examples below as a guide for establishing clear behavior expectations during different times of the day.

	WHOLE-CLASS INSTRUCTION	SMALL-GROUP INSTRUCTION	LITERACY CENTERS/ INDEPENDENT WORK
Be Respectful	• Listen with your whole body—eyes, ears, and heart. • Stay in your seat. • Use kind words.	• Use kind words. • Listen when classmates are speaking. • Keep hands and feet to yourself.	• Use a quiet voice. • Be kind to your classmates. • Share materials.
Be Responsible	• Follow the teacher's directions. • Take care of books and materials.	• Follow the teacher's directions. • Go to the small-group table quickly and quietly.	• Take care of books, materials, and devices. • Put away materials before moving to a new activity. • Help your classmates.
Do Your Best	• Participate in every lesson. • Speak loudly and clearly when you share. • Try new things.	• Participate in every lesson. • Complete work neatly.	• Help your classmates. • Complete work neatly. • Encourage others.

Support Positive Behaviors

Use these materials to remind children of positive behaviors and reinforce positive communication habits.

Anchor Charts

• Social Communication

• Ask and Answer Questions

• Give and Follow Instructions

• Collaborative Conversations

Teacher's Guides

Use lessons in the Teacher's Guides to teach and reinforce good communication habits.

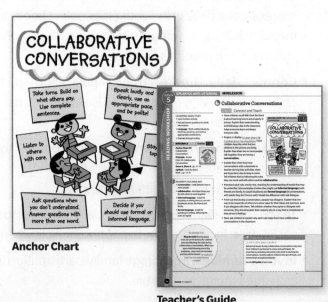

Anchor Chart

Teacher's Guide

Best Practices: Reinforcing Positive Behavior

Keep in mind these key points for promoting positive behavior in your classroom.

- **Teach and model expectations.** Start teaching classroom expectations and procedures on the first day of school. Model examples and non-examples for each behavior and give children opportunities to practice and for role play.

- **Give behavior-specific feedback.** For example, instead of saying *"Good job!"* try *"You were very responsible when you put away all the materials. Thank you!"*

- **Use positive language.** For example, use *"Be respectful"* in place of *"Don't be rude,"* or *"Use a quiet voice"* instead of *"Don't yell."*

- **Consider room arrangement.** Ensure that furniture placement promotes smooth transitions from one activity to the next and allows you ready access to a child to give a quick nonverbal reminder of expectations. Offer strategic seating choices to children, making sure that children with behavior challenges sit near you and not each other.

- **Create a quiet space.** Designate a place in the classroom for "peace and quiet," where children know they can go when their emotions get in the way of learning. Be clear that this space is not meant to be a "time out" or seclusion area.

- **Acknowledge positive behavior.** "Catch" children in the act of following expectations and acknowledge the behavior.

- **Communicate with families.** Share behavioral expectations with families early in the year with a note home and at back-to-school night. Throughout the year, touch base with families to let them know when their children succeed!

Social-Emotional Learning

¡Arriba la Lectura! cuenta con todo esto y más. En la sección ¡Viva el español! verá lo que distingue a este programa.

Support Social-Emotional Learning with Texts

Social-emotional development is key to the education of young children. Children develop social-emotional skills as they become more aware of their own feelings and needs as well as the needs and feelings of others. Books allow children to view others' experiences and emotions through the eyes of the people and characters in each text. In fact, research has shown that children who are read to the most understand others the most. Books help children analyze relationships, see how others handle problems, and make human connections.

Build a Social-Emotional Library

Help children develop social-emotional skills by using *Into Reading* literature to support the development of key social-emotional competencies.

SOCIAL-EMOTIONAL COMPETENCY	GRADE 1 TEXTS	GRADE 2 TEXTS
Self-Awareness	*The Nest; I am Amelia Earhart; Goal!; Pelé, King of Soccer; Blue Bird and Coyote; Step-by-Step Advice from the Animal Kingdom; Monument City; You're a Grand Old Flag; The Contest; Presidents' Day*	*The Great Fuzz Frenzy; Hollywood Chicken; The Important Book; The Puddle Puzzle; How to Read a Story; A Crow, a Lion, and a Mouse! Oh, My!; If the Shoe Fits; The Perfect Season for Dreaming*
Self-Management	*Chicken Little; Interrupting Chicken; The Grasshopper and the Ants; The Kissing Hand; So You Want to Grow a Taco?; The Talking Vegetables; The Curious Garden; What Can You Do?; Charlotte the Scientist Is Squished; Kids Are Inventors, Too!; Sky Color; Young Frank Architect*	*The Stories He Tells; Jackie and the Beanstalk; I Am Helen Keller; Drum Dream Girl; The Legend of the Indian Paintbrush; Miss Moore Thought Otherwise; Experiment with What Plants Need to Grow; The Patchwork Garden; My Dream Playground; Seed by Seed; Wilma Rudolph: Against All Odds; Whoosh!; Stand Tall, Molly Lou Melon*
Social Awareness	*Who Put the Cookies in the Cookie Jar?; Maybe Something Beautiful; Places in My Neighborhood; Dan Had a Plan; Sam & Dave Dig a Hole; Whose Hands Are These?; On Meadowview Street; Grand Canyon; Do You Really Want to Visit a Wetland?; I am Amelia Earhart; Pelé, King of Soccer; Goal!; Try This!*	*Clark the Shark; Spoon; The Name Jar; Where on Earth Is My Bagel?; Dreams Around the World; Being a Good Citizen; The William Hoy Story; May Day Around the World; Goal!; Cloudette; Whatever the Weather; Freddy the Frogcaster; We Are Super Citizens; Hello, World!*
Responsible Decision-Making	*Blackout; Waiting Is Not Easy!; Suki's Kimono; Maybe Something Beautiful*	*Big Red Lollipop; Clark the Shark; Pepita and the Bully; I Am Helen Keller; Wilma Rudolph: Against All Odds; Gingerbread for Liberty!; Great Leaders*
Relationship Skills	*Good Sports; Goal!; A Big Guy Took My Ball!; If You Plant a Seed; Pete the Cat: Rocking in My School Shoes; Baseball Hour; The Great Ball Game; Color Your World with Kindness; Do Unto Otters; You Will Be My Friend!; My School Trip; Kids' Guide to Friends; Suki's Kimono*	*Gingerbread for Liberty!; Be a Hero! Work It Out!; Nature's Patchwork Quilt; Sea Otter Pups; The Great Kapok Tree; Meet Me Halfway; Working with Others; Big Red Lollipop; Pepita and the Bully; The Best Habitat for Me*

Make Learning Stick

Books are powerful tools for teaching social-emotional skills because they serve as examples of important behaviors, actions, and emotions. Here are some ways to help children develop social-emotional competencies as they read.

- Use a question to prompt children to respond to social-emotional aspects of the book. Ask: *How did the character show kindness? What was the girl determined to do _____? What problem did the character face? How did he/she handle the problem?*

- Prompt children to recognize and discuss a character or narrator's emotions. Ask: *If you were _____, how would you feel?*

- Use the book to help children build understanding and empathy for others. Discuss differences between the people and communities children meet in the book, as well as how they are similar to or different from the children in the class.

- Point out examples of characters who do and don't show self-regulation, kindness, or empathy. Then model or role-play the situation with children to help them learn about social cues or how to discuss their own feelings and behaviors.

- Oftentimes it's easier to talk about a difficult situation as it happens to characters in a book rather than in children's own lives. Talk about how the people or characters in the book handled a tricky situation. Then ask children if they've ever had a similar experience. Allow them time and space to share.

- As children move through the rest of their day, pay attention to children's interactions with one another. Comment when you see children helping one another, developing friendships and solving problems together, or when they develop and carry out plans. Connect these observations to texts you've read together.

● *Professional Learning*

BEST PRACTICES

❝ *Each child demands from us an individualized and differentiated approach with regard to the reading instruction we offer and the personal connection we make.* ❞

— Collins & Glover (2015)

Engaging Families as Learning Partners

Building partnerships with families and engaging them in their children's literacy learning can lead to a lifetime of benefits.

¡Arriba la Lectura! cuenta con todo esto y más. En la sección ¡Viva el español! verá lo que distingue a este programa.

A Culture of Collaboration

When families participate in their child's literacy development, children have improved achievement, better school attendance, and reduced dropout rates (Segal & Martin-Chang, 2018). Begin building home-school literacy partnerships by working to initiate a culture of collaboration with families:

- Communicate early in the year with parents and caregivers and work to build trusting relationships so you can leverage their ongoing support.

- Focus initial communications on accomplishments and positive observations.

- Provide clear paths and options for family engagement that are sensitive to constraints families may be experiencing.

- Take into account local considerations and collaborate with families to make plans for connecting school to home that work for your community.

The Role of Families

One of the most impactful practices is to encourage children's parents and caregivers to think of themselves as educators. In addition to providing opportunities for families to become involved within the school day, we can partner with them to support their children beyond the classroom.

Share key practices with families to support their children's literacy success:

- Inform parents and caregivers of the cumulative effect of missing school and intervene to support families facing challenges with **regular attendance**.

- Provide strategies for working with children to develop their **oral language**.

- Model how to interact with children while **reading together**.

- Send home ideas for **authentic reading and writing opportunities**.

Professional Learning

RESEARCH FOUNDATIONS

66 *The most important practice in any family engagement initiative is to link that initiative to student learning and development.* 99

—Thiers (2017)

Let's Talk

Through conversations with their children, parents and caregivers help them understand word meanings, sentence structure, and social language. Strong oral language skills are critical for reading success.

Encourage families to support oral language development by:

- Playing with language, singing songs, and telling stories.
- Talking with their children throughout the day—on the way to school, at the grocery store, and during shared meals.
- Modeling the social aspects of language, such as greeting people, taking turns speaking, and speaking politely.

Read It Again!

Reading together is a powerful mechanism for promoting literacy development. When parents and caregivers make shared reading time interactive and fun, children become successful, motivated readers.

Promote effective strategies for families to read together:

- Demonstrate fluent reading with prosody, expression, and enthusiasm. Show how to interact with children while reading together and sounding out words.
- Give family members ideas for types of questions to ask while reading.
- Provide ideas for types of books to read across genres, both for children to read independently and for families to read aloud. Reading aloud books two years above children's reading level exposes them to vocabulary and more complex syntax that they will need in later years and develops comprehension.

Be a Bookworm

The amount that children read by themselves and with others strongly contributes to how well they read and how much they enjoy reading (Cunningham & Zibulsky, 2014).

To promote reading volume:

- Ensure that families have access to an abundance of books during the school year and over the summer.
- Coach parents and caregivers on how to consider children's interests and allow them to select related texts, including magazines, graphic novels, and online resources.
- Encourage families to gradually stretch reading sessions over time.

Communicating with Families

Keep families informed of their child's progress and communicate ways you can work together to meet children's learning needs throughout the year.

A Great Start

For some children, starting a new school year can be both exciting and stressful. The first day of school can also be emotional for children's families.

Consider these suggestions for welcoming new families into the school community:

- Mail a personal letter or post card to children and let them know you are looking forward to the first day of school.

- Call children's parents or caregivers to introduce yourself and answer any questions they may have about the first week of school.

- Make sure to translate any communication or handouts and have translators available for meetings or conferences, if needed.

Meet the Families

Use your time at back-to-school night to meet children's family members and set the tone for the year.

- Let parents know how often they should expect to hear from you, and how and when they can reach you.

- Convey your homework policy, making sure to stress the importance of allowing for unstructured play, talking with children, reading together, spending family time together, and getting enough sleep.

- Display *Into Reading* or *¡Arriba la Lectura!* books for parents to browse, and explain the curriculum.

- Inform parents of volunteer opportunities and how they can get involved at the school or in the classroom throughout the year.

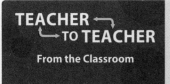

TEACHER ↪ TO TEACHER

From the Classroom

66 *I have each child write a letter or draw a picture for their parents to read at Back to School Night, and I encourage parents to write a letter back to their child. The class is thrilled to come in and find their parents' responses the next day!* 99

Foster Ongoing Outreach

Communicating to families that they can be active participants in their child's learning and identifying specific ways for them to participate help families understand expectations and feel confident about their role.

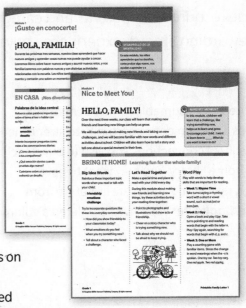

- Send home the Printable: **Family Letter** at the beginning of each module to inform family members about what their children are learning and to offer practical ideas for reinforcing skills.

- Post family letters and other communications on a board outside or just inside the classroom door.

- Work with other teachers to host family workshops that focus on specific aspects of support for children at home, such as social- emotional learning, oral language development, shared reading strategies, writing opportunities, and summer learning.

- With appropriate permission, take photos or videos of children and their work to share with parents through text, email, or on a secure class website.

- Invite families to special events where they can view children's projects and watch their performances!

Share Progress

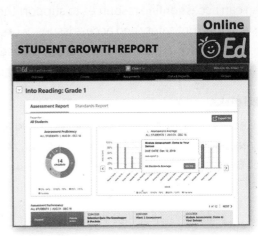

Hold conferences with parents or caregivers to share observations about children's development and discuss strategies for working together.

- Start with the positive, focusing on the child's particular strengths or progress since your last meeting.

- Share the child's reading and writing goals.

- Review the child's portfolio with classwork that shows growth and includes samples of children's work.

- Share assessment scores and individual reports, making sure to explain where the data come from and what they mean.

- Print a copy of the **Student Growth Report** to point out and discuss the child's growth in reading ability.

- Print a copy of the **Standards Report** to discuss the child's proficiency in areas such as listening comprehension, decoding, and recognizing high-frequency words.

- Provide specific strategies and resources for family members to support their child's learning outside of school.

- Keep a log to record important notes about parent communications and areas that require follow-up.

FAMILY AND COMMUNITY

Learning Beyond the Classroom

Provide resources for parents and caregivers to engage in rich and rewarding literacy experiences beyond the classroom.

¡Arriba la Lectura! cuenta con todo esto y más. En la sección ¡Viva el español! verá lo que distingue a este programa.

*my*Book

The write-in, consumable format of ***my*Book** provides a convenient opportunity to strengthen home-school connections and also to build each child's home library. You may want to have children take home and share literature from their ***my*Book** after you have completed a volume in class.

Online Resources

Provide parents, caregivers, and after-school staff with login information so children can access online resources to support their learning. Make sure to be sensitive to Internet safety and access issues, working with caregivers to provide resources that work in their personal circumstances.

Online Ⓔd eBooks

Provide access to a library of eBooks where children can listen to and read along with the **Read Aloud Books, *my*Book** texts, Grade 1 **Big Books,** and **Start Right Readers** they are using in class.

Online Ⓔd *iRead*

Encourage families and caregivers to access ***iRead*** outside of school so children can practice foundational reading skills at their "just right" level.

Online Ed Printable Resources

Based on children's individual needs, email or provide copies of Printable Resources available online for family members to use outside of school.

Handwriting Practice

Support letter formation with the **Handwriting Practice** printables. Use assessment data to target specific letters for children who need to practice.

Start Right Readers

Share printable versions of **Start Right Readers** available online for children to take home to practice decoding and fluent reading.

- Encourage children to read the texts to different family members, favorite dolls or stuffed animals, or family pets.

- Share the focus sound-spellings and High-Frequency Words with families so they can reinforce them while reading.

- Have children do the activities on the pages that precede and follow each **Start Right Reader** text with a family member to review foundational and comprehension skills.

Word Lists

Give family members the weekly printable list of **High-Frequency Words** and **Spelling Words** available online, and highlight particular words for the child to practice. Provide ideas for working with the words. For example:

- Play games using the words, such as Tic-Tac-Toe and Go Fish.

- Make a word ring or flashcards to practice reading and spelling the words.

- Have children practice writing the words and writing sentences that use the words.

Celebrating Success

Communicate children's successes to their families and celebrate their efforts throughout the year.

¡Arriba la Lectura! cuenta con todo esto y más. En la sección ¡Viva el español! verá lo que distingue a este programa.

Reach Out to Families

Consider your children's family members and caregivers when choosing the best strategies for keeping them informed of their children's successes at school.

• During drop-off or pick-up time, make a brief connection to verbally share targeted feedback.

• Designate a board near the classroom to display children's writing, projects, or other work for families to view.

• Make a call or send a text, email, or note.

• Share pictures or videos of children's work via text, email, or a secure class website, making sure that you have appropriate permissions.

Share Accomplishments

Create or print certificates and send them home to share children's accomplishments with their families. Use Printable: **Learning Mindset Certificate** to recognize children who demonstrate the learning mindset focus for each module. Additional possibilities for certificates include:

• Remarkable Reader

• Word Wizard

• Wonderful Wordsmith

• Handwriting Hero

• Special Speller

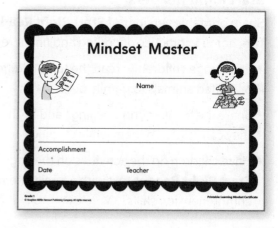

TEACHER → TO TEACHER
From the Classroom

❝ *I try to visit each of my students' homes at least once during the school year. It's usually just a quick check-in, but it strengthens my relationship with the entire family and helps me better understand the whole child.* ❞

Supporting Summer Learning

At the end of the school year, offer families strategies and resources to keep children's growing minds active during the summer.

Beat the Summer Slide

Give families ideas and resources to support children's literacy development over the summer.

- Encourage families to visit the local library to sign children up for library cards, browse books, and participate in summer reading programs.

- Provide a summer reading list with suggested titles across a variety of genres for families and children to read together.

- Give families a list of questions to ask children before, during, and after reading fiction and nonfiction books.

- Send home printable **Start Right Readers** that focus on sound-spellings children need to practice more.

- Share login information for appropriate literacy apps that children can access.

- Inform families of literacy games they can play together.

● **Professional Learning**

RESEARCH FOUNDATIONS

❝ *During the summer months, young children lose literacy gains made during the school year, a phenomenon known as "summer slide." The most important thing teachers can do to reverse this trend is to help families adopt family literacy routines and promote opportunities for families to talk, read, and write together throughout the school year.* ❞

— Hoisington (2017)

Get Out and About

With sensitivity to families' circumstances, suggest accessible experiences and local events that will support children to build knowledge, language, and literacy over the summer.

- Participate in story time or other events at the library or in a bookstore.

- Grow a garden or cook a family recipe together.

- Take a walk around the neighborhood, explore a local park, or join a community garden.

- Visit an art or science museum, the zoo, or an aquarium.

- Attend a concert, play, or performance for children.

- Look out for announcements from the local library or department of parks and recreation for more recommendations for events and activities in your area.

Family and Community

Connecting with the Community

Connect children and their families to the larger community to make learning meaningful, teach important skills, and access resources.

Take a Trip

Field trips can bring learning to life and provide some of the most memorable learning experiences from the year. Remember that field trips don't have to involve big expenses. There are often destinations within walking distance that allow children to learn more about the community around them. Make the most of a field trip:

• Prepare by reading books, asking questions, and planning focused activities.

• Invite family members to chaperone: to observe their child in a new context, connect with classmates and teachers, and learn about community resources.

• Take photos during field trips to share on a class website or in a family newsletter.

• Reflect after the trip by writing, drawing, and discussing what was learned.

Invite Classroom Visitors

Reach out to children's family members and other community members to share resources or discuss their expertise. For example, the local librarian can visit to tell children about summer reading programs, or firefighters can visit to answer questions about fire safety. When logistics make a visit unfeasible, set up a video chat to bring the community to the classroom.

Brainstorm questions to ask visitors, take photos, and record what you learn. If visitors wear a uniform or use special tools in their work, invite them to share these items or do a hands-on demonstration of their work for the class.

Give Back to the Community

Engage children in service projects to develop social awareness, responsibility, and citizenship. The community can also be a powerful audience. For example, children can do the following:

• Share books at a local preschool or write cards to people at a senior center.

• Write letters to local representatives or their favorite authors.

• Display writing or art at the local library, bookstore, or grocery store.

• Send thank you notes to classroom visitors or field trip coordinators.

• Draft emails to expert sources for research writing and projects.

Community Connections

Consider these ideas to plan meaningful experiences with the community beyond school.

CLASSROOM VISITORS	FIELD TRIPS
School workers, such as a principal, crossing guard, custodian, nurse, or cafeteria worker, can talk about their role in the school community.	Tour the different areas of school to help children understand the various jobs that people do there.
Family members can share photos and stories or read their child's favorite book.	Arrange a class picnic at a local park with children's families.
Local community heroes, such as police officers, sanitation workers, or artists can answer questions about their important jobs and the tools they use.	Take a walk to tour a local fire station, post office, police station, or library.
A dentist, doctor, nurse, P. E. teacher, or nutritionist can answer questions about dental hygiene, eating right, exercising, and staying healthy.	Plan a "get fit" day on the schoolyard or at a local park with fitness activities and healthful snacks.
A person living with a disability can discuss overcoming challenges, or former students who are now in high school or college can come back to tell children about their successes.	Visit the local library where the librarian can help children sign up for a library card, engage them in selecting and reading books, and tell them about available resources.
Local leaders can talk about their work in the community and address children's questions or concerns.	Plan a visit to a local historical landmark or attend a local sports team's game.
A scientist, detective, or anyone whose work involves looking closely can share discoveries that came from close examination.	Explore the schoolyard or nearby park with a focus on learning through looking closely.
A farmer or gardener can share how they grow plants for food.	Walk to a local grocery store, farmer's market, or community garden.
A zoologist or biologist can discuss habitats and ecosystems and answer questions about things animals need to survive.	Take a nature walk to a nearby stream, pond, or city park to observe local wildlife habitats.

TEACHER → TO TEACHER
From the Classroom

"At Back-to-School Night, I survey children's families to ask if they have a job or hobby related to the topics we're going to study. My students are so motivated to learn when family members visit!"

Assessing Children Throughout the Year

Follow this suggested timeline to administer assessments and monitor children's learning over the course of the school year.

BEGINNING OF YEAR				MIDYEAR	
Module 1	Module 2	Module 3	Module 4	Module 5	Module 6

Module 6

	WEEK 1					WEEK 2	
	Lesson 1	Lesson 2	Lesson 3	Lesson 4	Lesson 5	Lesson 6	Lesson 7
Daily Formative Assessment	● ●	● ● ●	● ● ●	● ● ● ●	● ● ● ●	● ● ●	● ● ● ●
Guided Reading Benchmark Assessment Kit							
Intervention Assessments							
Selection Quizzes			●				●
Weekly Assessments					●		
Module Assessment/ Inventory							

Daily Formative Assessment

Use embedded opportunities for daily formative assessment along with Selection Quizzes. Then support or extend learning during Small-Group Instruction.

- Foundational Skills
- Vocabulary
- Reading Workshop
- Writing Workshop

Intervention Assessments

- Use **screener assessments** at the beginning of the year and again at mid-year in Grade 1.
- Follow up with **diagnostic assessments** for select children.
- Use **progress-monitoring assessments** every two weeks as needed.

Guided Reading Benchmark Assessment Kit

Use Benchmark Leveled Readers and oral reading records on an ongoing basis to assess children's reading skills.

| Module 7 | Module 8 | Module 9 | Module 10 | Module 11 | Module 12 |

			WEEK 3				
Lesson **8**	Lesson **9**	Lesson **10**	Lesson **11**	Lesson **12**	Lesson **13**	Lesson **14**	Lesson **15**
• • •	• • • •	• • • •	• • • •	• • • •	• • • •	• • • •	• • •

ASSESS LEARNING

Weekly Assessments

Assess understanding of reading comprehension, vocabulary strategies, generative vocabulary, grammar, and foundational skills (in Grade 1) each week.

● 36 Weekly Assessments per year

Module Assessments

Assess understanding of reading comprehension, vocabulary strategies, generative vocabulary, writing and grammar, and foundational skills (in Grade 1) each module.

● 12 Module Assessments per year

Module Inventories (Grade 1 only)

Assess select children's progress with foundational skills at the end of each module for more information.

● 12 Module Inventories per year

Assessment and Differentiation

Screening, Diagnostic, and Progress-Monitoring Assessments

¡Arriba la Lectura!
cuenta con todo esto y más.
En la sección ¡Viva el español!
verá lo que distingue a
este programa.

Use these assessments to identify areas for intervention, plan flexible groups for teaching, and monitor progress throughout the year.

Grades 1 and 2 Intervention Assessments

ASSESSMENT TYPE	FREQUENCY	ASSESSED IN GRADE 1	ASSESSED IN GRADE 2
Screening	• Beginning of year • Midyear (Grade 1)	• Letter Identification • Phoneme Segmentation • Nonsense Word Reading • Word Identification • Oral Reading Fluency	• Word Identification • Oral Reading Fluency
Diagnostic	• Follow-up, as needed	• Print Concepts Inventory • Phonological Awareness Inventory • Letter-Sound Correspondence	• Print Concepts Inventory • Phonological Awareness Inventory • Letter-Sound Correspondence
Progress Monitoring	• Every two weeks, as needed	• High-Frequency Words • Decoding • Sentence Reading • Oral Reading	• Oral Reading Fluency

Screening Assessments

Use these assessments early in the school year to:

- obtain preliminary information about children's performance

- screen all children for intervention

- determine flexible groups for foundational skills instruction

Letter Identification

Administer the **Letter Identification** assessment individually to assess a child's facility with naming the letters of the alphabet.

Phoneme Segmentation

Use the **Phoneme Segmentation** oral assessment to individually assess a child's ability to identify the individual sounds in a spoken word.

Nonsense Word Reading

Use the **Nonsense Word Reading** assessment to individually assess a child's ability to read nonsense words using letter-sound associations.

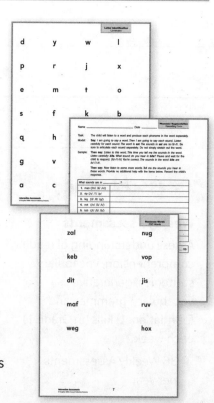

Word Identification

Use the **Word Identification** assessment to individually assess a child's ability to read high-frequency and multisyllabic words.

Oral Reading Fluency

Use the **Oral Reading Fluency** assessment to assess a child's oral reading fluency, accuracy, and rate as well as information about decoding strategies using specific grade-level targeted vocabulary. Use the results to determine whether children would benefit from intervention instruction or require additional diagnostic testing.

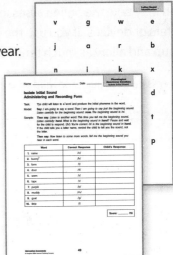

Diagnostic Assessments

Administer the diagnostic assessments as needed to:

- follow up with children who score below expectation on screening assessments
- obtain information to inform skills-based flexible groups and targeted instruction

Print Concepts Inventory

Use the **Print Concepts Inventory** with children who struggle with Letter Identification to determine whether they would benefit from instruction in concepts of print. Then re-administer it to monitor progress throughout the year.

Letter-Sound Correspondence

The **Letter-Sound Correspondence** assessment determines a child's ability to associate letters with sounds.

Phonological Awareness Inventory

Administer the **Phonological Awareness Inventory** to children who struggle with phoneme segmentation to determine whether they would benefit from additional phonological awareness instruction. The skills assessed include words in a sentence; blending, segmenting, and deleting syllables/phonemes; adding/substituting phonemes; rhyme; onset and rime blending and segmentation; and phoneme isolation.

Progress-Monitoring Assessments

Administer these three- to five-minute oral assessments to individuals approximately every two weeks to measure growth in reading skills; identify challenging areas for reteaching, review, and extra practice; provide checks on children's beginning reading skills; monitor progress of children who are receiving intervention; and help determine when children are ready to exit intervention.

 Access the Intervention Assessments and more information online.

Formative Assessments

Use formative assessments to determine children's mastery of skills and to plan for review, reteaching, or differentiation.

¡Arriba la Lectura!
cuenta con todo esto y más.
En la sección ¡Viva el español!
verá lo que distingue a
este programa.

Weekly and Module Assessments

The **Weekly and Module Assessments** measure children's understanding of major comprehension, vocabulary, foundational, and writing/grammar skills at the end of each week and module.

In Grade 1, each assessment has three sections:

- The **Reading** section assesses comprehension and vocabulary skills.
- The **Foundational Skills** section assesses phonics skills and high-frequency words.
- The **Writing** section assesses grammar and writing skills.

In Grade 2, each assessment has two sections:

- The **Reading** section assesses comprehension and vocabulary skills.
- The **Writing** section assesses grammar and writing skills.

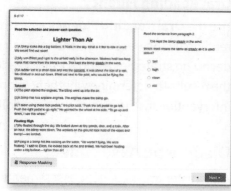

Children may take the online assessments flexibly, depending on your access to computers or devices. If you use the paper-and-pencil assessment, administer it to a group and allow as much time as children need to complete it.

Online
🙂**Ed** *Access detailed guidelines and answer keys for the Weekly and Module Assessments online.*

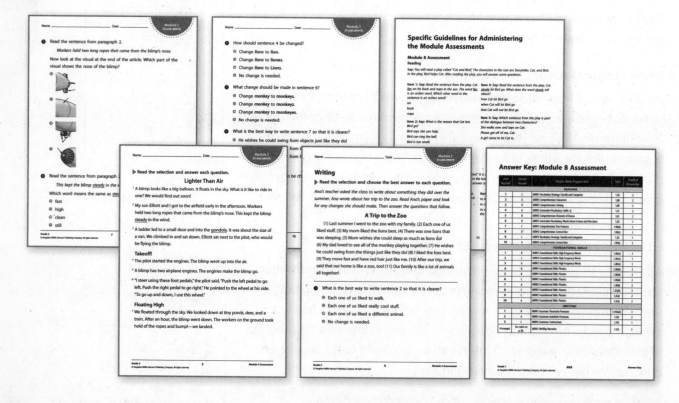

Data Reports

When children take the Weekly and Module Assessments online, you can access **data reports** to analyze gaps and gains, form groups for differentiated instruction, and locate resources to target children's needs.

- **Assessment Report:** View class scores for each assessment and analyze student proficiency data.

- **Standards Report:** Follow children's progress in standards proficiency and access resources that support learning those skills.

Use data from the reports to:

- determine if children have met learning objectives for the week or module

- look for patterns in children's errors to choose concepts and skills for reteaching or additional practice

- decide if children are ready to advance to the next week or module of instruction

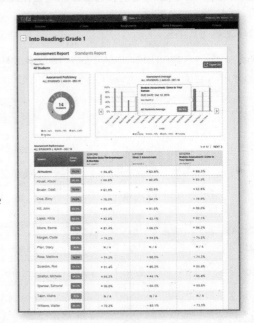

Grade 1 Module Inventories

Administer the one-to-one **Module Inventory** to assess foundational skills in more depth as needed. Use some or all parts of the inventory depending on children's needs:

- **Part 1: Phonological Awareness** Orally prompt the child to demonstrate phonological awareness skills, such as producing rhymes and blending phonemes to say words.

- **Part 2: High-Frequency Words** Point to high-frequency words from the module and prompt the child to read each word with automaticity.

- **Part 3: Decoding** Point to nonsense words and prompt the child to decode the words to demonstrate an understanding of target sound-spellings taught in the module.

- **Part 4: Print Concepts** Use a familiar book from the module and prompt the child to demonstrate an understanding of concepts of print taught in the module, such as book parts or directionality.

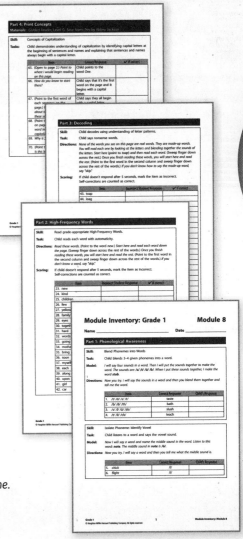

 Access the Module Inventories, detailed guidelines, and answer keys online.

Assessment and Differentiation

Formative Assessments

¡Arriba la Lectura!
cuenta con todo esto y más.
En la sección ¡Viva el español!
verá lo que distingue a
este programa.

Targeted Skills

Grade 1 and 2 lessons include embedded opportunities for formative assessment during daily instruction, as well as Selection Quizzes.

WEEK 1	WEEK 2	WEEK 3	TARGETED SKILLS
Lesson 1	Lesson 6	Lesson 11	Foundational Skills
Lesson 1	Lesson 6	Lesson 11	Reading Skills and Strategies
	Lesson 6	Lesson 11	Vocabulary
		Lesson 11	Writing and Grammar
Lesson 2	Lesson 7	Lesson 12	Foundational Skills
Lesson 2	Lesson 7	Lesson 12	Vocabulary
Lesson 2	Lesson 7	Lesson 12	Reading Skills and Strategies
	Lesson 7	Lesson 12	Writing and Grammar
Lesson 3	Lesson 8	Lesson 13	Foundational Skills
Lesson 3	Lesson 8	Lesson 13	Vocabulary
Lesson 3	Lesson 8	Lesson 13	Reading Skills and Strategies
	Lesson 8	Lesson 13	Writing and Grammar
Lesson 4	Lesson 9	Lesson 14	Foundational Skills
Lesson 4	Lesson 9	Lesson 14	Vocabulary
Lesson 4	Lesson 9	Lesson 14	Reading Skills and Strategies
Lesson 4	Lesson 9	Lesson 14	Writing and Grammar
Lesson 5	Lesson 10	Lesson 15	Foundational Skills
Lesson 5	Lesson 10	Lesson 15	Vocabulary
Lesson 5	Lesson 10	Lesson 15	Reading Skills and Strategies
Lesson 5	Lesson 10	Lesson 15	Writing and Grammar

Use each lesson's Independent Practice and Engage and Respond work to determine whether children are meeting the learning objectives. Depending on your observations, provide either support or extensions during Small-Group Instruction.

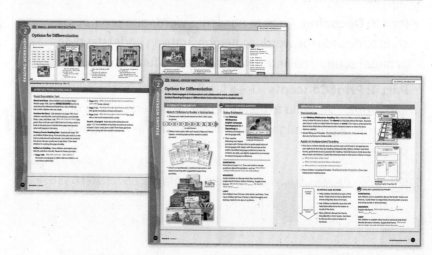

Guided Reading Benchmark Assessment Kit

Use the primary **Guided Reading Benchmark Assessment Kit** to determine children's Guided Reading levels and make instructional decisions.

The kit includes a paired fiction and nonfiction **Benchmark Leveled Reader** for Guided Reading levels A–N. Including this range of levels allows you to assess accelerated learners in your class beyond grade-level expectations.

Follow the Teacher Directions in the corresponding **Benchmark Evaluation Guide** for guidance with:

- providing an overview of the selections
- assessing oral reading by having the child read aloud while you mark errors
- prompting the child to retell the selections
- reading aloud comprehension questions and marking the child's responses
- using results to determine the child's Guided Reading level

Every **Leveled Reader** also has a corresponding **Oral Reading Record** so you can monitor children's reading as frequently as needed.

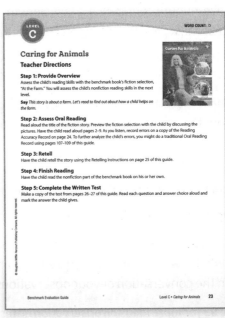

Conferring with Writers

Circulate as children write independently to ask questions, provide targeted feedback, and take notes to inform your teaching.

Encourage Writing Independence

Here are some suggestions for ensuring children are engaging in writing so you are freed up to have meaningful conversations.

- Talk about the expectations for independent writing with the class, and revisit them if there is a breakdown during a session.

- Anticipate issues that may arise and draw you away from conferring or distract children from their writing. For example, have a system in place for when a child needs a sharpened pencil.

- Provide accessible, motivating, and developmentally appropriate materials.

- Teach children a set of **SILENT SIGNALS** (p. 55) to express their needs while you are conferring without interrupting a conference in progress.

- Encourage children to solve problems on their own and how to use their peers as a resource using **ASK THREE, THEN ME** (p. 57).

Conference Basics

Take a set of portable materials along as you meet with individuals, such as a clipboard or notebook, sticky notes, pencils, highlighters, and a stapler. Let children know that you may stop to talk to them about their writing.

Circulate and confer with a few children every day. A focused four- or five-minute conference is sufficient to deliver personalized instruction. When you approach a child to confer:

1 **Listen** Find out what the child is doing well, ask about the writing, and pay close attention to the child's response.

2 **Affirm** Based on what you hear, tell the child something about the writing that is working well to reinforce the child's strengths.

3 **Teach** Focus on a general principle rather than a specific correction. Use the focal text, writing model, or other familiar text for examples of the principle.

4 **Apply** Suggest that the child try it out for himself or herself.

Document your conversations with children using a system that works for you. Include what is working in the child's writing and a focus for the child to work on based on the conversation or your observations.

See page 93 for more ideas on observation notes.

Choosing Children for Conferences

You will likely have writers at different stages of the writing process at any one time. So how do you decide which children to confer with? Here are some ideas:

- Make a list of a few children, including those you haven't conferred with recently or who need a follow-up from a previous conference.

- Allow for some flexibility to confer with children who signal for help. Scan work areas to ensure children are engaged.

- Use children's questions during independent writing to inform your teaching. When you notice that there are a few children with similar needs, consider pulling them together for a small-group conference.

Language for Conferring

It can be challenging to think of meaningful feedback on the spot. You may find it helpful to compile a sheet of sample prompts, positive statements, questions, and teaching focuses based on your class's writing goals to keep handy while you confer with children.

The Writing Workshop lessons for Revising offer ideas for focused discussion based on the writing form and the topic of a day's lesson, but you can reference other lessons for ways to support children who are working on a different step in the writing process.

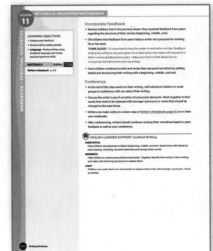

Writing Workshop Teacher's Guide

Early in the Year

At the beginning of the year, especially in Grade 1, conferences with writers may mostly serve to reinforce expectations for writing time or to model how to access and share materials. For children who are more comfortable drawing than writing, focus on aspects of their work that will transfer to writing:

- Reinforce that pictures convey meaning and tell stories.

- Ask children about their drawings. Point out significant details in their pictures, and encourage them to add details.

- Remind children of what you are working on as a class.

● Professional Learning

BEST PRACTICES

❝ *If a teacher can listen to a writer talk about her writing, and then can skim what the child has done so far and intervene in ways that lift the level not only of this piece of writing but of that child's work on future pieces, that teacher's conferences are a Very Big Deal.* ❞

— Calkins, Hartman & White (2005)

Assessing Writing and Projects

Use clear evaluation criteria to assess children's writing and project work and to provide actionable feedback.

Writing Rubrics

Use rubrics in the Resources section of the **Writing Workshop Teacher's Guide** or online to assess children's published opinion, narrative, informational text, and research writing in these areas:

- Organization and Presentation
- Development of Ideas
- Use of Language and Conventions

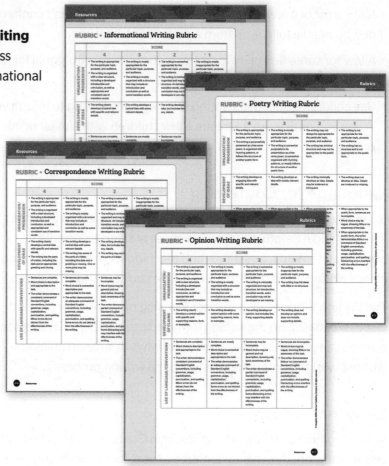

Inquiry and Research Project Rubric

Locate the rubric in the Resources section of the main **Teacher's Guide** or online to assess children's project work from each module in four key areas:

- Collaboration
- Research and Text Evidence
- Content
- Presentation

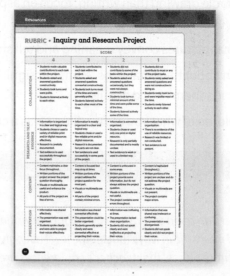

How to Use the Rubrics

Use specific criteria to monitor children's growth in writing types and project work throughout the year.

1. Print the rubric from *Ed* and use a copy to score each child's work, or copy the rubric from the Writing Workshop Teacher's Guide.

2. Review criteria for each area one at a time as you consider children's work.

5. Record notes to clarify scores and reference during conferences.

3. Record a score for each criterion. Read the descriptors for each score and consider which score best matches the child's performance.

4. Average scores for all of the criteria to determine an overall score of one to four.

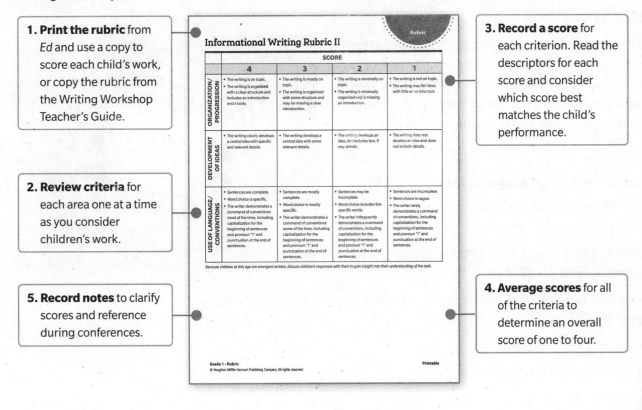

Informational Writing Rubric II

	SCORE			
	4	**3**	**2**	**1**
ORGANIZATION/ PROGRESSION	• The writing is on topic. • The writing is organized with a clear structure and includes an introduction and a body.	• The writing is mostly on topic. • The writing is organized with some structure and may be missing a clear introduction.	• The writing is minimally on topic. • The writing is minimally organized and is missing an introduction.	• The writing is not on topic. • The writing may list ideas with little or no structure.
DEVELOPMENT OF IDEAS	• The writing clearly develops a central idea with specific and relevant details.	• The writing develops a central idea with some relevant details.	• The writing develops an idea, but includes few, if any, details.	• The writing does not develop an idea and does not include details.
USE OF LANGUAGE/ CONVENTIONS	• Sentences are complete. • Word choice is specific. • The writer demonstrates a command of conventions most of the time, including capitalization for the beginning of sentences and pronoun "I" and punctuation at the end of sentences.	• Sentences are mostly complete. • Word choice is mostly specific. • The writer demonstrates a command of conventions some of the time, including capitalization for the beginning of sentences and pronoun "I" and punctuation at the end of sentences.	• Sentences may be incomplete. • Word choice includes few specific words. • The writer infrequently demonstrates a command of conventions, including capitalization for the beginning of sentences and pronoun "I" and punctuation at the end of sentences.	• Sentences are incomplete. • Word choice is vague. • The writer rarely demonstrates a command of conventions, including capitalization for the beginning of sentences and pronoun "I" and punctuation at the end of sentences.

Because children at this age are emergent writers, discuss children's responses with them to gain insight into their understanding of the task.

Best Practices: Rubrics

- **Use anchor papers.** Identify work samples that exemplify particular scores for different rubric criteria, and reference these "anchor papers" if scoring questions arise.

- **Monitor growth.** Use rubric scores to track children's progress and monitor their understanding of new skills and development of longer-term goals.

- **Be transparent.** Let children know the rubric criteria, and point out specific examples of what you will be looking for when you review their work.

- **Inform families.** Share children's work with families to highlight areas of growth and give concrete examples of how they can provide support.

Documenting Children's Growth

Use informal assessment tools to gather data and gain a more complete picture of children's growth and instructional needs.

Portfolios

At the beginning of the year, set up portfolios for all the children in your class. Some teachers compile portfolio contents in a binder for each child and designate a shelf in the classroom to store them. Other teachers use a hanging file folder for each child and house the portfolios in a storage crate.

Formal and Informal Assessments

Consider these suggestions for assessments to include in children's portfolios:

- Screening, Diagnostic, and Progress Monitoring Assessments (see pp. 82–83)

- Weekly Assessments, Module Assessments, and Grade 1 Module Inventories (see pp. 84–85)

- Oral Reading Records (see p. 87)

- Writing and project rubrics (see pp. 90–91)

- Observation notes

Work Samples

Collaborate with children to select work samples for their portfolios that showcase their best work and document growth over the year. These may include:

- copies of **myBook** work, such as response to text or comprehension skills pages

- Reading or Language **Graphic Organizers** children have completed

- handwriting samples from the beginning, middle, and end of year

- writing samples for different writing types over the course of the year

- photos of children's inquiry and research projects or other collaborative work

Reading Surveys

Survey children and their families at the beginning and middle of the year to gather information about their reading interests, attitudes, and preferences.

Use the information from surveys to inform instructional planning, support children with self-selected reading, and recommend books or literacy routines to families.

Have children complete a **Reading Log** for their independent reading, and monitor how frequently they are reading and what they record about the books they read.

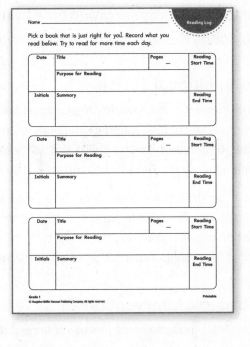

Observation Notes

Observe children closely and take notes during individual conferences, guided reading groups, small-group instruction, and independent reading and writing.

Set up a system for recording and organizing observation notes that works for you. One option is keeping a clipboard handy to take notes throughout the day. Another option is using a file folder with sticky notes to record observations for each child. Once you have recorded observations, transfer your notes to children's individual portfolios.

You may consider observing and noting:

- reading behaviors children show during guided reading, such as pointing to words, rereading, or self-correcting

- writing strategies children use independently, such as adding details, applying grammar skills, or spelling known or unknown words

- foundational skills understandings children demonstrate during small-group instruction

- examples of children displaying social-emotional competencies, such as responsible decision-making, social awareness, self-awareness, and self-management, or using relationship skills

Forming Flexible Groups

Make the most of small-group time by using data to thoughtfully form groups that will optimize student growth.

¡Arriba la Lectura! cuenta con todo esto y más. En la sección ¡Viva el español! verá lo que distingue a este programa.

Foundational Skills

Children come to school with a range of foundational skills knowledge. Using assessment data to plan foundational skills lessons will allow you to provide targeted attention based on children's needs and will help prevent advanced learners from becoming fatigued during lessons on skills they have already mastered.

Assess all children at the beginning of the year using Intervention Assessments and use the data to plan flexible groups for foundational skills lessons. Use whole-class instruction to teach skills that the majority of children have not mastered. Form small groups to teach skills that a cohort of children in the class need to learn or review.

Strategic Intervention

Use data from multiple measures to implement daily targeted Tier 2 and Tier 3 interventions during designated times. Strategic intervention may be a combination of pull-out, push-in, small-group, or one-to-one time.

For more information on assessment and resources for intervention, see pages 82–83 and 106–109.

Small-Group Instruction

Use data to form flexible small groups and locate resources for differentiating instruction.

SMALL GROUP	ASSESSMENT DATA	INSTRUCTIONAL RESOURCE
Guided Reading	• Guided Reading Benchmark Assessment Kit • Oral Reading Records • Adaptive Growth Measure and Student Growth Report • Leveled Reader Quizzes	• Rigby Leveled Readers • Take and Teach Lessons • Tabletop Minilessons: Reading
English Language Support	• State English Language Development Assessments	• Tabletop Minilessons: English Language Development • English Language Support lessons • Language Graphic Organizers
Skills and Strategies	• Daily Formative Assessments • Weekly Assessments	• Tabletop Minilessons: Reading • Reinforce Skills and Strategies lessons • Reading Graphic Organizers
Foundational Skills	• Daily Formative Assessments • Weekly Assessments	• Start Right Reader • Reinforce Foundational Skills lessons • Learning Cards • Foundational Skills and Word Study Studio

Small-Group Weekly Schedule

Plan a weekly schedule for small-group instruction based on the individual needs of children in your classroom. Every school and class is different, so no two small-group schedules will be alike. Use the sample below as a model for creating your own.

SMALL GROUPS	MONDAY	TUESDAY	WEDNESDAY	THURSDAY	FRIDAY
🕐 **Guided Reading**	Level E	Level F	Level G	Level H	Level J
🕐 **English Language Development**	Persuade	Persuade	Persuade	Persuade	Persuade
🕐 **Reinforce Skills and Strategies**	Ideas and Support	Text Organization	Make Inferences	Point of View	Gather Information
🕐 **Reinforce Foundational Skills**	Reinforce Skills and Read Decodable Text	Reinforce Skills and Read Decodable Text	Reinforce Skills and Read Decodable Text	Reinforce Skills and Read Decodable Text	Review and Make Text Connections

Online Ed Customized Groups

Create and track small groups online based on assessment and observational data.

- *Ed* **will automatically group children** based on *Into Reading* assessment results.

- **Customize** your groups using drag and drop functionality.

- **See more information** about each child by clicking his or her name.

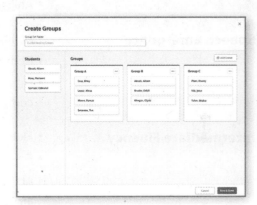

Online Ed Resources for Small-Group Instruction

Access recommended resources online for each group or search for your own based on individual needs. Then assign resources to groups to create a customized small-group plan.

- **View** recommended resources for each group.

- **Search** for additional resources as needed.

- **Assign** resources to groups or individuals.

Supporting English Learners

Build understanding of children's first languages and the stages of second language acquisition to support decisions about providing appropriate levels of scaffolding and targeted language support.

¡Arriba la Lectura!
cuenta con todo esto y más.
En la sección ¡Viva el español!
verá lo que distingue a
este programa.

Stages of Second Language Acquisition

Language learners progress through five stages as they acquire English language skills.

STAGE	CHARACTERISTICS OF LEARNERS
❶ **Preproduction**	• Silence or speaking exclusively in first language • Ability to mimic but not produce original thoughts in new language • Characterized by observing and listening • Learn through gestures, images, or other visual aids
❷ **Early Production**	• Use of simple sentences and phrases • Repetition of learned phrases or "headlines" • Use of verbs in present tense • Ability to answer simple questions
❸ **Speech Emergence**	• Ability to use English to communicate and learn • Communication in simple sentences with frequent errors • Dependence on context clues and familiar subject matter for comprehension
❹ **Intermediate Fluency**	• Fluent communication in academic and social settings • Few grammatical errors but some vocabulary gaps • Ability to understand some figurative language, make predictions and comparisons, and formulate explanations
❺ **Advanced Fluency**	• Effective communication about a variety of subjects • Vocabulary comparable to that of a native speaker • May still use idioms incorrectly or speak with an accent

⊙ *Professional Learning*

RESEARCH FOUNDATIONS

❝ *Children's language skills in kindergarten predict their performance in other areas, including math and reading, throughout school. Not only does a child's use of vocabulary and grammar predict future proficiency with the spoken and written word, but it also affects performance in other subject areas.* ❞

—Echart (2018)

English Learner Support

Into Reading lessons have embedded **English Learner Support** for multiple language proficiency levels across instructional contexts. Look for the recurring feature along the bottom section of your Teacher's Guide lessons.

Preview the strategies before teaching a lesson, and select the level of support and strategy that best targets the needs of the English learners in your class.

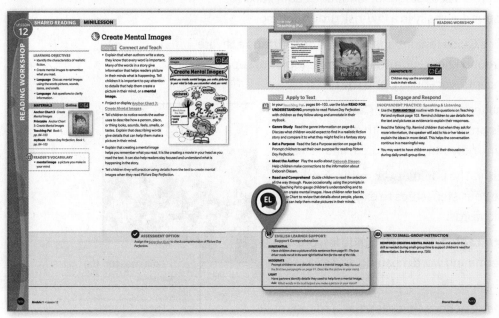

Small-Group Support

Form small groups for English Learner Support based on the number of English learners in your class and the level of support they require.

If most children in your class are English learners, and the level of support they need is different, you may decide to form multiple small groups. If you have six or fewer English learners, you may decide to form one group but provide different levels of support within the group.

During daily small-group English Learner Support:

- Use the **Tabletop Minilessons: English Language Development** to introduce, review, and practice a particular language function.

- Use the text-based prompts in the Teacher's Guide to practice the language function in the context of the daily reading.

See page 31 for more information about materials for English language support.

Supporting English Learners

Effective Instruction to Build Language

Into Reading for Grades 1–2 embeds evidence-based strategies and practices that contribute to all children learning while also accelerating English learning.

¡**Arriba la Lectura!**
cuenta con todo esto y más.
En la sección ¡Viva el español!
verá lo que distingue a
este programa.

- **Engage children.** Use the **ENGAGEMENT** routines (pp. 154–161) embedded throughout the lessons in the Teacher's Guides to provide frequent opportunities for English learners at all stages of language acquisition to actively participate and respond verbally in a low-risk group setting.

- **Build knowledge.** Teacher's Guide lessons and **Get Curious Videos** activate and build children's background knowledge about module topics to support their understanding of concepts, vocabulary, and the texts.

- **Make learning visual.** Images on **Vocabulary Cards, Anchor Charts,** and **Picture Cards** provide children with a visual reference to support learning new concepts, words, and skills.

- **Teach vocabulary explicitly.** The **VOCABULARY** routine and **Vocabulary Cards** include consistent steps to explicitly teach module topic and academic words.

- **Bolster word-learning strategies.** Teacher's Guide lessons focus on strategies for determining word meaning and exploring word relationships.

- **Read texts multiple times.** Teacher's Guide lessons and routines engage children in multiple readings of texts with the whole class and in smaller group settings.

- **Provide sentence frames.** Teacher's Guide lessons include sentence frames to support children as they structure their verbal and written responses.

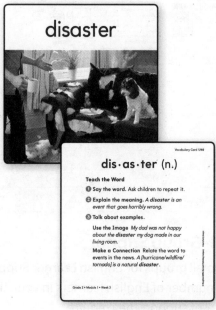

Vocabulary Cards

Best Practices: English Learners

Keep these best practices in mind as you plan how to best meet the needs of the English learners in your class:

- Include English learners in all lessons and class activities. Ensure that children who receive "pull-out" services don't miss critical content.

- Demonstrate respect for and interest in children's first languages—for example, by asking children to share the equivalent of an English word.

- Work to build a non-intimidating environment in which children feel comfortable taking risks and experimenting with language.

- Use pictures, visual aids, and gestures paired with words whenever possible, especially when giving directions and when teaching new content.

- Demonstrate or act out procedures, vocabulary, and stories as a class to help English learners access information. For example, have children practice prepositions for location with an object, such as an eraser, at their desks. Tell children to put the eraser *on* the desk, *in* the desk, *under* the desk, *above* the desk, and *beside* the desk.

- Make the most of teachable moments by pointing out differences in pronunciation, meaning, and spelling of words when children encounter them: for example, minimal pairs (e.g., *check, chick*), multiple-meaning words (e.g., *sink*), and homophones (e.g., *pear, pair*).

- Take children's efforts to communicate seriously and assure them that making mistakes is to be expected and is part of the learning process.

> **● Professional Learning**
>
> RESEARCH FOUNDATIONS
>
> 66 *Making the core curriculum comprehensible is central to preventing new English learners from becoming long-term English learners.* 99
>
> — Echevarria, Frey & Fisher (2015)

Supporting English Learners

¡Arriba la Lectura! cuenta con todo esto y más. En la sección ¡Viva el español! verá lo que distingue a este programa.

Addressing Language Differences

Children who speak a language other than English bring with them knowledge of language to use as building blocks for learning English. Understanding similarities and differences between a child's first language and English can help guide and tailor your instruction to meet children's individual needs.

Helpful Similarities

Children will naturally compare and contrast English with their first language and use that knowledge to develop English language skills. Children's first language can provide useful tools to help them learn English and act as a familiar frame of reference.

Learning cognates is one way to draw on a shared element to help strengthen children's vocabulary. Cognates are words that are written and pronounced similarly between languages, like *attention* in English and *atención* in Spanish. Shared letter-sound correspondences (e.g., the letter *d* stands for the sound /d/ in both Spanish and English) are another example of a shared element that can help children as they learn to read and write.

Contrasting Differences

When elements of a child's first language conflict with elements of English, it can cause confusion that may impede English learning. For example, false cognates can lead to attributing incorrect meaning to words. False cognates are words that are spelled or pronounced very similarly across languages but mean very different things, such as *exit* in English and *éxito*, which means *success* in Spanish. Those are two very similar words with two very different meanings!

Non-Correlated Elements

When language learners encounter a feature of English that is not present in their first language, or vice-versa, it neither helps nor harms their acquisition of English. For example, articles do not exist as parts of speech in Vietnamese, so children whose first language is Vietnamese will have no frame of reference for using the word *the*. Some sounds in English may not exist in a child's first language. In those cases, children may need additional practice with mouth positions and articulating sounds.

As you consider how to best support English learners in your class, keep in mind that young children are language learners in both their first language and English. They may not have developed the particular knowledge in their first language to support learning in English. For example, cognates are only useful if children already have an understanding of the word in their first language.

Building Cross-Linguistic Connections

Use *Into Reading* resources to build cross-linguistic connections between English and children's first languages.

The **Language Differences** online Teacher's Guide resource can help you understand differences between children's first languages and English. These languages are featured in the online resource:

- Spanish

- Vietnamese

- Cantonese and Mandarin

- Filipino

- Hmong

- Korean

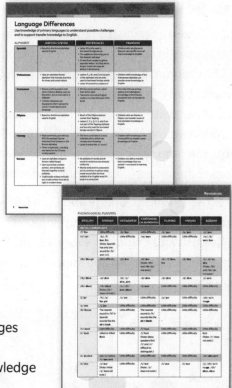

This resource gives specific examples to show how these languages compare to English. It can help you target specific areas that are challenging and identify areas where children can leverage knowledge from their first languages.

Use the resource to become familiar with ways that each language aligns with or differs from English in the following areas:

- Alphabet (Writing System)

- Phonological Features (Consonant and Vowel Sounds)

- Grammatical Features (Parts of Speech, Verb Tenses, Sentence Structure and Syntax)

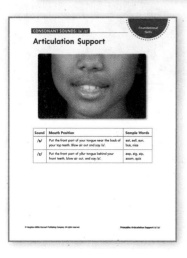

There are also resources available online to support English learners with articulating challenging sounds. Model the mouth positions for making particular sounds using the **Articulation Videos,** and access Printables: **Articulation Support** for model language you can use to describe the mouth positions to children.

Dual Language and Biliteracy

Purpose-Built Equity and Support

¡*Arriba la Lectura!* is a Spanish Reading and Language Arts program intentionally created to be used in conjunction with *Into Reading* in dual language and biliteracy settings. The program is designed around high-interest, knowledge-building module topics that follow a parallel structure to the modules in *Into Reading*. This provides teachers with complementary resources to reinforce students' content and language learning in English and Spanish. Skill and concept development align across the programs, except where linguistic differences call for appropriate instructional differences (such as for foundational skill development).

The daily Cross-Linguistic Bridge and Dual Language Settings features in the *¡Arriba la Lectura!* **Teacher Guide** support teachers in establishing connections between Spanish and English in every lesson. These resources provide tools to encourage bilingual learning and support students' cognitive development in both languages.

**Dual Language
Implementation Guide**

Guia del maestro

Teacher's Guide

miLibra

myBook

Dual Language Implementation Guide

The **Dual Language Implementation Guide** was conceived by program author Dr. Elena Izquierdo, an expert in dual language and biliteracy. Its purpose is to help teach and implement dual language and biliteracy programs. It gives teachers opportunities to combine material from *¡Arriba la Lectura!* and *Into Reading* efficiently and easily with great flexibility, following the goals of their selected dual language model. The guide is divided into three parts, designed to provide easy access for teachers to consult on an ongoing basis, with an attractive bilingual design for ease of reading and navigation.

Part 1: Language Acquisition in Bilingual Environments

This section introduces basic concepts in biliteracy, such as the various models of bilingual education and their common principles, the development of cultural awareness, and translanguaging. It introduces a theoretical framework for teachers that provides the rationale for the relevance of dual language instruction and informs the overall instructional approach. This section also includes a bilingual glossary of professional terms and a bibliography of relevant research related to Spanish learning, bilingualism, dual language, and biliteracy.

Support for district leaders and teachers in maintaining and extending an inclusive, student-centered culture in which biliteracy can thrive.

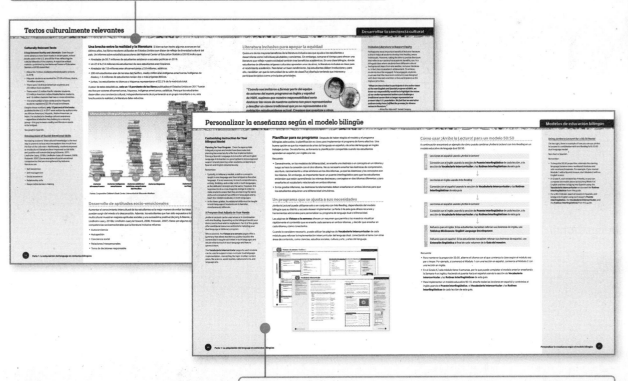

Practical suggestions for classroom management in dual language and other bilingual settings.

Part 2: Planning for the Grade

Part 2 provides grade-specific resources for efficient lesson planning.

Dual Language Across the Curriculum Cross-Curricular Vocabulary sections for each module include definitions, examples of usage, and suggested activities. Suggested activities are designed to expand vocabulary, to further develop module-specific content knowledge, and to support cross-curricular connections in both languages.

> Many dual language programs extend across the curriculum; the Dual Language Implementation Guide supports vocabulary bridging science, health, social studies, and the arts.

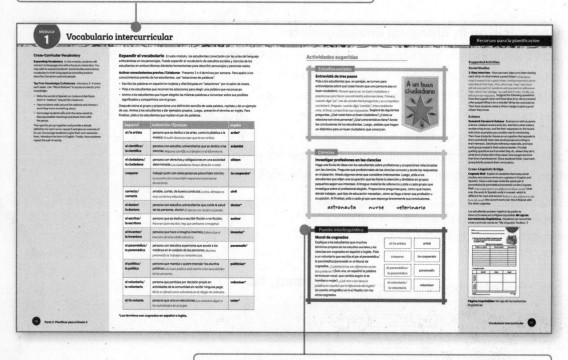

> The Cross-Linguistic Bridge section suggests ideas for cognate walls that support students in making connections between the two languages.

> 66 *Academic language is different from everyday language.* 99
> — Dr. Elena Izquierdo

Week at a Glance The At a Glance section provides an easy-to-read display of the content taught every week in both languages. This resource supports teachers in the intentional selection of instructional topics for each language and in the design of the connections between the English and Spanish instruction.

> Week at a Glance provides a dual scope and sequence from which teaching teams (Spanish and English) can decide what to teach in Spanish, what to teach in English, and how to bridge between the two. An overview of each week's Cross-Linguistic Bridges is included.

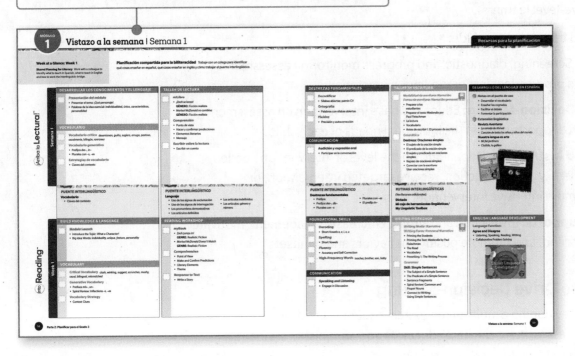

Additional Resources

The third part of the **Dual Language Implementation Guide** contains routines, rubrics, and planning templates to support the implementation of *¡Arriba la Lectura!* and *Into Reading* in dual language and biliteracy programs. This section also provides the resources to support the implementation of a dictation routine. The dictation routine provides structured and controlled practice in which students apply the language arts content that they have learned each week. The dictation routine also provides the opportunity for students to reflect on their language learning and compare and contrast the two languages to develop their metalinguistic awareness.

Implementing a Multi-Tiered System of Supports

A strong, multi-tiered system of supports ensures that all children receive the support they need to be successful learners.

What Is a Multi-Tiered System of Supports?

A multi-tiered system of supports (MTSS) is a systematic framework for allocating instructional services and resources to support all children—from children who struggle to above-level learners.

Successful MTSS frameworks include:

- **Assessment:** Screening, diagnostic, and progress monitoring assessments track children's progress against grade-level expectations.

- **Data-Driven Decision-Making:** Educators base intervention on assessment data and select supports to meet the individual needs of each child.

- **Differentiated Instruction:** Depending on the level of intervention needed, children may review core instruction, receive targeted intervention, or participate in more intensive intervention.

- **Behavioral Supports:** Instruction and support increase engagement, motivate children to succeed, and promote positive behaviors and mindsets.

Using Data to Drive Decision-Making

The first step in developing a multi-tiered system of support is assessment. Different types of assessment can help educators and administrators identify areas in which children need additional support.

- **Screening:** Screen children to assess their academic performance against grade-level standards.

- **Diagnostic:** For children whose initial assessment scores show areas of concern, administer assessments to determine the focus for intervention.

- **Progress Monitoring:** Use ongoing progress monitoring to measure the effectiveness of instruction or intervention.

For more information about intervention assessments, see pages 108–109.

◦ Professional Learning

RESEARCH FOUNDATIONS

❝ *Tier-2 interventions produce meaningful effects on student reading achievement in schools experiencing persistently low reading achievement and across very different school districts.* ❞

— Coyne et al. (2018)

Determining the Appropriate Level of Intervention

Response to Intervention (RtI) is a critical part of the larger MTSS framework. RtI is a multi-level system for maximizing student achievement by using assessment data to help determine the appropriate level of intervention for each child.

RtI organizes intervention into tiers of increasingly intense interventions for children who are not making adequate progress with core instruction or after changes in instruction. The level of interventions is intensified as needed by:

- the amount of instructional time dedicated to intervention
- decreasing group sizes
- appropriately matching materials to children's skill levels
- providing corrective feedback

Three Tiers of Intervention Support

TIER III

Intensive Intervention

- Individualized instruction and pacing
- High-intensity, longer-duration intervention in a small-group, one-to-one, push-in, or pull-out setting

TIER II

Strategic Intervention

- Supplemental curricula for children who need support beyond Tier I
- Explicit, rapid-response, short-term instruction in a small-group setting

TIER I

Core Instruction

- Differentiated support for all students
- Small-group instruction for key grade-level skills

Providing Differentiated Support and Intervention

Choose flexible resources based on children's assessed needs to provide the appropriate level of support.

Guided Reading Groups

Choose books that match children's instructional levels and target specific reading behaviors to reinforce whole-group skills.

- Use the **Guided Reading Benchmark Assessment Kit** to determine children's instructional level for guided reading groups.

- Reinforce or intervene by choosing just-right books from a library of 570 **Leveled Readers** across the spectrum of guided reading levels.

- Select flexible teaching sessions from **Take and Teach Lessons** to deliver scaffolded instruction to guided reading groups.

Reading Skill and Strategy Support

Teach a skill or strategy that children have not yet mastered or connect to the day's whole-group skill with scaffolded support to reinforce learning.

- Reinforce the skill from whole-group Reading Workshop lessons using the **Scaffold and Extend** options in your Teacher's Guide.

- Intervene based on data and reteach grade-level skills or strategies using accessible texts and the Almost There prompts on **Tabletop Minilessons: Reading** or in your Teacher's Guide.

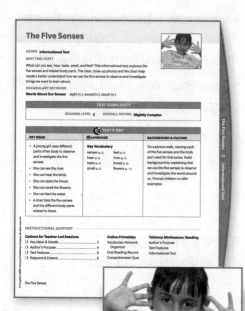

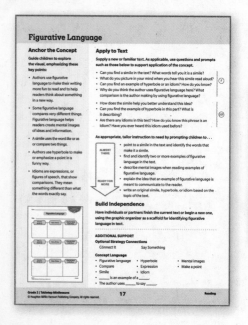

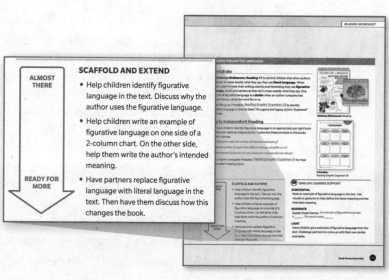

Foundational Skills Support

Teach prerequisite foundational skills or reinforce daily foundational skills lessons during small-group or one-on-one time.

- Use the **Intervention Assessments** to determine which prerequisite foundational skills children need to learn or review.

- Reinforce whole-group foundational skills lessons using the daily small-group reinforcement options in your Teacher's Guide.

- Intervene using the appropriate lessons from the **Foundational Skills and Word Study Studio**.

- Support children whose spelling is below grade-level, using **Differentiating Spelling Instruction: Placement Support and Differentiated Lists**, located in the online Teacher's Guide Additional Resources.

- Implement *iRead* to provide children with personalized and individually paced intervention for learning foundational skills.

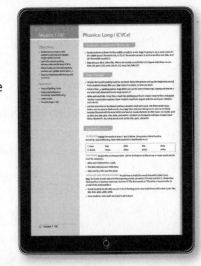

Best Practices: Intervention Support

Follow these best practices to plan and provide differentiated support and intervention.

- **Screen and diagnose.** Screen children at the beginning of the year to identify any areas for which they may need additional support. Then follow up with diagnostic assessments for select children.

- **Assess.** Use frequent and multiple measures to guide instructional decisions and monitor progress throughout the year.

- **Individualize.** Provide individualized support and learning strategies based on the child's needs and most successful learning approaches.

- **Set goals.** Establish goals for children and track progress. Discuss goals with children and their families, and celebrate achievements along the way.

- **Locate resources.** Use *Ed: Your Friend in Learning* to find resources recommended based on children's assessment data. Search for resources by skill or standard.

- **Provide feedback.** Whenever possible, provide children with immediate corrective feedback.

- **Share information.** Connect with other teachers, administrators, and families to build a team of support for each child. Meet regularly to share assessment data and discuss progress.

Using Digital Features for Accessibility

Activate digital features to provide access to program texts to children with impairments to vision, hearing, mobility, or cognition.

Content Accessibility

Features in *Ed: Your Friend in Learning* comply with Web Content Accessibility Guidelines (WCAG) 2.0 AA to meet the needs of diverse learners.

ACCESSIBILITY FEATURE	IMPAIRMENT			
	Visual	Hearing	Cognitive	Mobility
Closed captioning for videos		•	•	
Transcripts for audio	•	•	•	
Contrast and color compliance	•		•	
Screen reader compatibility (keyboard operability) for platform and content	•		•	•
Keyboard encoding for compatibility with many assistive technologies	•	•		
Responsive, reflowable design	•	•	•	•
Pedagogically equivalent alternatives for components and resources	•		•	•

Inclusive Design and Compassionate Innovation

Additional built-in features create an engaging and instructionally effective experience for all children. These features include:

- Read-along audio with synchronized text highlighting
- Tools for student highlighting and note-taking
- Point-of-use glossary entries
- Custom planning features
- Spanish language
- Pedagogical text alternatives
- Curiosity-provoking and engaging text alternatives
- Grade- and level-appropriate text alternatives

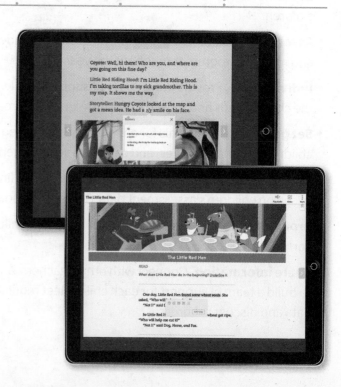

Text Alternatives

The *Into Reading* and *¡Arriba la Lectura!* digital content is built to ensure that children using accessibility features, such as screen readers, have a seamless experience. Built-in text alternatives for images provide experiences for children using screen readers that are comparable to those of their peers.

Informational Texts

Informational texts often include diagrams and other images. In this example from the Grade 4 **myBook,** the screen reader text is enhanced to allow children with visual impairments to access the information.

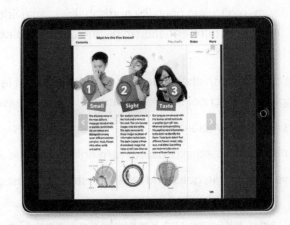

1 In the diagram for "Smell," the accompanying text does not convey the positional relationships, so the text alternative provides information: *In this cross-section of a human head, an aroma is shown entering the nose. Deep inside the nose is the olfactory nerve. Deeper still is a nasal cavity.*

2 The text above the diagram for "Sight" includes the positional information shown in the diagram, so the text alternative is more general: *A diagram of an eyeball showing lens, retina, and optic nerve.*

3 The text in the "Taste" section doesn't describe the positions of the labels in the diagram, so the text alternative provides that information: *This diagram shows areas of the tongue where specific flavors are tasted. Sweet is picked up by the tip of the tongue, salty by the sides in front, sour by the sides in back, and bitter at the very back of the tongue.*

Literature

In literature, illustrations often convey details about the story that aren't in the text. Text alternatives describe these details for children who are unable to see them.

In this example from the Grade 1 **myBook,** the illustration conveys important information about the story setting. The text alternatives describe these details from the illustration:

Tall city apartment buildings crowd together. Below, a taxicab honks. Music plays from an open window, and an air conditioner hums. The people who live in the apartments are talking, eating, and watching television with their windows open. An ice cream shop is open for business.

Assessment and Differentiation

Meeting the Needs of Special Populations

Building understanding of the unique challenges some children face will help you make decisions about how to best support their learning.

Understand and Address Challenges

Many districts use a multi-tiered system of supports, which is designed to ensure timely, targeted interventions for students who struggle. The first requirement for all children, regardless of ability or disability, is an evidence-based, engaging core curriculum, with differentiation in pacing and grouping strategies for those who need more support.

While children with challenges may require different levels of intervention throughout the school day, ensure that *all* children have opportunities to:

- participate in whole-class discussions and projects
- demonstrate standards-based learning via multiple assessment measures
- strive for learning goals and receive instruction based on achievement data

Challenge: Concept Knowledge and Oral Language

Some children have limited concept knowledge or oral language, which may be a result of weak word-reading skills. Children who struggle to read read less and do not reap the knowledge and language growth that come from extensive reading.

INSTRUCTIONAL FOCUS	SUPPORT IN *INTO READING* AND *¡ARRIBA LA LECTURA!*
• Build background knowledge around concepts and content-area topics. • Conduct interactive read alouds and shared reading to involve children in high-quality discussions about texts. • Directly teach academic vocabulary related to a topic or theme. • Encourage children to interact and play with words. • Provide scaffolds, such as sentence frames, to facilitate children's participation in class discussions. • Honor and validate children's home languages, and explicitly teach and model the language of school.	• **Get Curious Videos, Knowledge Maps,** and lessons for building knowledge and language support children as they build knowledge networks for module topics. • Interactive read aloud lessons and **BookStix** include dialogic reading prompts for discussion. • A **VOCABULARY** routine and lessons using **Vocabulary Cards** provide consistent steps to teach and practice using topic-related and academic words from texts. • Generative vocabulary and vocabulary strategy lessons help build word knowledge. • Lessons guide children to practice using topic and academic words in speaking and writing and include sentence frames to support children as they structure oral and written responses. • Social communication and collaborative discussion lessons explicitly teach and guide practice of speaking and listening skills.

Challenge: Dyslexia and Word-Reading Skills

Some children have dyslexia, a specific learning disability that involves difficulties in phonological processing. These difficulties make it hard for children to develop phonemic awareness, or the ability to identify and manipulate the smallest sounds of speech, which makes decoding extremely difficult. A lack of fluent decoding, in turn, generally leads to low levels of academic vocabulary and understanding of language structures because of insufficient exposure to academic texts.

Children who do not have a diagnosed disability may *also* have difficulties with phonological processing and word-level reading, which are the most common impediments to fluent word reading. *Into Reading* and *¡Arriba la Lectura!* include instruction and supports to address challenges children may have with these skills.

INSTRUCTIONAL FOCUS	SUPPORT IN *INTO READING* AND *¡ARRIBA LA LECTURA!*
<ul><li>Provide daily, engaging instruction in phonological awareness.</li><li>Systematically work with children on phoneme segmenting and blending.</li><li>Support children with mouth positions for pronouncing sounds.</li><li>Directly build automatic recognition of high-frequency words.</li><li>Practice new skills and review previously learned ones through daily reading of connected texts.</li><li>Include daily opportunities for small-group instruction and practice to differentiate instruction for the range of student needs in the class.</li></ul>	<ul><li>Daily foundational skills lessons based on children's assessed needs build phonological awareness, including blending and segmenting phonemes.</li><li>**Articulation Videos** and online Printables: Articulation Support provide models and guidance for pronouncing particular sounds.</li><li>A consistent HIGH-FREQUENCY WORDS routine, systematic lessons, varied daily practice, and Literacy Center activities for reading, spelling, and writing high-frequency words reinforce word learning.</li><li>Decodable **Start Right Reader** texts (four per week at Grade 1, two per week at Grade 2) provide practice reading high-frequency words and words with target sound-spellings in context.</li><li>Daily small-group instruction for Foundational Skills and Guided Reading provide options for teaching and practicing various skills in small groups.</li><li>**Foundational Skills and Word Study Studio** provides opportunities for strategic intervention in phonological awareness and phonics based on children's needs.</li><li>*iRead* assesses each child's foundational reading skills and then delivers personalized instruction and practice based on specific needs.</li></ul>

Meeting the Needs of Special Populations

Challenge: Children with Disabilities

You may have children in your class with disabilities that make it challenging for them to fully take part in the curriculum. Supports throughout *Into Reading* and *¡Arriba la Lectura!* allow children with visual, hearing, physical, or cognitive impairments to access the content and participate in learning.

INSTRUCTIONAL FOCUS	SUPPORT IN *INTO READING* AND *¡ARRIBA LA LECTURA!*
• In general, provide multiple options for children to understand, participate, respond, and express themselves.	• The instructional model includes whole-class lessons, small-group instruction, and options for building independence.
• Allow for variations in the pace of lessons and in the length of time spent on a given skill or concept.	• Daily lessons are organized so teachers can adjust pacing and schedules as needed.
• Establish routines and set goals to support children as they build executive function skills.	• Consistent routines and procedures across lessons help children know what to expect.
• Vary options for expressing understanding and ideas: verbal and nonverbal, visual and nonvisual.	• Resources allow children to set and monitor reading and writing goals.
• Limit the amount of sensory stimulation in the classroom.	• Engagement and classroom routines provide options for expression. For example, **WRITE AND REVEAL** and **SILENT SIGNALS** routines allow children to respond and demonstrate understanding nonverbally.
• When available and appropriate, provide children with Braille formats and supports using American Sign Language.	• Suggestions for setting up the classroom include minimizing artificial light and unnecessary visual stimulation.
• Provide features to make all content, including videos and eBook texts, accessible to children with disabilities.	• Printed materials are compliant with NIMAS and can be output in Braille.
	• The digital content on *Ed: Your Friend in Learning* includes WCAG 2.0 AA compliance features, such as closed captioning for videos, contrast and color compliance, responsive and reflowable design, and pedagogically equivalent text alternatives.

See pages 110–111 for more information about accessibility features available online.

Challenge: Engagement in Learning

Children who struggle with reading may cope by not engaging and may appear unmotivated—especially if they perceive there is no possibility of success. All children, without exception, need encouragement and validation to become successful, lifelong learners. *Into Reading* and *¡Arriba la Lectura!* include content and instruction that strive to engage and nurture the whole child in learning.

INSTRUCTIONAL FOCUS	SUPPORT IN *INTO READING* AND *¡ARRIBA LA LECTURA!*
• Consider the whole child and infuse teaching with social-emotional learning that is critical for young children's development. • Ensure that children participate in whole-class and small-group instruction. • Actively engage children through interactive reading and writing strategies. • Explore topics and provide texts that are suited to children's skill levels and interests. • Provide clear and specific feedback. • Guide children to set goals. • Promote choice to build autonomy, decision-making skills, and independence.	• Lessons make connections to social-emotional learning and include embedded support for fostering growth mindset beliefs. • Engagement routines such as **ECHO READING** and **TURN AND TALK** allow all children opportunities to participate and respond. • Shared reading, dialogic reading, and group projects involve children in actively responding to texts and working together to contribute to shared written texts. • Captivating content and high-quality, grade-appropriate texts seek to strengthen children's skills and ignite a lifelong love of learning. • Foundational Skills and Writing Workshop lessons include model language for conferring with children and giving immediate, targeted feedback. • Children set and monitor their own reading and writing goals. • Literacy Centers provide opportunities for children to make choices about activities, materials, partners, and seating.

● Professional Learning

RESEARCH FOUNDATIONS

❝ *Differentiation addresses the wide range of needs presented by the students, who will have vastly different backgrounds, ways of learning, strengths, and areas in need of intensive support.* ❞

—Hougen (2012)

Meeting the Needs of Accelerated Learners

Provide targeted support to children who are exceeding grade-level expectations to keep them engaged and thriving.

Who Are Accelerated Learners?

Accelerated learners are children whose skills are above grade-level. They may not have been identified as "gifted," but they're clearly ready for accelerated learning experiences, such as more challenging books, opportunities to read to their peers, and leadership roles in group projects.

With heavy emphasis placed on reaching children who are trailing behind their peers, high achievers—or accelerated learners—sometimes sit through day after day of lessons for skills they have already mastered. When accelerated learners are disengaged, they can become restless, act out, and even begin to dislike school, making it critical to provide them with learning opportunities matched to their abilities.

Ready for More

Daily options for differentiation in *Into Reading* and *¡Arriba la Lectura!* provide support for above-level learners who are ready for more, including:

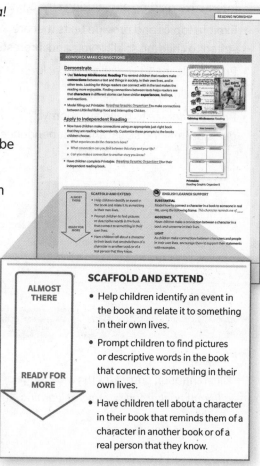

- Teaching support labeled **Ready for More** that extends skill and strategy work during small-group lessons and provides daily opportunities for those children who need a challenge.

- **Rigby Leveled Readers** and **Take and Teach Lessons** that may be used to support Guided Reading Groups.

- **Tabletop Minilessons: Reading** that provide support as children apply comprehension skills to higher-level texts they are reading independently.

- **Differentiated Spelling Instruction: Placement Support and Differentiated Lists** that determine children's stage of spelling development and access to spelling lists appropriate to their level.

- *iRead* adaptive software that adjusts to children's particular learning needs and provides fast-track assessments and individualized pacing.

- **Inquiry and Research Projects** and **Reading Remake** activities in every module that provide enrichment opportunities.

- **Flexible grouping** for foundational skills lessons that provides for children who have mastered skills.

Avoid Assumptions

Carefully consider ways to avoid making incorrect assumptions that could impact accelerated learners in your class.

- Advanced abilities may not cut across all content areas. For example, a child who reads above level may need scaffolding in math or be a reluctant writer.

- Having classroom library books that span the expected range for your grade-level is not enough. Provide a range of texts that mirror the range of reading abilities of the children in your class.

- Assigning more work to accelerated learners, for example, asking them to write more than classmates, will not effectively meet their needs. Instead, provide an alternate, more challenging version of the activity for enrichment.

- Unexpected or challenging behaviors may be a result of an accelerated learner lacking engaging work at the appropriate level.

- Differentiation doesn't have to happen in small groups. While small-group time might be the most obvious setting for supporting accelerated learners, increase engagement and minimize behavioral challenges by looking for opportunities to differentiate for accelerated learners in whole-class settings as well.

Best Practices: Accelerated Learners

Remember these best practices when working with accelerated learners:

- Ensure that children's "advanced" beginning literacy skills continue to progress in all aspects of reading, especially comprehension.

- Use flexible grouping and avoid forming fixed groups for extended periods of time. Children may be above level for particular skills and not others, or be above level at one point in the year but not remain so.

- Provide opportunities for children to make their own decisions whenever possible. Think of ways for accelerated learners to take on leadership roles and assist classmates, when appropriate.

- Provide targeted feedback to accelerated learners based on their learning goals—just as you do with their peers.

⊸● Professional Learning

BEST PRACTICES

❝ *Teachers must observe and note the progress of students to know how to adjust instruction to keep the accelerated students engaged and motivated while providing additional support as needed.* ❞

— Hougen (2012)

Building Knowledge Networks

Children build networks of knowledge that help them construct meaning.

What Is a Knowledge Network?

A **knowledge network** is a set of interconnected ideas that work together to build knowledge. As children learn, they build **schema**—that is, they connect new ideas to existing ones and map them onto a web of knowledge, holding them in their memory. Knowledge networks grow and change as children acquire new ideas and information.

Building knowledge is central to reading success. Children are more likely to comprehend what they are reading when the topic is part of their existing schema. Teachers can help children access texts by activating prior knowledge and building background before reading.

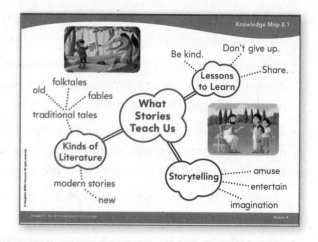

TYPE OF KNOWLEDGE	DEFINITION	EXAMPLE *from* Grade 1, Module 8: Tell Me a Story
		Essential Question: *What lessons can we learn from stories?*
Prior Knowledge	What children *already know* from prior academic, personal, or cultural experiences	Personal experience of being read to, reading, watching dramatic performances, or listening to stories; information learned from prior school experience, books, and media
Background Knowledge	What children *need to know* in order to access a topic or concept	Explicit instruction about story structure and elements common to traditional tales and other types of fiction

● Professional Learning

RESEARCH FOUNDATIONS

❝ *We must recognize that knowledge is not just accumulating facts; rather, children need to develop knowledge networks, comprised of clusters of concepts that are coherent, generative, and supportive of future learning in a domain.* ❞

—Neuman, Kaefer & Pinkham (2014)

Building Knowledge in *Into Reading* and *¡Arriba la Lectura!*

Use the Introduce the Topic lessons to build knowledge for each module topic.

- **Access prior knowledge.** At the beginning of each module, use the Introduce the Topic lesson to assess prior knowledge. Use the prompts in the Teacher's Guide to discuss the topic.

- **Build background.** Discuss the quotation and Essential Question, and have children view and discuss the **Get Curious Video** to build knowledge about the topic. Use the **ACTIVE VIEWING** routine to analyze and discuss the video. Use the **VOCABULARY** routine and **Vocabulary Cards** to introduce the module **Big Idea Words**.

- **Teach.** Use module texts, videos, and vocabulary to teach key aspects of the topic.

- **Make connections.** Throughout the module, use **Display and Engage: Knowledge Map** to review and connect the topic knowledge children are building.

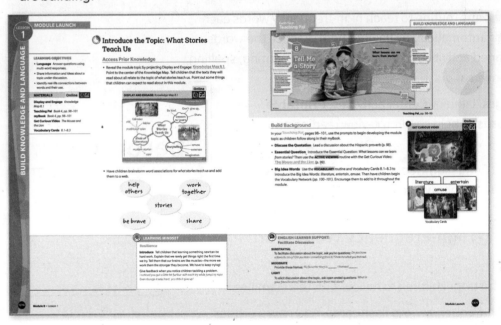

Best Practices: Building Knowledge

Consider these best practices for building knowledge.

- **Assess.** Before introducing a topic, ask children what they know about it.

- **Front-load vocabulary.** This is especially important for English learners and others who may not have the language to comprehend topic-based texts or discussions.

- **Make it visual.** Use a knowledge map, such as **Display and Engage: Knowledge Map**, to help children visualize how ideas are connected.

High-Frequency Words

Build children's vocabulary and reading fluency by helping them master reading and spelling high-frequency words with automaticity.

What Are High-Frequency Words?

High-frequency words are the most commonly used words in printed text. Children should memorize these words and recognize them by sight to build reading fluency. Because of their high utility, children benefit from knowing these words well.

- The high-frequency words taught in *Into Reading* were compiled from the following well-known sources:
  - » *Dolch Basic Sight Vocabulary* (Buckingham and Dolch, 1936)
  - » *1,000 Instant Words* (Fry, 2004)
  - » *The Educator's Word Frequency Guide Grade 1* (Zeno et al., 1995)
  - » *Eeds Word List*

- Use the **HIGH-FREQUENCY WORDS** routine to teach high-frequency words each week. Then build children's automaticity by having them practice the words throughout the week in varied activities that focus on reading, writing, spelling, and using the words in conversation.

- Use **Know It, Show It** pages, Literacy Center activities, **Printable Resources**, and **Word Cards** to help children review reading and spelling the words.

- Children can practice identifying high-frequency words in context when reading the **Start Right Reader** or *my*Book.

Best Practices: Making High-Frequency Words Part of Every Activity

- Send home printable word lists for children to review with their families.

- Create word rings with high-frequency word flash cards. Add new words as children learn them. Attach word rings to children's backpacks so they can practice reading and spelling the words outside the classroom.

- Display cloze sentences in a pocket chart with blanks for high-frequency words. Work with children to read the sentences and complete the blanks with word cards. For example:
  - » **Where** did you find your shoes?
  - » **When** did you eat lunch?

Phonological Awareness

Build children's phonological awareness skills to familiarize them with the sounds and sound patterns of the English language.

What Is Phonological Awareness?

Phonological awareness is the ability to identify and manipulate units of oral language, such as syllables and individual sounds in words. Developing phonological awareness builds children's understanding of the sound structure of language. Children will apply their understanding of the sounds of language to printed text as they learn how to read and write.

Phonological Awareness in *Into Reading* and *¡Arriba la Lectura!*

Develop children's phonological awareness in a way that is both structured and engaging.

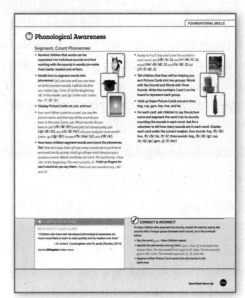

- Engage children to enhance their rhyme recognition skills. Help them produce rhymes using familiar songs, rhymes, and poems.

- Use **Picture Cards** to help children work with sounds without connecting the sounds to letters.

- Cycle through phonological awareness skills—as children develop decoding and encoding skills, they may become more attuned to the sounds in words. This type of spiraling review benefits children who didn't quite "get it" the first time the phonological awareness skill was introduced.

Best Practices: Make Phonological Awareness Fun!

- Pronounce phonemes precisely, being careful not to add sounds that make working with the sounds more difficult. For example, avoid adding a vowel sound after consonant stop sounds: saying "buh" for /b/ or "puh" for /p/.

- Keep activities brief and playful, using a lively and engaging pace. Vary activity types to help maintain children's engagement.

- Incorporate phonological awareness into transitions and activities throughout the day. For example, ask children who are wearing /r/ /ĕ/ /d/ to line up for lunch or call children to activities based on how many syllables are in their names.

Developmental Stages of Word Knowledge

Understand how research and children's word knowledge development have informed the sequence of lessons and skills in *Into Reading*.

How Do Children Develop Word Knowledge?

In *Into Reading*, our phonics/decoding and spelling instruction, from the level of foundational skills through the exploration of Latin and Greek word parts, is based on what we know about the stages of developing word knowledge. After leaving the **Emergent Stage**, there are four stages of word knowledge through which most learners pass in the elementary grades. In Grades 1 and 2, most children will be in the **Letter Name–Alphabetic** or **Within Word Pattern Stage**; a few will be in **Syllables and Affixes**. The table on the facing page shows the types and sequence of spelling features learners explore at each stage. Following are the important learner characteristics for each stage in Grades 1 and 2.

At the **Letter Name–Alphabetic Stage**, learners:

- attend much more closely to print.

- understand that units on the printed page or screen correspond to speech.

- develop a concept of *word in text:* the ability to point to each word accurately as they read lines of memorized text. This concept leads to full *phonemic awareness:* the ability to consciously attend to every consonant and vowel sound within a syllable and an understanding of the alphabetic principle, in which sounds and letters are matched in a left-to-right sequence within the printed word.

- begin to develop a *sight vocabulary*—words that the child recognizes immediately both in text and in isolation.

- read orally "word by word" in a new text, because they are spending so much of their "thinking space" focused on identifying the words on the page.

- write slowly, matching up letters with the sounds they want to represent, while still trying to hold onto the topic of their writing.

At the **Within Word Pattern Stage,** learners:

- dramatically increase their store of sight words.

- explore the range of spelling patterns in single-syllable words.

- apply this knowledge to decoding two-syllable words and words with simple prefixes and suffixes.

- move toward fluency in their reading, increasing their rate and expression, which allows them to comprehend more fluently.

- become more fluent in their writing, encoding words and ideas more rapidly.

- recognize, or *read*, more words correctly than they will be able to *produce*, or *spell*, correctly.

- enhance vocabulary through basic morphology: adding prefixes and suffixes to base words.

At the **Syllables and Affixes Stage**, learners:

- are able to spell most single-syllable words correctly, which allows them to explore multisyllabic words, applying knowledge of syllable division patterns to spelling and reading.

- are able to read on-level texts with appropriate fluency.

- write more fluently and extensively.

- develop vocabulary through morphological exploration; the most frequently-occurring Greek and Latin affixes and roots will be introduced and explored, for example *inter* (between) + *rupt* (break) = "break in between" someone else's words; *bio* ("life") + *logy* ("study of") = *biology*, "study of life."

- recognize, or *read*, more words correctly than they will be able to *produce*, or *spell*, correctly.

STAGE	DEVELOPMENTAL SPELLING	INSTRUCTIONAL FOCUS
Letter Name– Alphabetic Beginning Literacy: K to Grade 2	bed – **bad** ship – **shep** float – **fot** drive – **jriv**	• Beginning and ending single consonants • Short vowels • Consonant digraphs (*sh, th*) • Consonant blends (*bl, dr*)
Within Word Pattern Transitional Literacy: Late Grade 1 to Middle of Grade 4	float – **flote** spoil – **spoyle** table – **tabul** chewed – **chood** smudge – **smuge**	• Common long vowel patterns: vowel-consonant-*e*; vowel teams (*ai, oa,* etc.) • *r*- and *l*-influenced vowels • Three-letter consonant blends (*str, scr*) • Common spelling for diphthongs /ow/, /oi/ • Complex consonants: final sound of /k/, /ch/, /j/ • Compound words • Homophones: *sail/sale, beat/beet*
Syllables and Affixes: Intermediate Literacy: Grades 2 to 6	shopping – **shoping** capture – **capchure** serving – **surving** middle – **middel** fortunate – **forchinet**	• Base words + inflectional endings: *-ed, -ing; -s, -es* • Base words + common prefixes and suffixes • Syllable patterns: VCCV *bas/ket rab/bit;* VCV open: *hu/man;* VCV closed: *cab/in* • Less-frequent vowel patterns • Changing final *y* to *i* • Patterns in unaccented syllables • 2-syllable homophones and homographs: *peddle/ pedal, dual/duel; PRESent/present, REcord/reCORD*
Derivational Relationships Skilled/Proficient Literacy: Grades 5 and Up	opposition – **opisition** emphasize – **emphesize** conference – **confrence** commotion – **comotion** feasible – **feasable**	• Spelling/Meaning Relationships: *sign music ignite reside mental* *signature musician ignition resident mentality* • More advanced exploration of prefixes, suffixes, and Latin and Greek roots • "Absorbed" Prefixes: *in-* + *mobile* = **im**mobile

◯ *Professional Learning*

RESEARCH FOUNDATIONS

Children's understanding about how written words "work"—their spelling and how this spelling represents the sounds and meanings of language—is the foundation for reading and writing. This foundation supports children's fluency in word recognition and in writing, and its construction follows a developmental path that can be described in terms of stages of word knowledge.

— Templeton (2011); Templeton & Bear (2018)

Templeton, S. (2011). Teaching spelling in the English/language arts classroom. In Lapp, D., & Fisher, D. (Eds.), *Handbook of Research on Teaching the English Language Arts* (3rd ed.) (pp. 247-251). IRA/NCTE: Erlbaum/Taylor Francis.

Templeton, S., & Bear, D. R. (2018). Word study, research to practice: spelling, phonics, meaning. In D. Lapp & D. Fisher (Eds.), *Handbook of Research on Teaching the English Language Arts* (4th ed.) (pp. 207-232). New York: Routledge/Taylor & Francis.

Phonics and Decoding

Teach children to connect spoken sounds to written letters, and use that knowledge to decode words accurately and fluently.

¡Arriba la Lectura! cuenta con todo esto y más. En la sección ¡Viva el español! verá lo que distingue a este programa.

What Is Decoding?

Decoding is connecting word spellings to their pronunciations. It is the process of translating letters (graphemes) into sounds (phonemes) and then blending the sounds to read words.

Sounds and Letters

In English, there is not always a simple one-to-one correspondence between letters and sounds.

Consonants:

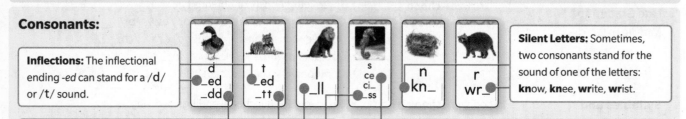

Inflections: The inflectional ending -ed can stand for a /d/ or /t/ sound.

d
_ed
_dd

t
_ed
_tt

l
_ll

s
ce
ci_
_ss

n
kn_

r
wr_

Silent Letters: Sometimes, two consonants stand for the sound of one of the letters: **kn**ow, **kn**ee, **wr**ite, **wr**ist.

Double Consonant (doublet): Two of the same letters stand for one sound: pu**ff**, fi**ll**, ki**ss**, bu**zz**.

Soft c /s/ and **Soft g** /j/: The letters c and g can stand for a soft sound when followed by e, i, or y: i**c**e, ca**g**e, e**dg**e.

Consonant Digraphs/Trigraphs: Two or three consonants together can stand for one sound.

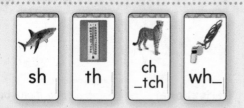

sh
th
ch
_tch
wh_

Short Vowels:

a
e
_ea
i
o
u

Long Vowels:

Vowel-Consonant-e (VCe or silent e): A vowel followed by a consonant and a silent e that stand for a long vowel sound: w**a**v**e**, b**i**k**e**, b**o**n**e**, c**u**b**e**.

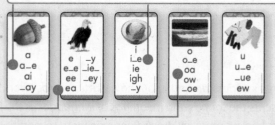

a
a_e
ai
_ay

e
e_e
ee
ea
_y
_ie_
_ey

i
i_e
ie
igh
_y

o
o_e
oa
ow
_oe

u
u_e
_ue
ew

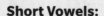

Vowel Digraph (vowel team): Two vowels that stand for a vowel sound: **ea**ch, qu**ee**n, h**ea**d, sn**ow**, g**oa**l.

r-Controlled Vowels:

or
ore

ar

eer
ear

ir
er
ur

Other Vowel Sounds:

_oy
oi

aw
au
al
all

oo

ow
ou

_le

Consonant + le: A syllable type in which the letters le stand for the sounds /əl/, or schwa + /l/.

Phonics in *Into Reading* and *¡Arriba la Lectura!*

Build children's skills to master the phonics focus each week.

- Early in Grade 1, use the **SOUND-BY-SOUND BLENDING** routine to help children connect letters to sounds and blend letter-sounds to read words. In late Grade 1 and in Grade 2, use the **CONTINUOUS BLENDING** routine to help children blend and read words. Then introduce more complex routines for syllabication.

- Practice blending words in isolation using **Display and Engage: Blend and Read** resources, so many children can participate at one time.

- Help children practice reading words with new phonic elements using the week's decodable texts in **Start Right Readers**.

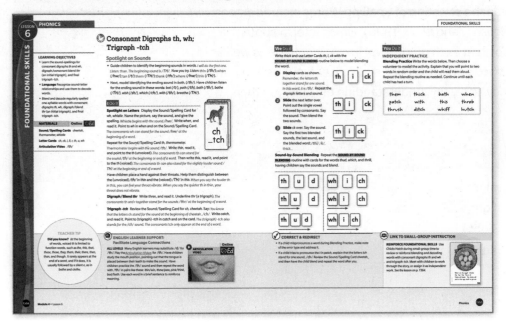

Best Practices: Steps for Teaching Phonics Lessons

- **Develop Phonemic Awareness:** Begin with a quick warm-up activity to focus children on the target skill, using the Spotlight on Sounds in phonics lessons.

- **Connect Sound to Spelling:** Teach the target sound-spelling and give examples in word context.

- **Decode Words:** Provide explicit instruction and practice blending sounds to read words with target phonic elements.

- **Work with Words:** Build transfer of skill knowledge with blending practice for additional words with a target element.

- **Read Decodable Text:** Children practice reading words with target elements and new high-frequency words using **Start Right Reader** texts. Send children home with copies of **Start Right Reader Printable Resources** so they can practice reading the texts with their families.

Spelling and Handwriting

Teach children to connect spoken sounds to written letters, and use that knowledge to encode words accurately and fluently.

¡Arriba la Lectura! cuenta con todo esto y más. En la sección ¡Viva el español! verá lo que distingue a este programa.

Spelling

Just as **decoding** is the process of translating letters (graphemes) into sounds (phonemes) and then blending them to read words, **spelling,** or **encoding,** is the reciprocal process of segmenting words into sounds and representing those sounds (phonemes) with written letters (graphemes).

Because of the reciprocal nature of decoding and encoding, each week's Spelling Words are often related to the phonics being taught. The research-based resources drawn upon to guide the selection of Spelling Words include extensive word frequency counts of English (Zeno et al., 1996), which inform about the most frequently occurring words at each grade level in oral language as well as in print. Through **interactive word sorting,** children discover features and patterns in the Spelling Words, and they apply this understanding efficiently in their reading and writing.

by	light	pie
dry	night	tie
fly	fight	lie
my	sight	
sky	tight	
try		

Handwriting

When children can form letters quickly and easily, the quality and quantity of their writing improves. Instruction for proper grip and paper position for right-handed and left-handed writers as well as legible letter formation and practice lead to children's handwriting development.

● Professional Learning

RESEARCH FOUNDATIONS

❝ *Handwriting is not merely a mechanical, motor skill, but rather a brain-based skill that facilitates meaning-making as writers externalize their cognitions through letter forms, the building blocks of written words and text.* ❞

—Richards et al. (2011)

Spelling and Handwriting in *Into Reading* and *¡Arriba la Lectura!*

Build children's skills to master the spelling focus each week. The letters for the Handwriting focus each week are drawn from the week's Spelling Words.

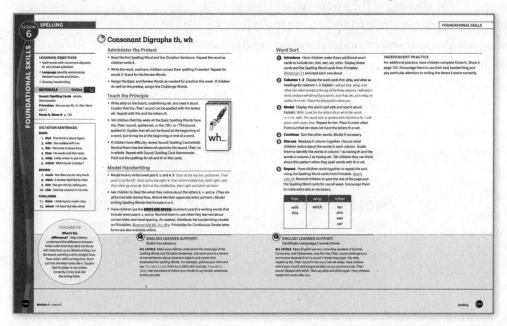

Best Practices: Spelling and Handwriting

- **Administer the Pretest:** Gauge children's knowledge of a week's spelling principle and assign Basic, Review, or Challenge Spelling Words accordingly.

- **Teach the Principle:** Teach the principle using Spelling Words as examples. Use **Sound/Spelling Cards**, **Picture Cards**, or **Letter Cards** to support children who struggle.

- **Model Handwriting:** Provide explicit instruction and have children practice using the **WRITE AND REVEAL** routine. **Handwriting Practice Printable Resources** are available for Manuscript, Continuous Stroke, and Cursive.

- **Word Sort:** Draw attention to spelling patterns by sorting Spelling Words by sound-spelling and then comparing and contrasting the words in each category. Have children practice using **Know It, Show It** pages.

- **Administer the Spelling Assessment:** Along with assessing the week's Spelling Words, use the Surprise Words each week to assess children's ability to apply the spelling principle to words they did not study and go beyond the memorization of specific words.

- **Reinforce in Small Group:** See the Make Minutes Count suggestions for Spelling and Handwriting to reinforce concepts or provide additional practice.

- **Differentiate Instruction:** Support children who are below- or above-level, using **Differentiating Spelling Instruction: Placement Support and Differentiated Lists**, located in the online Teacher's Guide Additional Resources.

Developing Oral Language and Vocabulary

What Are the Building Blocks of Language?

Language is a symbol system of rule-governed combinations of sounds, words, and sentences that create meaning. **Vocabulary** is the knowledge of words and their meanings—a building block of language. Understanding meaning is more than knowing a word's definition—it also requires an understanding of how the word is constructed and how it functions in relation to other words.

Knowing a Word

To recognize a word in context and use it flexibly, children use what they know about phonology, orthography, morphology, semantics, and syntax.

PHONOLOGY

Understanding the **sounds and pronunciations** of words.

MORPHOLOGY

Using morphemes, or **meaningful word parts** such as base words, prefixes, and suffixes, to understand words.

ORTHOGRAPHY

Understanding the **spelling** of words.

SEMANTICS

Understanding word **meaning** and how it's conveyed by the relationships between words, such as:

- synonyms and antonyms (*fast, quick/slow, fast*)
- shades of meaning (*jog, run, sprint*)
- multiple-meaning words (*bat, ring, wave*)

SYNTAX (grammar)

Understanding the **function** of words and how they relate to each other in a sentence by analyzing:

- the context in which a word is used. Some words only have meaning in sentence context (*and, the, of*)
- the word forms: base words with different suffixes (*walk/walked, hope/hopeful*)
- the word order

● *Professional Learning*

RESEARCH FOUNDATIONS

❝ *Children learn best when words are presented in integrated contexts that make sense to them. A set of words connected to a category such as 'energy' can help children remember not only the words themselves but the linkages in meaning between them.* ❞

— Neuman & Wright (2014)

Vocabulary in *Into Reading* and *¡Arriba la Lectura!*

There are two primary ways children develop oral language and vocabulary skills in the program.

Academic Word Instruction

Children learn general academic and domain-specific words using a consistent **VOCABULARY** routine and **Vocabulary Cards**. Instruction focuses on how to pronounce each word, understand its meaning, and use it in context.

Word-Learning Strategies

Vocabulary Strategy and **Generative Vocabulary** lessons allow children to see connections between words, deepen their understanding, and provide them with a growing bank of tools to help them unlock the meanings of unknown words.

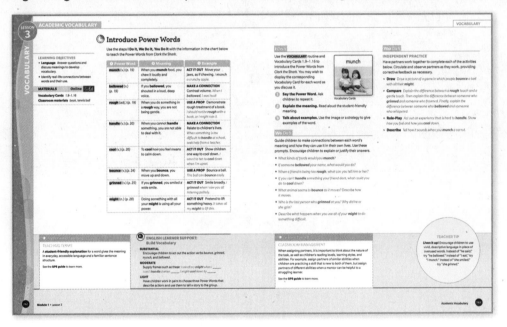

Best Practices: Oral Language and Vocabulary

Create a classroom environment rich in language and vocabulary.

- **Directly teach words.** Focus on sophisticated words that appear in a variety of texts and across content areas, using a consistent routine.

- **Address language differences.** Directly teach the language of school and make direct comparisons between "school language" and "home language."

- **Share words in context.** Provide repeated exposures to words. Find ways for the words to "crop up" throughout the year, to provide repeated exposure to them over time, and take note when children use the words.

- **Provide references.** Include print and digital dictionaries, glossaries, and thesauruses in the classroom to support children's word learning.

Engaging Children in Discussion

Carefully planned instruction can expand children's listening, speaking, and discussion skills across a variety of contexts.

What Are the Aspects of a Conversation?

Listening and speaking in different contexts means children can transition from informal to formal language situations. Children learn intentional listening and speaking skills through direct instruction and purposeful opportunities to hear language modeled in a variety of language situations.

CONTEXT
- *Is the setting formal (in school) or informal (on the playground)?*
- *What language should I use?*

CONTENT
- *What is the conversation about?*
- *What vocabulary do I need to know?*

CUES
- *What social norms are expected? (eye contact, turning toward the speaker)*
- *Am I listening actively?*
- *Are we taking turns?*

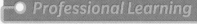

Professional Learning

RESEARCH FOUNDATIONS

❝ *[E]arly in the year when you set up class procedures, set up speaking procedures: "This is how we turn in papers; this is how we keep the assignment book; this is how we use hall passes; this is how we speak."...Make it known early in the year that speaking matters, and teach students all that is involved in even less formal public speaking.* ❞

— Palmer (2011)

Discussions Skills in *Into Reading* and *¡Arriba la Lectura!*

Discussion skills are developed through instruction for key listening and speaking skills. As children become more confident, they engage in deeper, more meaningful conversations, with many opportunities to practice. Discussion skills are classified as:

Social Communication

Early in the year, children practice listening and speaking skills for:

- greetings and introductions, initiating conversations
- following directions, asking for help
- practicing turn taking, active listening, making eye contact, and speaking audibly
- distinguishing between formal and informal language

Collaborative Conversations

Throughout the year, children collaborate to:

- speak with with partners
- respond to questions or prompts using complete sentences
- use formal and informal language
- practice intonation, phrasing, and speaking clearly
- extend conversations by adding details, using multiple exchanges, and practicing staying on topic

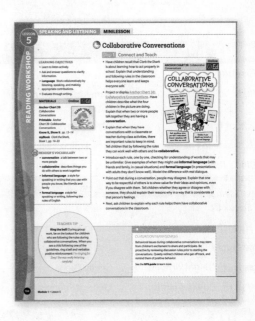

Best Practices: Collaborative Conversations

Help children build and strengthen their listening, speaking, and discussion skills.

- **Model new skills.** Have volunteers model the interaction with you; then have children practice with partners. Share examples and non-examples of appropriate tone, voice level, and body language.

- **Practice.** Encourage children to use skills across domains and settings. Remind children to use formal language when speaking with partners or in groups.

- **Make it routine.** Use discussion routines, such as **THINK-PAIR-SHARE** and **TURN AND TALK**, to structure conversations between partners.

- **Model appropriate body language.** Model appropriate body language during conversations. Remind children to make eye contact, face one another, and to listen with their whole bodies.

- **Be sensitive to cultural differences**. Social norms are not common to all cultures. For example, in some cultures it's a sign of disrespect for children to look an adult in the eye. Others may find it inappropriate to shake hands.

Leveraging Text Complexity

Use this table as a reference for the text complexity measures and build for the Grade 1 **myBook** texts.

Grade 1 *myBook*

TITLE	AUTHOR	GENRE	LEXILE	GR LEVEL	QUALITATIVE MEASURE
MODULE 1					
My First Day		Realistic Fiction	150L	E	Simple
Try This!	Pam Muñoz Ryan	Narrative Nonfiction	60L	D	Simple
My School Trip	Aly G. Mays	Realistic Fiction	140L	E	Simple
A Kids' Guide to Friends	Trey Amico	Informational Text	230L	F	Slightly Complex
Big Dilly's Tale	Gail Carson Levine	Fairy Tale	360L	F	Moderately Complex
MODULE 2					
Kids Speak Up		Opinion Writing	210L	D	Slightly Complex
Dan Had a Plan	Wong Herbert Yee	Realistic Fiction	250L	E	Slightly Complex
On the Map!	Lisa Fleming	Informational Text	240L	C	Simple
Places in My Neighborhood	Shelly Lyons	Informational Text	IG470L	I	Moderately Complex
Who Put the Cookies in the Cookie Jar?	George Shannon	Informational Text	420L	G	Moderately Complex
MODULE 3					
Animal Q & A		Informational Text	310L	E	Slightly Complex
The Nest	Carole Roberts	Realistic Fiction	260L	F	Slightly Complex
Blue Bird and Coyote	James Bruchac	Folktale	310L	F	Slightly Complex
Have You Heard the Nesting Bird?	Rita Gray	Narrative Nonfiction	AD430L	G	Moderately Complex
Step-by-Step Advice from the Animal Kingdom	Steve Jenkins and Robin Page	Procedural Text	480L	H	Moderately Complex
MODULE 4					
Good Sports		Opinion Writing	380L	G	Slightly Complex
Goal!	Jane Medina	Informational Text	480L	H	Moderately Complex
Get Up and Go!	Rozanne Lanczak Williams	Informational Text	370L	F	Slightly Complex
A Big Guy Took My Ball!	Mo Willems	Fantasy	AD270L	G	Slightly Complex
If You Plant a Seed	Kadir Nelson	Fantasy	AD340L	G	Moderately Complex
MODULE 5					
Super Shadows!		Informational Text	290L	G	Slightly Complex
Blackout	John Rocco	Realistic Fiction	330L	I	Moderately Complex
Day and Night	Margaret Hall	Informational Text	390L	J	Slightly Complex
The Best Season	Nina Crews	Opinion Writing	400L	I	Slightly Complex
Waiting Is Not Easy!	Mo Willems	Fantasy	250L	G	Simple

TITLE	AUTHOR	GENRE	LEXILE	GR LEVEL	QUALITATIVE MEASURE
MODULE 6					
State the Facts!		Informational Text	360L	H	Simple
Monument City	Jerdine Nolen	Drama	NP	L	Moderately Complex
The Contest	Libby Martinez	Opinion Writing	490L	J	Moderately Complex
The Statue of Liberty	Tyler Monroe	Informational Text	550L	N	Very Complex
Hooray for Holidays!	Pat Cummings	Realistic Fiction	450L	K	Slightly Complex
Patriotic Poems	various poets	Poetry	NP	K	Moderately Complex
MODULE 7					
Storm Report		Opinion Writing	430L	I	Moderately Complex
Sam & Dave Dig a Hole	Mac Barnett	Fantasy	450L	L	Moderately Complex
Deserts	Quinn M. Arnold	Informational Text	300L	H	Slightly Complex
Handmade	Guadalupe Rodríguez	Procedural Text	470L	K	Moderately Complex
Grand Canyon	Sara Gilbert	Informational Text	480L	H	Moderately Complex
MODULE 8					
Follow the Story Path		Informational Text	490L	H	Slightly Complex
Interrupting Chicken	David Ezra Stein	Fantasy	AD510L	L	Very Complex
Little Red Riding Hood	Lisa Campbell Ernst	Drama	NP	K	Moderately Complex
The Grasshopper & the Ants	Jerry Pinkney	Fable	470L	K	Moderately Complex
Thank You, Mr. Aesop	Helen Lester	Informational Text	520L	M	Very Complex
MODULE 9					
Plant Pairs		Poetry	NP	K	Very Complex
So You Want to Grow a Taco?	Bridget Heos	Procedural Text	510L	L	Moderately Complex
Which Part Do We Eat?	Katherine Ayres	Poetry	NP	K	Slightly Complex
The Talking Vegetables	Won-Ldy Paye and Margaret H. Lippert	Folktale	550L	K	Very Complex
Yum! ¡MmMm! ¡Qué rico!	Pat Mora	Poetry	NP	L	Moderately Complex
MODULE 10					
Kids Are Inventors, Too!		Informational Text	490L	J	Slightly Complex
Young Frank Architect	Frank Viva	Realistic Fiction	500L	K	Moderately Complex
Sky Color	Peter H. Reynolds	Realistic Fiction	AD550L	K	Very Complex
We Are the Future	various poets	Poetry	NP	J	Moderately Complex
Joaquín's Zoo	Pablo Bernasconi	Fantasy	580L	K	Very Complex

CONTENT CONNECTIONS | Science Connections | Social Studies Connections

Leveraging Text Complexity

Use this table as a reference for the text complexity measures and build for the Grade 2 **myBook** texts.

Grade 2 *myBook*

TITLE	AUTHOR	GENRE	LEXILE	GR LEVEL	QUALITATIVE MEASURE
MODULE 1					
We Are Super Citizens		Personal Narrative	530L	K	Slightly Complex
Clark the Shark	Bruce Hale	Fantasy	500L	M	Slightly Complex
Spoon	Amy Krouse Rosenthal	Fantasy	520L	K	Slightly Complex
Being a Good Citizen	Rachelle Kreisman	Informational Text	530L	N	Moderately Complex
Picture Day Perfection	Deborah Diesen	Realistic Fiction	570L	M	Moderately Complex
MODULE 2					
What's the Matter?		Informational Text	440L	L	Moderately Complex
Many Kinds of Matter	Jennifer Boothroyd	Informational Text	530L	M	Moderately Complex
The Great Fuzz Frenzy	Janet Stevens and Susan Stevens Crummel	Fantasy	420L	K	Slightly Complex
Water Rolls, Water Rises	Pat Mora	Poetry	NP	P	Moderately Complex
The Puddle Puzzle	Ellen Weiss	Drama	NP	L	Slightly Complex
Looking at Art	Andrew Stevens	Fine Art	630L	M	Moderately Complex
MODULE 3					
Meet Me Halfway		Informational Text	450L	K	Very Complex
Big Red Lollipop	Rukhsana Khan	Realistic Fiction	490L	M	Moderately Complex
Working with Others	Robin Nelson	Informational Text	490L	L	Slightly Complex
Gingerbread for Liberty!	Mara Rockliff	Biography	590L	M	Moderately Complex
Pepita and the Bully	Ofelia Dumas Lachtman	Realistic Fiction	530L	L	Slightly Complex
Be a Hero! Work It Out!	Ruben Cooley	Infographic	530L	L	Moderately Complex
MODULE 4					
Recipe for a Fairy Tale		Recipe	490L	K	Moderately Complex
How to Read a Story	Kate Messner	Informational Text	480L	L	Slightly Complex
A Crow, a Lion, and a Mouse! Oh, My!	Crystal Hubbard	Drama	NP	K	Moderately Complex
Hollywood Chicken	Lisa Fleming	Fantasy	600L	L	Very Complex
If the Shoe Fits: Two Cinderella Stories	Pleasant DeSpain	Fairy Tale	580L	M	Moderately Complex
MODULE 5					
What's Good to Read? Book Reviews for Kids by Kids!		Opinion Article	690L	L	Moderately Complex
Going Places	Peter and Paul Reynolds	Fantasy	480L	M	Moderately Complex
Wilma Rudolph: Against All Odds	Stephanie E. Macceca	Biography	570L	N	Moderately Complex
Great Leaders		Opinion Writing	520L	N	Moderately Complex
Who Are Government's Leaders?	Jennifer Boothroyd	Informational Text	580L	L	Moderately Complex

TITLE	AUTHOR	GENRE	LEXILE	GR LEVEL	QUALITATIVE MEASURE
MODULE 6					
Weather Through the Seasons		Informational Text	500L	L	Very Complex
Wild Weather	Thomas Kingsley Troupe	Narrative Nonfiction	590L	O	Very Complex
Cloudette	Tom Lichtenheld	Fantasy	590L	K	Moderately Complex
Get Ready for Weather	Lucy Jones	Informational Text	580L	L	Moderately Complex
Whatever the Weather	various poets	Poetry	NP	K	Moderately Complex
MODULE 7					
Get to Know Biographies		Opinion Essay	560L	L	Moderately Complex
I Am Helen Keller	Brad Meltzer	Biography	560L	O	Very Complex
How to Make a Timeline	Boyd N. Gillin	Procedural Text	530L	L	Moderately Complex
The Stories He Tells	James Bruchac	Biography	700L	M	Moderately Complex
Drum Dream Girl	Margarita Engle	Poetry	NP	L	Very Complex
MODULE 8					
The Growth of a Sunflower		Photo Essay	490L	J	Moderately Complex
Experiment with What a Plant Needs to Grow	Nadia Higgins	Informational Text	570L	M	Moderately Complex
Jack and the Beanstalk	Helen Lester	Fairy Tale	550L	M	Moderately Complex
Jackie and the Beanstalk	Lori Mortensen	Fairy Tale	660L	M	Very Complex
Don't Touch Me!	Elizabeth Preston	Informational Text	600L	M	Moderately Complex
MODULE 9					
The Best Habitat for Me		Opinion Essay	620L	L	Moderately Complex
The Long, Long Journey	Sandra Markle	Informational Text	610L	M	Very Complex
Sea Otter Pups	Ruth Owen	Informational Text	600L	I	Moderately Complex
At Home in the Wild	various poets	Poetry	NP	L	Moderately Complex
Abuelo and the Three Bears	Jerry Tello	Folktale	460L	L	Moderately Complex
MODULE 10					
Hello, World!		Informational Text	540L	M	Moderately Complex
Where on Earth Is My Bagel?	Frances and Ginger Park	Realistic Fiction	590L	L	Moderately Complex
May Day Around the World	Tori Telfer	Narrative Nonfiction	600L	L	Moderately Complex
Goal!	Sean Taylor	Informational Text	620L	M	Moderately Complex
Poems in the Attic	Nikki Grimes	Poetry	NP	N	Very Complex

CONTENT CONNECTIONS ▌ Science Connections ▌ Social Studies Connections

Teaching with Text Sets

Help children build and deepen their knowledge of specific topics through reading and discussion based on multi-genre text sets.

What Are Text Sets?

Text sets are collections of texts focused on a specific topic. When children read multiple texts on a topic, their understanding of that topic deepens, and they can use knowledge gained from reading one text to help them understand the next one, further building their topic knowledge and vocabulary. Text sets:

- are effective in building knowledge and vocabulary and as preparation for reading new texts about the same topic

- provide background knowledge that allows readers to make inferences, which aids comprehension and memory

- provide an avenue to focus study on ideas larger than the content of a single book; readers begin to think more critically and analytically because they have read multiple texts about a topic

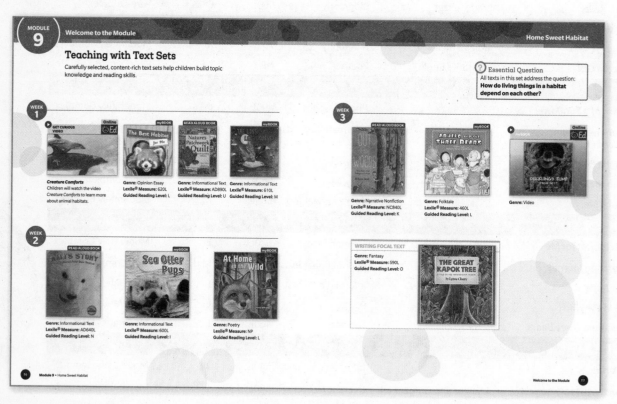

Teaching with Text Sets in *Into Reading* and *¡Arriba la Lectura!*

Each module in *Into Reading* and *¡Arriba la Lectura!* consists of a curated multi-genre collection of texts around a single topic. The texts for each module are arranged to contribute to children's content knowledge and knowledge of genres through these elements:

- a **Get Curious** video to spark interest in the topic

- an Essential Question that all the module texts address, which inspires inquiry and sets a purpose for reading

- a Short Read text to build and activate background knowledge around the topic

- read aloud texts for modeling fluent reading and promoting listening comprehension

- interaction with complex texts using annotation, note-taking, and marking text evidence in texts in the **myBook**

- a trade book to use as a model for Writing Workshop lessons

Best Practices: Teaching with Text Sets

- **Establish a purpose.** Use the Essential Question to guide children's work through the text set. Give children a purpose for reading each of the texts, for example, to note what details an author includes or the way an author organizes information in a text.

- **Note similarities and differences between texts.** Help children notice the ways a topic is presented by different authors and how the details in one text contribute to children's understanding of another text and of the overall topic.

- **Model making connections.** Support children as they begin reading and thinking across texts. For example, collaborate to build and discuss a Knowledge Map that shows what children have learned about the topic.

- **Facilitate discussions.** Model and provide opportunities for children to practice sharing responses to each text in the module and to discuss multiple texts. Prompt children to add to comments and the observations of others.

Dialogic Reading with Read Alouds

Use dialogic reading and the PEER sequence to engage children in text-based discussion during interactive read alouds.

What Is Dialogic Reading?

Dialogic reading is a research-based technique that creates a dialogue between the reader and the listeners, helping children become active participants in read alouds. A key technique used in dialogic reading is the **PEER** sequence of short interactions:

- **P**rompt children to say something about the book.
- **E**valuate the response.
- **E**xpand on the response by rephrasing and adding to it.
- **R**epeat the prompt to check understanding and give children additional opportunities for using language.

Research shows that dialogic reading and the PEER sequence increase attention, engagement with the text, understanding of plot or key details, and vocabulary. When children actively engage with books, their literacy skills improve along with their motivation to learn to read.

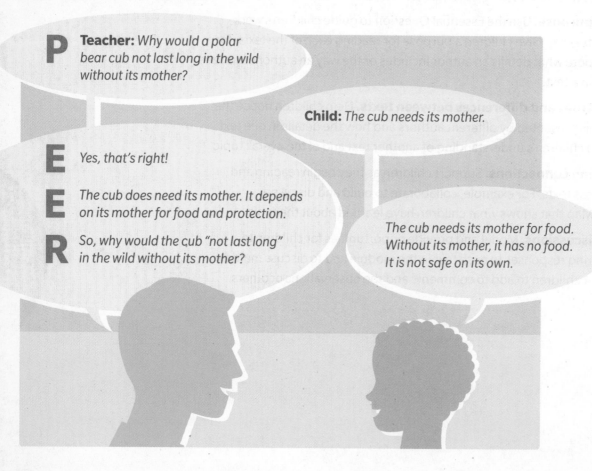

P **Teacher:** *Why would a polar bear cub not last long in the wild without its mother?*

Child: *The cub needs its mother.*

E *Yes, that's right!*

E *The cub does need its mother. It depends on its mother for food and protection.*

R *So, why would the cub "not last long" in the wild without its mother?*

The cub needs its mother for food. Without its mother, it has no food. It is not safe on its own.

Interactive Read Alouds in *Into Reading* and *¡Arriba la Lectura!*

Interactive read-aloud lessons provide a common foundation of experience for children at various levels of reading proficiency. Use **Read Aloud Books** and Grade 1 **Big Books, Anchor Charts,** and the questions and prompts on **BookStix** to encourage collaborative discussion. Read-aloud minilessons provide:

- genre instruction, a powerful tool to help children develop competencies as readers and writers

- focused instruction about a specific topic, literary concept, or skill using the Read Aloud text as the example to demonstrate

- discussion questions and prompts to spark children's thinking and discussion around the text, using literary academic language

- a purpose for reading and listening to the text

- a model of fluent, expressive reading

- engagement and response prompts alternating between spoken and written response types

Best Practices: Reading Aloud

Use the suggestions below to prepare for reading aloud and to engage children in informational and literary texts.

Before Reading

- Read the text and accompanying **BookStix.** Attach the **BookStix** to the back cover of the text.

- Notice words or phrases that might be tricky for your class, and prepare to teach them quickly while reading.

- Think about ways the text connects to other content areas, current events, or relevant activities in the classroom.

During Reading

- When you introduce a book, ask children to talk about the cover and predict what the book will be about.

- Read the text the first time with minimal interruptions. Stop only to briefly define unfamiliar words and at preplanned spots to check for understanding.

- Model fluent reading, using accurate pronunciation and appropriate pacing, rate, intonation, and expression.

Professional Learning

RESEARCH FOUNDATIONS

66 *[B]efore students can read substantive texts on their own, this content will be best conveyed orally. An important vehicle is teacher read-alouds, in which texts...are read aloud to children and followed by discussion and lessons that build children's understanding of the ideas, topics, and words in the story.* 99

— Hirsch (2003)

Shared Reading

Teach comprehension and literary analysis skills in Reading Workshop lessons and develop oral language skills through shared reading.

What Is Shared Reading?

Shared reading is an interactive reading experience in which children join in the reading of a text as guided by a teacher. Children learn and practice comprehension skills and strategies, speaking and listening, and literary analysis and response, using the Reading Workshop model.

Minilessons for a target skill or strategy in the Teacher's Guide set the stage for the day's lesson and provide a focus for the community shared reading experience of *myBook* texts. For the teacher, the **Teaching Pal** contains all the *myBook* texts and color-coded point-of-use questions and prompts to use while reading with children.

> **READ FOR UNDERSTANDING** During a first reading, guide children with questions and prompts to **get the gist** of the text.

> **TARGETED CLOSE READ** During rereading, children **closely analyze** parts of a text to apply skills and show understanding.

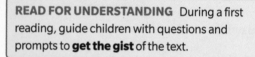

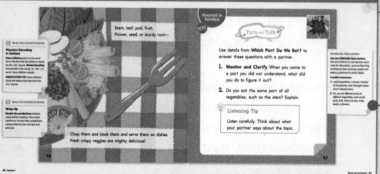

> **Notice ❷ Note** Use these notes to help children think more deeply about texts as they look for Signposts that help them create meaning.

> **Academic Discussion** Yellow notes contain instructional support for pages that precede and follow *myBook* texts.

Shared Reading with Big Books in Grade 1

The Grade 1 **Big Books** used in Week 1 of each module are excellent vehicles for instruction in print concepts, including:

- directionality
- letters, words, and sentences
- capitalization, punctuation, and dialogue

Text Direction
I will start reading at the top left and move across the line. When I get to the end, I move down to the next line.

Concept of a Word
Words are separated by spaces. Count the words on this page.

Turn Pages
Turn pages in a book from right to left.

Concept of a Sentence
Sentences start with a capital letter and end with punctuation. What is the first word in the sentence? What mark is at the end?

Shared Reading in *Into Reading* and *¡Arriba la Lectura!*

Shared reading lessons provide the tools for children to develop as readers, writers, and critical thinkers as they read common topic-related texts together.

- Minilessons before reading provide instruction in skills and strategies using visual **Anchor Charts** that help focus children's thinking and serve as reminders during and after reading.

- Use the **Teaching Pal** for:

  » **First readings.** Blue Read for Understanding notes in the **Teaching Pal** guide children's understanding of the text through think-aloud strategy modeling, text-based questions and annotation tips to promote active reading, phonics and decoding tips, and quick point-of-use explanations of specific words in a text that children may not know but are needed to understand the text.

  » **Strategies for close reading.** Promote deeper thinking about and understanding of texts using Notice & Note supports. Red notes in the Teaching Pal support children as they identify Signposts that frequently appear in texts and use them to create meaning.

  » **Targeted close reading.** During a second reading of specific pages or passages, purple notes identify opportunities for children to apply skills and demonstrate knowledge.

  » **Responding to texts.** Yellow notes provide instructional support for pre- and post-reading pages. These include guidance for academic discussions, writing to sources, and close reading practice pages.

Best Practices: Shared Reading

Use the suggestions below when you read with your class.

- Demonstrate behaviors of fluent and analytical readers, such as reading with expression and modeling think alouds.

- When children respond to questions or share ideas, ask them to support their thinking with evidence from the text.

- Prompt children to listen to and respond to each other. We can all develop fuller understanding when we have the benefit of others' interpretations.

- Use a gradual release model in which you teach a minilesson about a target skill or strategy, guide children to apply it to a common text, and have children practice independently through oral or written response activities.

Close Reading

Build children's reading comprehension and fluency through the close reading of texts.

What Is Close Reading?

Close reading involves the reading and rereading of a text to more deeply understand it. In close reading:

- Readers look at a text and examine what it explicitly says. Using prior knowledge, readers construct meaning based on the words in the text.

- Readers interact with the text to make logical inferences and to note how the text is constructed, or how it works.

- Readers use text evidence to support their conclusions and thoughts about it and come to a deeper understanding of the text's meaning.

Close Reading in *Into Reading* and *¡Arriba la Lectura!*

The write-in student ***myBook*** is designed to help children develop as readers and writers. Guided by the teacher using notes in the **Teaching Pal**, children reread ***myBook*** texts to apply skills and annotate the text to demonstrate their thinking. During rereadings, they look for specific evidence to support their understanding of the text, including:

- text structure and organization
- literary elements
- central idea
- ideas and support
- theme
- point of view
- figurative language and other literary devices

After reading, children turn and talk to a partner to answer questions about the text and use text evidence to respond in writing to prompts in the ***myBook.*** The student ***myBook*** also provides shorter texts for independent close reading practice and skill application.

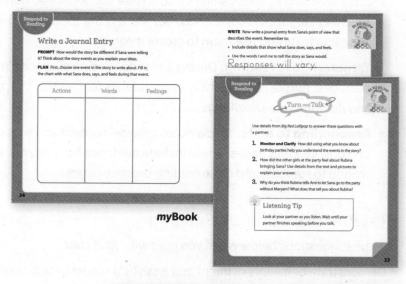

myBook

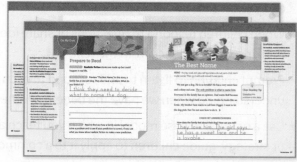

Teaching Pal

Using Notice & Note Signposts

Notice & Note Signposts are designed to help children think about texts in a deeper way. Through introduction of the Signposts in the **Teacher's Guide** and guided support in the **Teaching Pal,** children will come to understand when to stop and question a text, how the language of a text is meant to affect readers, or notice places where something that happens to make them wonder.

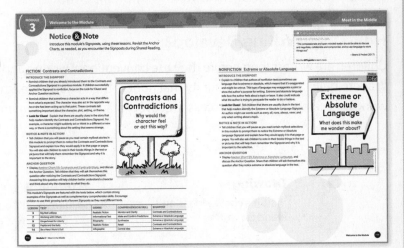

Signposts for works of fiction include:

- **Contrasts and Contradictions:** contrasts between what readers expect will happen and what a character says or does

- **Aha Moments:** moments when characters come to a realization about their situation and that help readers understand character development and internal conflict

- **Tough Questions:** the difficult questions a character asks him- or herself; noticing this signpost helps give insight into the character's internal conflict

- **Words of the Wiser:** the advice or insights that a wiser, usually older, character offers to the main character; these life lessons provide insights into the theme

- **Again and Again:** events, images, or words and phrases that recur often; noticing things that happen again and again helps readers to recognize symbolism, character development, and sometimes also theme

- **Memory Moments:** when a character shares a memory; these moments help readers understand character development or the relationship between the character and the plot

Signposts for nonfiction include:

- **Contrasts and Contradictions:** places where the author shows readers how things, people, or ideas contrast with or contradict one another or with what a reader knows

- **Extreme and Absolute Language:** language that leaves no doubt or seems to exaggerate or overstate a case

- **Numbers and Stats:** language an author uses to show specific quantities or to leave those vague; they can help readers visualize something in the text

- **Quoted Words:** language an author uses to support a point, either by a direct quote from a person or in a summary of what someone has said or written

- **Word Gaps:** vocabulary that is unfamiliar to readers, such as technical language, or discipline-specific or rare words

Establishing a Community of Writers

Build a classroom community in which all children see themselves as writers.

How Does Writing Develop?

Children are writers long before they use conventional writing and spelling. Work to build a writing community that honors their efforts, treasures their work, and celebrates their successes at every stage of development.

Drawing

Pictures convey ideas and stand for writing

Scribbling

Random marks represent ideas

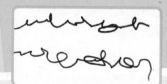

Letter-Like Forms

Shapes imitate or look like letters

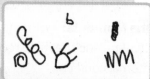

Letters: Initial Consonants

Uses a letter to represent the first sound of words

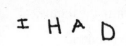

Letter Strings

Random long strings of letters, usually without spaces

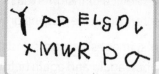

Letters: Initial and Final Consonants

Uses letters to represent the first and last letters of words

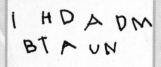

Letters: Vowel Sounds

Uses medial vowel sounds and some known words

I had a drem ubot a unicrn.

Conventional Writing and Spelling

Includes short and long vowel spellings

I had a dream about a unicorn.

● **Professional Learning**

RESEARCH FOUNDATIONS

❝ *Collaboration can increase the sense of community in a classroom, as well as encourage students to become engaged in the writing process with their peers.* ❞

—Graham et al. (2012)

A Classroom Writing Community

Use these various opportunities in *Into Reading* and *¡Arriba la Lectura!* to create a supportive classroom writing community.

- During independent writing time, encourage children to approach each other with questions about their writing using the **ASK THREE, THEN ME** routine (p. 57).

- Confer with children, ask questions, and listen to their responses to offer targeted feedback and build a relationship with each child around their writing.

- Engage children in using peer feedback to learn from other writers by sharing their writing and offering feedback.

- Help give writers a sense of purpose by offering regular opportunities to share writing ideas and drafts with small groups or the class.

- Bring together your community of writers and emphasize the value of writing using the **SHARE CHAIR** routine (p. 161) to celebrate published writing with the class.

Best Practices: Writing Community

Consider these best practices for building your community of writers throughout the year:

- Dedicate time to writing every day.

- Make intentional decisions about how to set up your classroom, including flexible seating for independent writers, areas for peers to collaborate, and a special chair to share writing.

- You know the children in your class best. Personalize your writing community, offer choices, and consider the interests of the writers in your classroom to help build agency and independence.

- Emphasize and model that your classroom is a place where writers can take risks and learn from mistakes.

- Ensure authentic audiences that matter to your children. For example, write an opinion letter and deliver it to the principal, make books to share with a younger class, or display writing in shared community spaces or at the local library.

- A few times a year, consider inviting families to school for special publishing parties where children read their writing and celebrate their efforts.

Reading-Writing Connections

Make frequent connections while teaching to reinforce the reciprocal relationship between reading and writing.

The Reading-Writing Relationship

There is a powerful and reciprocal relationship between reading and writing: students who read more write better, and students who write more read better.

I Can Read!

READING IMPACTS WRITING

- Reading builds background knowledge to use in writing.
- Decoding and sound-spelling knowledge support word writing.
- Reading expands vocabulary and leads to using new words in writing.
- Reading across genres supports writing different text structures.
- Analyzing and discussing texts support organization, voice, and word choice in writing.

WRITING IMPACTS READING

- Writing provides an authentic purpose and audience for reading.
- Sounding out words to write builds phonemic awareness skills and increases decoding fluency.
- Writing in response to reading deepens reading comprehension.
- Sharing writing with peers and reading one's own writing aloud builds reading fluency.

I Can Write!

Writing to Sources

Build strong connections between reading and writing using writing tasks that are embedded throughout *Into Reading* and *¡Arriba la Lectura!*

- Following each main text in *myBook* and in your **Teaching Pal,** have children complete the **Respond to Reading** task. Each task includes a writing prompt, planning space with a **graphic organizer,** and space to write, including reminders to go back into the text to **cite text evidence.**

- Following each On My Own text in *myBook* and in your **Teaching Pal,** have children demonstrate **increasing independence** with writing to sources by responding to the **Write About It** prompt. Children can complete these writing tasks during independent work time. Use the Scaffolded Support notes to guide children, as needed.

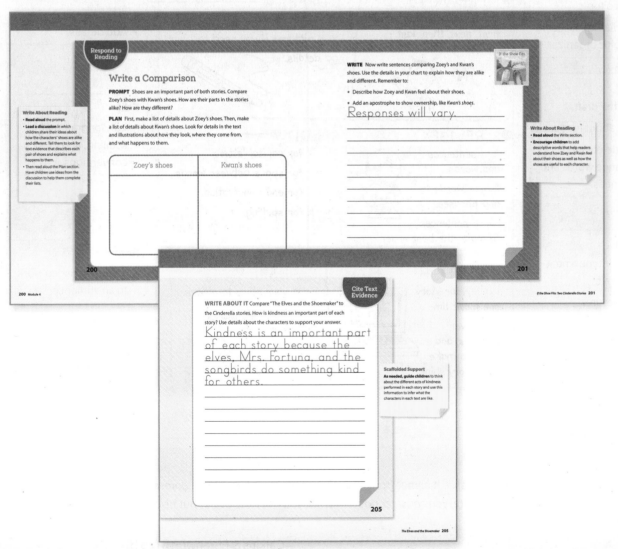

Teaching Writing as a Process

When children learn and practice a step-by-step way to write, they have an efficient formula to call on for turning ideas into published pieces of writing.

Stages of the Writing Process

Engage children in the writing process to generate ideas, organize drafts, revise and edit, and publish and share multiple texts.

Prewrite
- Decide on the audience.
- Brainstorm.
- Select a topic.
- Organize ideas, using a graphic organizer.

Revise
- Read the draft.
- Think about feedback.
- Add, delete, and rearrange words and sentences.

Publish
- Write or type a neat final draft.
- Add pictures.

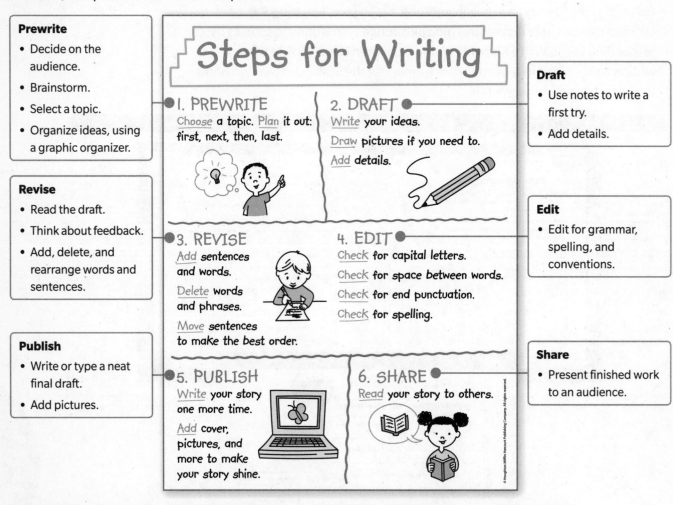

Draft
- Use notes to write a first try.
- Add details.

Edit
- Edit for grammar, spelling, and conventions.

Share
- Present finished work to an audience.

Professional Learning

RESEARCH FOUNDATIONS

"The writing process is a learned skill. It comes from many hours spent writing a lot. It comes from a mindset that whatever you write, you consider not only what you will write about but also how you will write well."

—Calkins & Ehrenworth (2016)

Writing Process in *Into Reading* and *¡Arriba la Lectura!*

Use the **Writing Workshop Teacher's Guide** lessons to provide explicit modeling and instruction for each stage of the writing process. In each Writing Workshop module, children focus on a particular writing mode and explore it through all stages of the writing process.

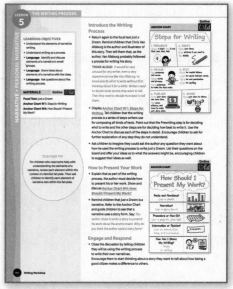

- Provide explicit modeling and instruction for the stages of the writing process early in the year. (See **Writing Workshop Teacher's Guide**, page W22 for either Grade 1 or Grade 2).

- Display <u>Anchor Chart W1: Steps for Writing</u> and point out the stages when you model tasks for each stage of the process.

- Teach the Writer's Vocabulary for each stage of the writing process, and reinforce the words when you teach and confer with children.

- Plan time to write every day, starting with shorter sessions initially, gradually building children's writing stamina through the year.

- Allow for flexibility in the writing process, acknowledging that children will often be at different stages of the process and supporting them accordingly.

- Offer choice whenever possible—in materials for writing, flexible seating for independent writing, and topics for writing. For example, use writing prompts as a starting point, knowing that they may help some children to get their ideas flowing, while others may respond well to having more choice.

Best Practices: Grammar Through Writing

Grammar, language, and conventions are taught most effectively in the context of authentic writing instruction, in the moment that a new skill or concept is useful to children. The **Writing Workshop Teacher's Guide** provides multiple paths for Grammar instruction, which you may use flexibly to best serve your students' needs.

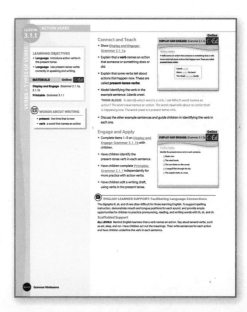

- **Integrated** Use the grammar instruction at point of use in the context of the revising and editing steps of the writing process.

- **Differentiated** Choose from the bank of grammar minilessons in the back of the **Writing Workshop Teacher's Guide** to provide targeted support for children who need something other than the integrated grammar lesson.

- **Systematic** For a systematic grammar scope and sequence, follow the recommended path on the Teacher's Guide Week at a Glance pages.

Facilitating Inquiry and Research Projects

Engage children in projects to allow opportunities to extend content knowledge while building research, writing, listening, speaking, and collaboration skills.

What Is Project-Based Learning?

Inquiry and research projects require children to work for an extended period of time to solve a problem, answer a question, or share information. Projects are most effective when they allow children to explore their interests or have real-world applications, such as solving a problem in the community.

Steps for Effective Project-Based Learning

STEP 3

REFLECT AND CELEBRATE
Children **share** what they learned with their audience.

STEP 2

TAKE ACTION
Children write, build, create, or **work toward** their project **goal.**

STEP 1

LAUNCH THE PROJECT
Connect the project to a topic children are learning.
Establish a real-world **purpose** and **audience** for the project.
Children **generate research questions** and **develop a research plan.**

● Professional Learning

RESEARCH FOUNDATIONS

❝ *When learners have a compelling purpose to achieve and a meaningful audience to reach, we see their attention to tasks, their willingness to persevere in reading challenging texts, and even their motivation to revise and edit their work increase. In fact, people seem to be built for learning through projects.* ❞

— Duke (2015)

Inquiry and Research in *Into Reading* and *¡Arriba la lectura!*

Children work on one three-week long Inquiry and Research Project per module.

- **Week 1: Launch the Project** Introduce the project and make connections to the module topic. Then have children work collaboratively to generate research questions, develop a research plan, and explore an area of curiosity about the topic. Provide accessible source material, including books, children's magazines, videos, and online resources.

- **Week 2: Take Action** Work toward the final goal. Allow time for children to write drafts and revise work as needed.

- **Week 3: Reflect and Celebrate** Have children practice listening, speaking, and presentation skills and share their final products with an audience. Then celebrate children's hard work!

Best Practices: Facilitating Inquiry and Research Projects

Help children make the most of project-based learning.

- **Identify a real-world problem or question.** The best projects have real-world applications. Have children brainstorm a problem or a question to explore.

- **Select an audience.** Have children present to people outside of their classroom, such as another class, family members, or community members.

- **Schedule project work.** Select a weekly time for project work.

- **Build research skills.** Model how to find and record information, including how to conduct an interview and how to make and record observations when exploring an environment or experimenting.

- **Allow time for revision.** Build in time for children to revise and finalize their final products. Encourage groups to work together to review and revise their work. Provide feedback as needed.

- **Consider the time of year.** Early in the year, children will need support with each step of the inquiry and research process. As children become more comfortable with the format, gradually transfer responsibility to children.

- **Support English learners.** Scaffold instruction and materials by allowing English learners to use illustrations, videos, and other media sources. Consider sharing written sources and samples in their home languages.

Teaching with Instructional Routines

Instructional Routines at a Glance

Into Reading and *¡Arriba la Lectura!* include support and suggestions for using these instructional routines.

ROUTINE	PURPOSE	ROUTINE IN ACTION
Active Viewing	Build and extend children's knowledge about the module topic by actively viewing and responding to Get Curious Videos.	• **GRADE 1** Teacher's Guide, Volume 3, p. T15 • **GRADE 2** Teacher's Guide, Volume 3, p. T15
Vocabulary	Explicitly teach the meaning of general academic and domain-specific words, provide examples, and practice using the words in context.	• **GRADE 1** Teacher's Guide, Volume 1, p. T259 • **GRADE 2** Teacher's Guide, Volume 2, p. T263
High-Frequency Words	Teach children to read and spell common high-frequency words with automaticity.	• **GRADE 1** Teacher's Guide, Volume 2, p. T15 • **GRADE 2** Teacher's Guide, Volume 1, p. T263
Blending: Sound-by-Sound Blending	Lead children to decode one-syllable words with target sound-spellings one sound at a time, and model precise and consistent hand motions.	• **GRADE 1** Teacher's Guide, Volume 1, p. T15
Blending: Continuous Blending	Lead children to practice blending words with target sound-spellings, without any break between the sounds, and model precise and consistent hand motions.	• **GRADE 1** Teacher's Guide, Volume 4, p. T15 • **GRADE 2** Teacher's Guide, Volume 1, p. T15
Blending: Vowel-First Blending	For children who have difficulty with Sound-by-Sound and Continuous Blending, lead them to decode by focusing on vowel sounds.	• **GRADE 1** Teacher's Guide, Volume 2, p. T263
Syllabication: VCCV Pattern	Explicitly teach children to decode two-syllable words with the VCCV syllable pattern.	• **GRADE 1** Teacher's Guide, Volume 4, p. T263 • **GRADE 2** Teacher's Guide, Volume 2, p. T15
Syllabication: VCV Pattern	Explicitly teach children to decode two-syllable words with the VCV syllable pattern.	• **GRADE 2** Teacher's Guide, Volume 5, p. T15
Syllabication: VCCCV Pattern	Explicitly teach children to decode two-syllable words with the VCCCV syllable pattern.	• **GRADE 2** Teacher's Guide, Volume 5, p. T263

KEY ▮ Build Knowledge and Language   ▮ Vocabulary   ▮ Foundational Skills

Embedded Instructional Routines

Instructional routines are embedded in *Into Reading* lessons to target the acquisition of key skills and to build structure and continuity between lessons.

Look for instructional routines highlighted in **GREEN** throughout the lessons in the Teacher's Guide.

Preview the consistent routine steps and model language before teaching a lesson.

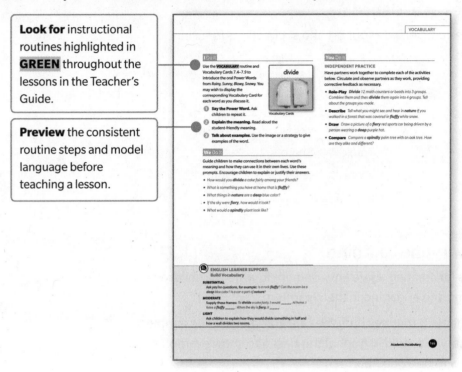

Take a Deep Dive

Each module in the Teacher's Guide spotlights one of the routines.

Learn why the routine is important and how it helps children build a foundation for literacy.

Access suggestions for using *Into Reading* materials to teach the routine.

Examine the consistent set of steps and model language for teaching the routine.

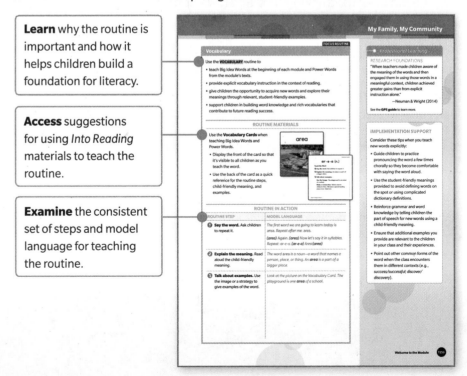

Engaging Children in Learning

Use routines to strategically structure student engagement so that all children are actively participating, thinking, and responding.

Engagement Routines at a Glance

Into Reading and *¡Arriba la Lectura!* include support and suggestions for using these engagement routines:

GRADES 1–2 ENGAGEMENT ROUTINES	
• Echo Reading	• Turn and Talk
• Choral Reading	• Think-Pair-Share
• Partner Reading	• Write and Reveal
	• Share Chair

Everyone Talking, Everyone Learning

Remember these key points for creating a safe environment in which all children feel comfortable participating and engaging in their learning.

- Model and practice engagement routines until they are automatic. For example, role-play **THINK-PAIR-SHARE** with a child in front of the class and show examples (and non-examples) of how to be a good partner.

- Provide thinking time for all children to consider responses.

- Use consistent nonverbal signals to let children know when it's time to think or respond. For example, raise your hand to signal thinking time and lower it to signal for children to respond at the same time.

- Check for participation by making eye contact to prompt children to respond or reminding the group that you expect everyone to respond.

- Follow up if not all children respond. Determine if children need additional support, a reminder, or a clear signal to respond together at the same time.

Professional Learning

RESEARCH FOUNDATIONS

66 *Master teachers create an active-learning environment in which students are on task in their thinking and speaking or are collaboratively working close to 100 percent of the time. Such teachers notice and measure not only when students are on task but also the quality of their engagement.* 99

—de Frondeville (2009)

ECHO READING

ECHO READING is an oral reading routine in which the teacher reads aloud phrase-by-phrase and children repeat each phrase. Use this routine for reading directions, books with one or two sentences per page, or short lines of a shared text.

ROUTINE IN ACTION

1 Read along.

- Display a book, short text, or directions.
- Tell children to listen as you read aloud one sentence or phrase at a time.
- Point to the words as you read aloud, modeling fluent reading.

2 Repeat together.

- Ask children to "echo" you, imitating your pronunciation and expression. *Let's pretend we're in a cave and you all are my echo. So, when I pause, everyone repeats what I read at the same time.*
- Read aloud the text, pointing to the words and pausing at natural intervals for children to chorally repeat each sentence or phrase.
- Check for participation. Make eye contact with children who are not repeating or stop to cue the whole group. *I think we were missing some voices that time. Let's try again with everyone repeating after me.*

CHORAL READING

CHORAL READING engages children with reading aloud a text multiple times in a group setting. Use this routine with small chunks of text, short lines of shared or familiar text, and procedures or directions.

ROUTINE IN ACTION

1 Read along with a text.

- Display a short text or provide copies, and ask children to follow along silently as you read aloud the entire text. *Listen while I read this poem. Follow along as I point to the words.*
- Point to the words and model fluent reading. *Notice how my voice changes to go with different parts.*

2 Read aloud together.

- Tell children that everyone will read together, starting at the same time and reading at the same rate.
- Point to the words as everyone reads together. *Remember to start at the same time and read at the same speed. Try to match your voice to mine.*

3 Listen as you read.

- Check for participation. *I didn't hear all of you. Let's try again with everyone reading.*
- If children read at different rates, provide immediate modeling and practice. *We were reading at different times. Let's read again and try to sound like we are one voice!*

PARTNER READING

PARTNER READING engages pairs of children with reading a familiar text multiple times. Use this routine to reread texts children have already read with teacher guidance.

ROUTINE IN ACTION

1 Partner up.

- Pair children and assign numbers (1/2), and make sure partners know their numbers. *Partner 1's are closest to the calendar. Partner 2's are closest to the clock. Partner 1's, hold up one finger. Partner 2's, hold up two fingers.*

2 Take turns reading.

- Tell partners who will read first and how much of the text to read. *Partner 1 reads first. Partner 2 listens and follows along. Read one page. Then switch so that the other partner reads the next page.*

3 Read the text again.

- Have children read the text again, starting with the other partner. *This time, Partner 2 reads first.*

PICK AND POINT

PICK AND POINT engages a group of children in responding to a question or task by pointing together at the same time. Use this routine to respond to visual discrimination tasks about letters, sounds, or word meaning.

ROUTINE IN ACTION

1 **Listen to the task.**

- Display two or three responses, spaced out horizontally across the board, and review each response. *See the letters* s-h. *What sound do these letters stand for? (/sh/). See the letters* c-h. *What sound do these letters stand for? (/ch/).*

- Explain to children that you will give them a task and they will pick and point to one of the responses. *I'm going to say a word. If you hear the sound /sh/ in the word, point to the letters* s-h. *If you hear the sound /ch/ in the word, point to the letters* c-h.

- Model and practice how to point to a response. *Let's practice pointing. I'll say the sound and you point to the letters: /ch/. Very good! I see everyone pointing to* c-h.

- Ask a question or give a task that children can respond to using Pick and Point. *Now let's try it with words. Point to the sound you hear at the beginning of the word* shark.

2 **Think about the answer.**

- Raise one hand up to allow children a few seconds of thinking time. *When my hand is up, think about your answer.*

- Ensure that children wait to point until you lower your hand. *Wait until I put my hand down, and point to your answer.*

3 **Point to the answer.**

- Lower your hand to signal for children to point at the same time. *Now let me see everyone pointing.*

- Check for participation. Use eye contact to prompt children to respond or remind the group verbally that you expect everyone to respond. *I don't see everyone pointing. Let me repeat the word and give you more time to think.*

- Provide immediate modeling and practice if children respond incorrectly. *I see most fingers pointing to the letters* s-h. Shark *begins with the sound /sh/. It begins with the letters* s-h. *Let's try another word:* ship. *Yes, I see all fingers pointing to* s-h *because* ship *begins with the /sh/ sound.*

- Follow up with more tasks, making sure to keep the pace engaging. *Let's try more words:* chin, chip, shop, chalk, shoe.

TURN AND TALK

TURN AND TALK is a routine that gives all children the opportunity to briefly share ideas with a partner. Use this routine as an alternative to hand raising to allow all children to respond to an open-ended question or to "get their ideas out."

ROUTINE IN ACTION

1 Turn toward your partner.

- Ask an open-ended question. *Let's turn and talk to retell the end of the story in your own words.*

- Use the **PARTNER UP** routine to pair children and assign numbers. *Make sure you are next to your "rug buddy." Partner 1's, hold up one finger. Partner 2's, hold up two fingers.*

- Tell partners to face each other. *Turn your body toward your partner to show that you are listening and want to know what your partner has to say.*

2 Look your partner in the eye.

- Remind children to look at their partners when speaking and listening. *Remember to look at your partner when you share and when you are listening.*

3 One partner talks. One partner listens.

- Provide a model response or response frame to help children understand the task and articulate their thinking. *You can start by saying: In the end, the family _____. Then tell what happened.*

- Tell partners who will start sharing. *Partner 1 shares first. Partner 2 listens.*

4 Switch!

- Let partners know to switch roles. *Now partner 2 shares and partner 1 listens.*

- Use a signal to bring children's attention back to the whole group, if needed.

- Briefly acknowledge ideas you heard from various partners.

THINK-PAIR SHARE

THINK-PAIR-SHARE engages children in a collaborative conversation in response to a question that children think about, share ideas with a partner, and then share with the whole group. Use this routine to ask open-ended questions that are personal or text-based.

ROUTINE IN ACTION

1 Think

- Use the **PARTNER UP** routine to pair children and assign numbers. *If you're sitting closest to the door, you will be Partner 1. If you're sitting closest to the cubbies, you will be Partner 2. Partner 1's, raise your hand. Partner 2's?*

- Ask an open-ended question. *Get ready to talk about this question with your partner: What is something you want to practice?*

- Display a response frame and model using it. *You can start with this sentence: I want to practice _____.*

- Allow children several seconds to think and have them show thumbs up when they are ready. *Think quietly about your answer. Put your thumb up when you are ready.*

2 Pair

- Tell children which partner will respond first and allow time to share. *Partner 1's share first. Partner 2's, your job is to listen. Now the Partner 2's share while Partner 1's listen.*

- Listen to children's responses to their partners, and ask a few children with strong responses to share. *That is a very thoughtful response, Rigo. I'm going to ask you to share with the whole group.*

3 Share

- Ask children you identified to share first. *I heard a lot of different responses. Rigo, what do you want to practice?*

- Continue the sharing by asking for volunteers. *Raise your hand if you have a different idea.*

WRITE AND REVEAL

WRITE AND REVEAL is a routine that allows all children to write a short response and reveal it to the teacher at the same time. Use this routine to write upper- or lowercase letters, sound-spellings, high-frequency words, and words for spelling dictation.

ROUTINE IN ACTION

1 **Listen to the task.**

- Make sure children have small dry-erase boards and markers or paper and pencils.

- Give children a writing task. *Write the letter that stands for the sound /m/ in* mop.

2 **Write your answer.**

- Raise one hand up to allow children a few seconds of writing time. *When my hand is up, write your answer. When I put my hand down, turn your board around.*

3 **Reveal your answer.**

- Lower your hand to signal for children to show their responses.

- Do a quick check of children's responses and write the correct response on your own board. *Check to make sure you wrote the letter* m.

- Provide immediate feedback if children respond incorrectly. *The letter* w *stands for the sound /w/ in the word* win. *The letter* m *looks similar, but it is the letter that stands for the sound /m/.* Follow up with more practice. *Now, write the letter that stands for the sound /s/ in* sun.

SHARE CHAIR

SHARE CHAIR is a special routine for presenting writing or other work to the class. Use this routine to share published writing, final projects, or reading responses.

ROUTINE IN ACTION

1 Present your work.

- Reserve a special chair for this purpose and involve children in decorating it.
- Select children who will share or choose children based on a predetermined schedule, ensuring that all children have opportunities to share over time.
- Consider having partners rehearse before sharing with the class.
- Remind the children who are presenting to use their "sharing voices." *When it's your turn to share, make sure to use a voice that is loud enough for everyone to hear.*
- Allow presenters to select one or two classmates to give feedback.

2 Listen to your classmates.

- Review the expectations for listening respectfully to fellow writers as they share. *Remember to listen with your whole bodies.*
- Provide a few sentence starters to focus children's feedback. *You can use one of these sentence starters to give feedback: I like _____. My favorite part is _____.*
- Keep Share Chair sessions short, especially at the beginning of the year.

Building Reading Independence

Give children the tools they need to become independent—and enthusiastic—readers.

Organizing Your Classroom's Reading Corner

Guiding children to choose books they'll enjoy reading—to themselves and to others—can help to lay the groundwork for a lifetime of happy reading.

The Reading Corner can be one of the most exciting places in a classroom—a candy store of books, where children choose what looks best. Here they can find a sense of agency and community—*they* choose what to read, *they* work together to help grow the collection. Use these tips for building a little corner of literary heaven:

- Don't organize the library by reading level. Instead, group books by content. This could mean by genre—nonfiction, fables, poetry, and so on—or by subject area, for example, sports, art, and science. Think of how bookstores are laid out.

- Bring children together to help decide exactly how to organize the library. This fosters feelings of investment and community.

- You don't need to have your Reading Corner perfectly assembled on the first day of school. In fact, it's better for it not to be. Start off with a small set of great titles, including the *Into Reading* **Student Choice Library.** Survey children to find out what else they're interested in. Then, let the collection grow organically throughout the year, adding books from the school library, from donations, or from other sources.

- Create a display of a few featured books and change them periodically to keep the Reading Corner new and interesting throughout the year.

- As the library grows, make sure it reflects the diversity of the class. For more on this, see "Creating a Culturally Responsive Environment," on pages 60–61.

GRADE 1
Student Choice Library

GRADE 2
Student Choice Library

Self-Selecting Books

Okay, the class Reading Corner is set up and ready to grow. Now, what to read? Consider the following in supporting children's selection process:

- Model choosing a book. Pick one up and check out the cover. "This book is about planets. I love outer space! I'm going to read this." Or, "I like cats, but I'd rather read about something else. I'll put this book back and keep looking."

- Early in the school year, assure children that even looking at a book's pictures is a form of reading!

- Have children conduct short Book Talks to recommend books they have read to their classmates.

Setting Goals and Responding to Reading

When it comes to the time children read in one sitting, starting small is key. At the beginning of the year, that could look something like this:

- 5 to 10 minutes of reading

- A body break

- Another 5 to 10 minutes of reading

Of course, the more children read, the more they'll be able to read. Encourage them to set goals, like reading to themselves for 10 minutes. Get them involved in tracking their progress by using Printable: **Reading Log** or by making a graph. As children move into reading time, have them set goals based on their history and how they're feeling in the moment.

Remember, while goals can be motivating, don't let children get the idea that reading is a slog, something you have to push through. Instead, they should think of their time target as how long they get to do this really fun thing!

Have children create a Response Journal in which they can draw or write about their independent reading books. Allow them to create a cover that makes it their own. Review children's journals occasionally to see what interests them and to talk with them about the books they are reading.

TEACHER → TO TEACHER
From the Classroom

" You know how kids love to keep track of their height on the wall? Approach tracking reading the same way. Make it visual. You could do a colorful graph. Letting them literally see their progress is a game changer. "

¡Viva el español!

Bienvenidos a ¡Arriba la Lectura!

¡Arriba la Lectura! proporciona una amplia gama de recursos paralelos al programa *Into Reading* en inglés, potenciando así una experiencia educativa equitativa para todos los estudiantes. Además, estos recursos se ven enriquecidos por herramientas y componentes exclusivos del programa en español. En estas páginas, podrá obtener un panorama general de los recursos que distinguen a *¡Arriba la Lectura!*

Literatura hispana y universal

Desarrolle los conocimientos a través de colecciones temáticas de distintos géneros.

- *¡Arriba la Lectura!* ofrece una rica variedad de literatura hispana y universal para todos los gustos e intereses.

- La exposición a una amplia gama de literatura hispana y universal amplía los horizontes intelectuales y culturales de los estudiantes hacia una sociedad global.

- Alma Flor Ada y F. Isabel Campoy revisaron todos los poemas, selecciones y traducciones literarias para garantizar la excelencia en el uso del lenguaje y la literatura en español.

- Puede usar la **Revista Aventuras** para el tiempo de lectura y conversación en grupos pequeños.

- En **"Nuestra lengua es arte"**, encontrará experiencias culturales y lingüísticas relevantes.

Las **obras premiadas,** relevantes y culturalmente significativas, tanto de autores hispanos como de diversas partes del mundo, son una herramienta fundamental para enriquecer los conocimientos y destrezas de lectoescritura de todos los estudiantes, así como su herencia cultural.

> 66 *Una lengua necesita a su literatura para sobrevivir* 99.
>
> — F. Isabel Campoy y Alma Flor Ada

Lecciones de destrezas fundamentales

¡Arriba la Lectura! desarrolla las destrezas de audición, expresión oral, lectura, escritura y reflexión que preparan a los estudiantes para una lectoescritura exitosa de por vida.

- Involucre activamente a los estudiantes en el **desarrollo de la conciencia fonológica** a través de una secuencia desarrollada especialmente para el español.

- Brinde una **enseñanza explícita de la fonética** para conectar la escritura con el habla, para leer y combinar sílabas y palabras.

- Enseñe a los estudiantes a leer y escribir **palabras de uso frecuente** específicas de la lengua española.

- Use **textos decodificables** para aplicar las destrezas aprendidas, practicar las palabras de uso frecuente en contexto y ayudar a los estudiantes a tener éxito en sus primeras experiencias de lectura independiente.

- Despierte el interés de los estudiantes por el **desarrollo de las destrezas fundamentales** con poemas originales en español.

Extensión lingüística

Apoye el lenguaje académico y promueva el aprecio de los estudiantes por la lengua y la cultura.

- Desarrolle la **conciencia metalingüística** con la sección **"Extensión lingüística".**

- Comience a desarrollar la **alfabetización académica en español** con "Extensión lingüística".

Taller de escritura

- A medida que exploran y aplican el proceso de escritura, use las notas a la mano para brindar apoyo a los estudiantes de enseñanza dual.

- Observe que ciertos textos modelo están escritos originalmente en español.

Evaluación que toma en cuenta el lenguaje

- Estrategias, formularios y herramientas que ayudan a los maestros a interpretar e informar sobre los datos de una forma adecuada para los estudiantes de idiomas

- Consejos claros y útiles de parte de la Dra. Elena Izquierdo en el recurso **Lenguaje dual: Guía de implementación**

- Listas de comprobación observacionales, formularios de informe de lenguaje dual y pautas de calificación del desarrollo del lenguaje

- Herramientas simples para ayudar a los estudiantes a monitorear su propia biliteracidad

Equidad y más

¡Arriba la Lectura! ofrece gran variedad de **literatura y materiales de enseñanza** especiales para el español, desarrollados y revisados por nuestras autoras.

Materiales para estudiantes

- Todas las selecciones de las **Lecturas en voz alta** y los **Superlibros** fueron revisadas por Alma Flor Ada y F. Isabel Campoy para asegurar la excelencia en el uso del lenguaje y la literatura en español.

- Los estudiantes podrán leer **poemas** divertidos y originales de Alma Flor Ada, F. Isabel Campoy y otros autores hispanohablantes para que las lecciones de destrezas fundamentales resulten entretenidas y apropiadas.

- Los **Alfamigos** incluyen canciones pegadizas que serán un éxito entre sus estudiantes. Tanto los **Videos** como las **Tarjetas de Alfamigos** brindan una amplia gama de posibilidades para la enseñanza de la lectoescritura.

- Los **Superlibros de rimas** fueron desarrollados por Alma Flor Ada y F. Isabel Campoy especialmente para *¡Arriba la Lectura!*

- La **Revista Aventuras** está compuesta por seis libros con literatura de calidad para enriquecer el desarrollo del lenguaje en español y la comprensión.

Materiales para maestros

- **"Nuestra lengua es arte",** un tesoro de la literatura en español creado por Alma Flor Ada y F. Isabel Campoy para la lectura en voz alta

- **"Extensión lingüística",** una sección pensada para enriquecer y ampliar la lectoescritura en español que contiene lecciones para la **Revista Aventuras** y "Nuestra lengua es arte"

- **Lecciones de destrezas fundamentales** especialmente diseñadas para el español

- **Notas especiales** para los contextos de enseñanza dual en cada lección

- **"Puente interlingüístico"** para desarrollar los conocimientos metalingüísticos en cada lección y conectar el aprendizaje en ambas lenguas

- El recurso **Lenguaje dual: Guía de implementación,** para facilitar el uso de *¡Arriba la Lectura!* e *Into Reading* en contextos de enseñanza dual

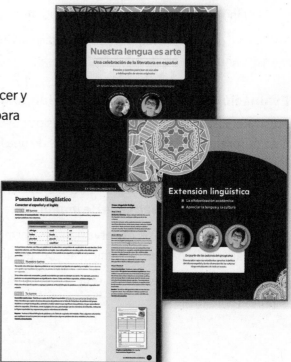

Destrezas fundamentales

Los materiales en los que se basa la enseñanza de las destrezas fundamentales fueron creados específicamente para el aprendizaje del idioma español.

Lecturas iniciales

Aprende y demuestra

Tarjetas de fotos

Tarjetas del abecedario

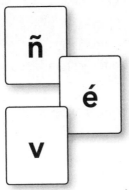

Tarjetas de letras

Tarjetas de Alfamigos

Tarjetas de palabras

Tarjetas de sílabas y ortografía

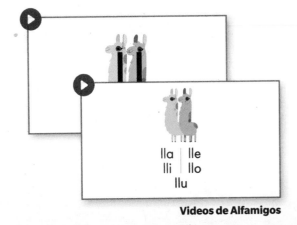

Videos de Alfamigos

Equidad y más *(cont.)*

Diseñado para la enseñanza bilingüe y de lenguaje dual

¡Arriba la Lectura! fue especialmente diseñado para su utilización en contextos de enseñanza dual, con secciones especiales que incluyen estrategias fáciles de usar y basadas en la investigación, tanto durante el tiempo de trabajo en grupos como durante el tiempo de trabajo de toda la clase.

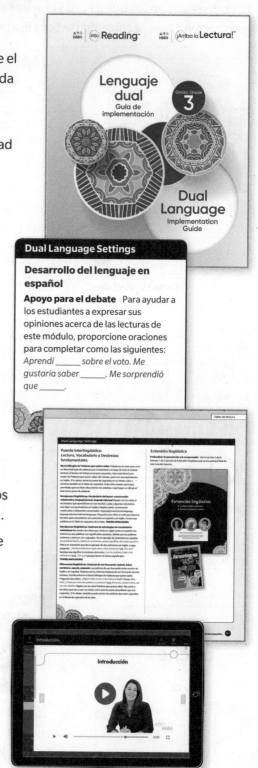

- Los **materiales** han sido desarrollados con el asesoramiento de la Dra. Elena Izquierdo, profesional con vasta experiencia y especialidad en el desarrollo de programas bilingües y duales exitosos.

- El recurso de educación dual **Lenguaje dual: Guía de implementación,** desarrollado con el asesoramiento de la Dra. Izquierdo, ofrece guías de planificación sugerida, buenas prácticas y otros recursos útiles para potenciar el progreso de los maestros junto con sus estudiantes.

- La sección **"Análisis lingüístico contrastivo"** del recurso **Lenguaje dual: Guía de implementación** brinda información de fácil acceso y consejos de enseñanza para fomentar el desarrollo paralelo del español y el inglés.

- Las **estrategias** de **"Dual Language Settings"** ayudan a los maestros a implementar buenas prácticas justo donde y cuando las necesitan.

- Las notas en el punto de uso están destinadas a brindar apoyo a toda la diversidad de estudiantes.

- Cada lección incluye un **"Puente interlingüístico"** para ayudar a los estudiantes y maestros a desarrollar la comprensión metalingüística.

- Este programa brinda apoyo a los estudiantes, tanto en contextos de un idioma como en contextos de enseñanza dual.

- El programa está basado en un **modelo de enriquecimiento** y desarrollado en función de los conocimientos previos de los estudiantes.

- Los **videos de desarrollo profesional** ofrecen modelos de enseñanza de distintos aspectos del lenguaje dual que los maestros pueden aplicar en su propio salón de clases.

Nuestras autoras

El programa *¡Arriba la Lectura!* fue creado en conjunto por el mismo grupo de autores que elaboró el programa *Into Reading*. Sin embargo, las autoras que aparecen en esta página estuvieron involucradas de forma particular en el desarrollo de *¡Arriba la Lectura!* desde un principio para garantizar su calidad literaria, educativa y lingüística en el idioma español y para planificar las oportunidades de implementación junto con *Into Reading* para los contextos de enseñanza dual.

F. Isabel Campoy, M.A., Lic.

Autora bilingüe que ha recibido múltiples premios por sus más de 150 libros para niños, que incluyen poesía, teatro, cuentos, biografías, arte y cultura. Académica de reconocimiento internacional, docente y traductora. Miembro de la Academia Norteamericana de la Lengua Española.

Alma Flor Ada, Ph.D.

Profesora Emérita de la Universidad de San Francisco. Experta de renombre internacional en literatura y lectoescritura bilingües. Autora de más de 200 libros premiados, tanto académicos como para jóvenes lectores, y consejera líder en educación transformadora.

> **❝*Una lengua necesita a su literatura para sobrevivir*❞**.
>
> — F. Isabel Campoy y Alma Flor Ada

Elena Izquierdo, Ph.D.

Profesora asociada de formación docente en la Universidad de Texas, en El Paso. Investigadora y profesional cuyos focos son la enseñanza dual, la lectoescritura bilingüe y la equidad educativa para estudiantes de inglés.

> **❝*Los programas duales bien implementados ayudan a los niños a ser exitosos a través de ambos lenguajes y además, a desarrollar habilidades meta cognitivas y meta lingüísticas*❞**.
>
> — Dra. Elena Izquierdo

¡Viva el español!

Literatura hispana

¡Arriba la Lectura! contiene obras originales en español, seleccionadas por su calidad literaria y relevancia cultural. La exposición a una amplia gama de literatura escrita originalmente en español es fundamental para desarrollar la riqueza lingüística de los estudiantes y expandir sus horizontes intelectuales y culturales hacia una sociedad global.

Lecturas para desarrollar la comprensión

Las lecturas de *mi***Libro**, los **Superlibros**, los **Libros para la lectura en voz alta,** los **Textos de enfoque** y las **Lecturas iniciales** presentan contenidos multiculturales que despiertan el interés de los estudiantes y son una herramienta imprescindible para enriquecer los conocimientos y desarrollar la comprensión.

Se han desarrollado especialmente para el programa textos de diversos géneros, como el *Superlibro de rimas* y la selección *El alegre abecedario*, y muchos otros títulos de F. Isabel Campoy y Alma Flor Ada, además de las **Lecturas iniciales,** escritas en su mayoría por autores hispanos específicamente para este programa.

Lecturas para desarrollar las destrezas fundamentales

Las **Lecturas iniciales** fueron cuidadosamente desarrolladas para este programa. Estos textos decodificables contienen exclusivamente los elementos de fonética, las sílabas y las palabras de uso frecuente que han sido enseñados previamente e incluyen un tema o un argumento presente en todos los textos de la semana para desarrollar la expectativa y despertar el interés de los estudiantes. Su principal objetivo es afianzar la comprensión lectora, dado que en español la decodificación no representa un reto significativo.

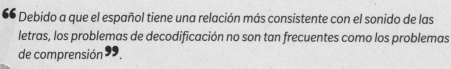

> 66 *Debido a que el español tiene una relación más consistente con el sonido de las letras, los problemas de decodificación no son tan frecuentes como los problemas de comprensión* 99.
>
> — Dra. Elena Izquierdo

Poesía

¡Arriba la Lectura! incluye poesía escrita originalmente en español, la cual resulta esencial para el desarrollo de las destrezas fundamentales, el enriquecimiento del lenguaje y la comprensión.

Se puede hallar poesía escrita originalmente en español como práctica oral en las lecciones de fonética de la **Guía del maestro** y en las páginas de **Mostrar y motivar** de los Grados K–2. También se encuentran poemas originales en español en las **Ediciones del estudiante** y en los **Textos de enfoque** de los Grados 3–6.

Selecciones multimedia

Videos de cierre y de selección

Los videos creados exclusivamente para *¡Arriba la Lectura!* proporcionan un modo diferente y entretenido de presentar contenidos para que los estudiantes comenten y desarrollen las habilidades para participar en conversaciones.

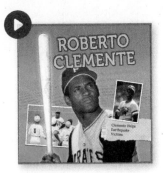  

Videos de Alfamigos

Los **Videos de Alfamigos** fueron creados especialmente para este programa por músicos profesionales, utilizando diferentes ritmos musicales y canciones pegadizas. Su propósito es enseñar a los estudiantes las letras, los dígrafos y las sílabas de una forma atractiva.

Los **Alfamigos** son amenos y divertidos, por lo que llaman la atención de los estudiantes al tiempo que fortalecen sus destrezas de lectoescritura y los ayudan a decodificar las sílabas que están aprendiendo.

¡Más literatura hispana!

Revista Aventuras

Los textos de la **Revista Aventuras,** escritos originalmente en español, cuentan con bellas ilustraciones y se pueden usar para enriquecer el lenguaje académico, la comprensión y la apreciación literaria. Estas lecturas incluyen cuentos, textos informativos, biografías, artículos, novelas históricas, poemas, etc. Su propósito es inspirar a los estudiantes y despertar en ellos el placer de la lectura.

Nuestra lengua es arte

Esta sección presenta literatura original en español de gran relevancia cultural, seleccionada por las autoras Alma Flor Ada y F. Isabel Campoy, para que el maestro comparta con la clase en voz alta al finalizar cada módulo de la **Guía del maestro** de los Grados K–6.

En "Nuestra lengua es arte", los estudiantes encontrarán experiencias culturales y lingüísticas relevantes, ya que la celebración de las diversas culturas del mundo está muy presente en los temas abordados. Incluye una sección de libros recomendados de autores de diversos orígenes hispanos para que los estudiantes exploren nuevas lecturas.

Superlibros de apoyo

Los **Superlibros de rimas** de los Grados K-1 y *El ABC de Culebra* fueron creados especialmente en español para *¡Arriba la Lectura!* Las rimas ayudan a desarrollar las destrezas fundamentales y permiten a los estudiantes compartir lecturas y mejorar la comprensión auditiva, mientras que *El ABC de Culebra* ofrece un repaso de las letras del abecedario acompañadas de bellas imágenes que les permiten establecer asociaciones útiles.

Interacción con *Into Reading*

Temas culturalmente relevantes

Los estudiantes tienen acceso a lecturas en inglés sobre temas relevantes relacionados con la cultura hispanoamericana, como "Pepita and the Bully", *Mango, Abuela, and me* y "Safeguarding the California Coast".

Paridad temática

Los temas cubiertos mediante la literatura original en español y en inglés se corresponden entre sí, lo cual potencia la implementación de programas de educación de lenguaje dual. Asimismo, los apartados de lenguaje dual brindan consejos de enseñanza para fomentar el desarrollo paralelo del español y el inglés y permiten comparar y contrastar ambos idiomas.

Versiones en español de excelencia

Todas las lecturas han sido cuidadosamente revisadas por Alma Flor Ada y F. Isabel Campoy para asegurar la excelencia en el uso del lenguaje y la literatura en español y para garantizar que las traducciones literarias son de gran calidad, escritas con un lenguaje auténtico y natural.

Literatura universal

Asegurar la diversidad cultural de la literatura que leen los estudiantes es de suma importancia. Por ello, *¡Arriba la Lectura!* incluye lecturas escritas por autores de los más diversos países y culturas y los temas tratados responden a esa diversidad.

La multiculturalidad de los autores hispanos se ve reflejada en sus variados orígenes, con autores de Argentina, México, Chile, El Salvador, Nicaragua, Puerto Rico, España, Estados Unidos y Cuba, entre muchos otros. Esta diversidad proporciona una mayor riqueza al lenguaje aprendido por los estudiantes y una visión del mundo más amplia y libre de prejuicios.

Lecturas bilingües

Las lecturas bilingües son de gran importancia para el desarrollo de las destrezas lingüísticas de los estudiantes tanto en inglés como en español, ya que les permiten establecer conexiones entre ambos idiomas y apoyarse en el dominio de la lengua nativa para fortalecer las destrezas de lectoescritura en la lengua que aprenden.

¡Viva el español!

Enseñanza especializada

Currículo especializado para el español

Para desarrollar una buena alfabetización en español, la educación debe basarse en las características específicas de la lengua española. La enseñanza de la lectura y escritura en español no puede ser una réplica o una traducción directa de la enseñanza en inglés.

¡Arriba la Lectura! está especialmente diseñado para abordar las particularidades de la lengua española y cumplir con los estándares de enseñanza. Este diseño educativo comienza con las destrezas fundamentales de lectura y escritura.

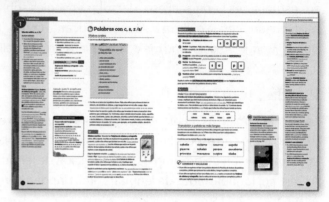

Aprendizaje inicial de los sonidos de las letras

En español, es fundamental aprender primero los sonidos de las letras, en lugar de los nombres de las letras. Como los sonidos de las vocales en español son los mismos que los nombres de las vocales, y los nombres de las consonantes incluyen sonidos de vocal que pueden contaminar la correspondencia entre letras y sonidos, la enseñanza de los nombres de las letras debe posponerse hasta que los lectores dominen las relaciones grafema-fonema.

¡Arriba la Lectura! presenta los nombres de las letras gradualmente mediante una rutina de conocimiento de las letras cada dos semanas para exponer a los estudiantes a la noción del abecedario. Los nombres de las letras y el abecedario se refuerzan aún más durante la semana dedicada al abecedario.

Para el Grado 1, se entiende que los estudiantes tienen el suficiente conocimiento previo de los nombres de las letras en español y los sonidos aprendidos durante el kínder para continuar reforzándolos semanalmente.

El español es una lengua basada en sílabas

Una vez que los estudiantes han aprendido las vocales y sus sonidos correspondientes, aprenden a formar sílabas. *¡Arriba la Lectura!* combina el método silábico, que se enfoca en la unidad más amplia de la sílaba, con el

> ❝ *Enseñar los fonemas de las consonantes individuales tiene sentido en inglés, pero en el español hablado, los fonemas de consonantes nunca se pronuncian sin vocales, por lo que enseñar consonantes de forma aislada suena artificial y es ajeno a nuestro idioma* ❞ .
> — Alma Flor Ada

método global, que presenta contextos significativos a través de palabras, frases, rimas u oraciones para luego enfocarse en sus elementos: sílabas, sonidos y letras.

La ortografía transparente del español

La lengua española tiene una ortografía transparente. Cada una de las cinco vocales tiene siempre el mismo sonido y la mayoría de las consonantes representan un solo sonido. Debido a esto, la adquisición de destrezas de decodificación ocurre más rápidamente en español que en inglés.

Debido a la ortografía transparente del idioma español, los estudiantes que trabajan con ¡Arriba la Lectura! comienzan a dominar la decodificación en el kínder y pueden aprender eficazmente todas las sílabas y los patrones de ortografía de los sonidos para el final del Grado 1. En el Grado 2, la enseñanza se centra en dominar los patrones dentro de las palabras polisílabas y enfocarse en la comprensión en español durante todo el proceso de lectura.

La ortografía transparente es una correspondencia prácticamente perfecta entre las letras y los sonidos en un idioma. Hace que sea fácil para el lector saber cómo se pronuncia una palabra escrita.

Palabras de uso frecuente en español

La ortografía transparente de la lengua española produce patrones fácilmente decodificables, de modo que la lectura no requiere de tanta práctica en la construcción de la memoria visual para las palabras vistas. Las palabras de uso frecuente en ¡Arriba la Lectura! han sido seleccionadas en base a listas de palabras de uso frecuente en español y a una sección transversal de listas investigadas específicamente para el aprendizaje de las artes del lenguaje en español. Aprender a reconocer fácilmente estas palabras promueve la fluidez.

Las palabras polisílabas (de varias sílabas) son comunes en español, pero son fácilmente decodificables para los estudiantes.

Literatura escrita originalmente en español

Los cuentos, las selecciones de no ficción y los poemas originales con gran riqueza de vocabulario de ¡Arriba la Lectura! constituyen una parte crucial de la educación especializada para el español. A medida que los estudiantes entran en contacto con esta literatura escrita y cuidadosamente seleccionada para representar la variedad y riqueza del idioma español, amplían la comprensión, el repertorio de vocabulario, las expresiones idiomáticas y los modismos en español.

Ortografía y gramática específicas del español

La **Guía del maestro** de ¡Arriba la Lectura! aborda temas de ortografía y gramática que son específicos del idioma español, entre ellos el uso de mayúsculas, la puntuación en los diálogos y la concordancia de pronombre-sujeto. Dentro del **"Taller de escritura"**, ¡Arriba la Lectura! ofrece enseñanza adicional sobre la ortografía y gramática específicas del idioma español en el contexto de la escritura, que incluye acentuación, conjugaciones de verbos, concordancia de género y sujeto tácito.

Pedagogía intercultural

El programa ¡*Arriba la Lectura!* se fundamenta en la pedagogía intercultural como modo de integrar a todos los estudiantes de cada salón de clases, sea cual fuere el entorno cultural del que procedan.

¿Qué es la pedagogía intercultural?

La pedagogía intercultural está diseñada intencionalmente para acoger el trasfondo cultural de todos los estudiantes. Se basa en la profunda comprensión del papel fundamental que desempeña la cultura en el proceso de aprendizaje. Todos los componentes de ¡*Arriba la Lectura!* están diseñados especialmente para plasmar la interculturalidad de los salones de clases.

La pedagogía intercultural comienza cuando vemos como ventajas las diferencias que nuestros estudiantes aportan a los salones de clases. Para los estudiantes bilingües emergentes, esto significa que consideramos su idioma principal como un atributo. Buscamos siempre oportunidades para incrementar las destrezas y el conocimiento que nuestros estudiantes han desarrollado en su idioma primario y diseñamos un currículo que los ayude a reconocer estos atributos y a progresar a partir de ellos. Motivamos el uso del repertorio completo que cada estudiante tiene en ambos idiomas con el propósito de que puedan comunicarse, aprender y expresar su identidad al máximo.

El maestro actúa principalmente como facilitador del aprendizaje, seleccionando oportunidades enriquecedoras para que los estudiantes colaboren y participen en conversaciones con sus compañeros.

¡*Arriba la Lectura!* sugiere actividades de aprendizaje que ayudan a los maestros a conocer a cada uno de sus estudiantes como individuo (sus puntos fuertes, sus dificultades, sus intereses y su trasfondo familiar y cultural) a través de proyectos y propuestas de escritura. A lo largo del programa, los estudiantes pueden elegir entre actividades, textos y proyectos, lo que les permite explorar sus intereses individuales y aprender dentro del contexto de su cultura y sus experiencias previas.

Las actividades de ¡*Arriba la Lectura!* están diseñadas para brindar a los estudiantes oportunidades para conectar su aprendizaje con su propio trasfondo a través de distintas secciones que los ayudan a relacionar el texto que leen con la comunidad, con sus propias experiencias y con su cultura.

Una clase con sensibilidad intercultural se focaliza en los estudiantes.

Los esfuerzos por incluir a la familia van mucho más allá de la tradicional reunión de padres y maestros, en la cual el papel del maestro es compartir información con los padres sobre el desempeño del estudiante en la escuela. En las escuelas con sensibilidad intercultural, los maestros buscan aprender activamente sobre la familia de cada estudiante y sus tradiciones, creencias y perspectivas en torno a la educación y el aprendizaje. Se comprometen con las familias como miembros del mismo equipo para apoyar el desarrollo académico y socioemocional del estudiante.

¡Arriba la Lectura! incluye varios recursos para ayudar a los maestros a involucrar a las familias, como parte del equipo, en el proceso educativo. Estos recursos incluyen las **"Cartas para la familia"** y las **Páginas imprimibles** de la sección **"Relacionarse con las familias"** que los estudiantes pueden llevarse a casa. Las "Cartas para la familia" recomiendan lecturas adicionales escritas originalmente en español.

La cuidadosa y atenta selección de los materiales de enseñanza es un componente esencial de una clase con sensibilidad intercultural. Es crucial que los estudiantes se vean a sí mismos reflejados en los libros que leen. Los estudiantes se benefician de la lectura habitual de textos que incluyan sucesos con los que se puedan identificar y personajes que compartan sus trasfondos culturales y hablen su mismo idioma. Lo ideal es que los materiales de enseñanza incluyan selecciones escritas por autores diversos, incluidos aquellos que compartan los trasfondos lingüísticos y culturales de los estudiantes de la clase.

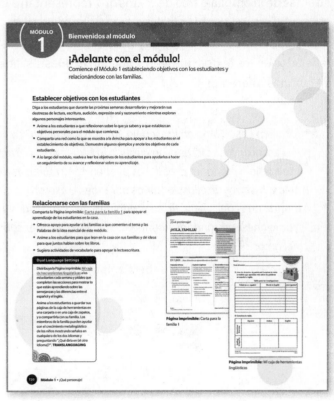

Página imprimible: Carta para la familia 1

Página imprimible: Mi caja de herramientas lingüísticas

En los entornos de lenguaje dual, esto significa que los materiales en español deben incluir una abundancia de textos escritos originalmente en español por autores que representen la diversidad de la comunidad hispana. Tanto los materiales como la enseñanza con sensibilidad intercultural desafían los estereotipos predominantes y fomentan perspectivas positivas.

¡Arriba la Lectura! celebra la riqueza de la literatura hispana. Los textos de autores hispanos representan casi el 60% de los textos en todos los niveles de grado, entre ellos canciones y cuentos tradicionales, así como textos de autores reconocidos como Graciela Montes, José Martí, Amado Nervo, Suni Paz, Rubén Darío, Georgina Lázaro, María Elena Walsh y Jorge Urgueta.

Los autores de *¡Arriba la Lectura!* provienen de una variedad de países de habla hispana, entre ellos Argentina, España, Cuba, México, Puerto Rico, Nicaragua,

Pedagogía intercultural *(cont.)*

Chile, Colombia, Ecuador y El Salvador. La **Revista Aventuras** y la sección "Nuestra lengua es arte" contienen literatura escrita en español que expone a los estudiantes a la riqueza y diversidad de vocabulario y contenidos que representan al mundo de habla hispana.

Además de la amplia gama de textos que representan a las culturas hispanas, *¡Arriba la Lectura!* también incluye una variedad de textos que representan la diversidad de nuestras escuelas y nuestra nación. Así, los estudiantes se ven reflejados en los textos que leen y quedan expuestos, además, a una variedad de culturas diferentes.

>  *Tanto en casa como en la escuela, los libros se eligen con cuidado: libros que representan los valores de la cultura, la riqueza del patrimonio, la universalidad de la experiencia humana. Esos libros pueden contribuir a enriquecer las identidades de los niños. A través de ellos, los niños aprenden a explorar quiénes son y a comprender el mundo en el que viven. En esas páginas, ven similitudes y diferencias entre sus comunidades, tradiciones y visiones del mundo. Y pueden aprender sobre la igualdad, la justicia, la libertad y el amor* .
>
> — F. Isabel Campoy

> **❝** *Una pedagogía que reconoce, responde y celebra culturas fundamentales ofrece un acceso pleno y equitativo a la educación para estudiantes de todas las culturas* **❞**.
>
> — Brown University Education Alliance, Culturally Responsive Teaching

¿Por qué planificar una pedagogía intercultural?

Cuando la enseñanza y los materiales responden principalmente a la cultura dominante de Estados Unidos y esperan que los estudiantes vean la escuela y el aprendizaje desde esa perspectiva, se les niega a los estudiantes de diversos orígenes el mismo acceso a todo lo que la escuela tiene para ofrecer.

Al diseñar intencionalmente escuelas y salones de clases que reciban con los brazos abiertos a todas las culturas de nuestra comunidad, creamos las condiciones para que todos los estudiantes tengan las mismas oportunidades para aprender y prosperar.

La educación con sensibilidad intercultural es el vehículo a través del cual logramos la equidad.

Las investigaciones demuestran el impacto positivo de la enseñanza con sensibilidad intercultural en la motivación y el compromiso de los estudiantes.

Cuando los estudiantes pueden conectar su aprendizaje en clase con sus experiencias personales fuera de la escuela, el aprendizaje se vuelve relevante y ameno.

> **❝** *Las investigaciones han demostrado que ninguna estrategia de enseñanza involucrará sistemáticamente a todos los estudiantes. La clave es ayudar a los estudiantes a relacionar el contenido de las lecciones con sus propios orígenes* **❞**.
>
> — Wlodkowski, R. & Ginsberg, M. (1995). A Framework for Culturally Responsive Teaching. *Educational Leadership, 53*(1), 17–21.

La participación y la motivación de los estudiantes son factores críticos en la persistencia y el éxito escolar a largo plazo. Al diseñar intencionalmente una enseñanza con sensibilidad intercultural, comenzando en los primeros grados, creamos las condiciones para que los estudiantes sientan una firme conexión con la escuela y sigan participando en el aprendizaje a lo largo de su experiencia escolar.

Puentes interlingüísticos

Cuando a los estudiantes se les brinda la oportunidad de utilizar toda la gama de recursos lingüísticos que poseen, aprenden de manera significativa y aprovechan al máximo su potencial.

Todos los estudiantes bilingües emergentes llegan a la escuela con la capacidad de usar lo que saben sobre el lenguaje para apoyar el proceso que los convertirá en completamente bilingües. De hecho, cada estudiante posee un conjunto particular de recursos lingüísticos que no se limitan a un idioma u otro. Cuando consiguen hacer conexiones entre idiomas, los estudiantes pueden usar los recursos lingüísticos que ya tienen para ampliar el aprendizaje en ambos idiomas.

>
> **❝** *Cuando los estudiantes pueden reflexionar sobre todas sus prácticas lingüísticas es cuando se desarrolla el lenguaje* **❞**.
> — Joanna Yip y Ofelia García

Sin embargo, no podemos esperar que los estudiantes reconozcan automáticamente las conexiones entre los idiomas. Una estrategia importante basada en la investigación es el puente interlingüístico. El puente es un paso crucial en el desarrollo de la alfabetización bilingüe de los estudiantes.

Los "Puentes interlingüísticos" de *¡Arriba la Lectura!*

Cada lección de *¡Arriba la Lectura!* cuenta con páginas dedicadas al "Puente interlingüístico", sección que brinda oportunidades de enriquecimiento del idioma basadas en el contenido de la lección específica trabajada. Estos puentes interlingüísticos resaltan las similitudes y diferencias entre los temas concretos del inglés y del español cubiertos en esa lección. Sirven como una base que los maestros pueden utilizar para incorporar más oportunidades de realizar conexiones en sus grupos.

> *El puente interlingüístico alude a la práctica de poner ambos idiomas uno junto al otro e identificar y enseñar explícitamente los puntos en común y las diferencias que existen entre ellos.*

> *El translenguaje es el uso fluido de todos los recursos lingüísticos presentes en el repertorio de un estudiante para comunicarse y aprender, independientemente del idioma utilizado.*

>
> **❝** *La enseñanza basada en el translenguaje también debe desarrollarse. Esto incluye tener el material multilingüe apropiado para que los estudiantes aprendan en ambos idiomas, preparar el salón de clases como un espacio multilingüe y agrupar a los estudiantes según el idioma que hablan en casa para que puedan ayudarse mutuamente y profundizar el significado del aprendizaje. E implica, también, diseñar intencionalmente lecciones con un lenguaje, un contenido y unos objetivos específicos. Una lección y un diseño de unidad de translenguaje no pueden generarse por casualidad, sino que deben integrarse plenamente en la lección* **❞**.
> — Joanna Yip y Ofelia García

A los estudiantes se les presentan las similitudes y diferencias entre el inglés y el español relacionadas con un tema de la lección.

Los estudiantes reconocen e identifican las similitudes y las diferencias entre el inglés y el español, guiados por el maestro.

Los estudiantes tienen la posibilidad de participar según el nivel de adquisición del lenguaje que posean.

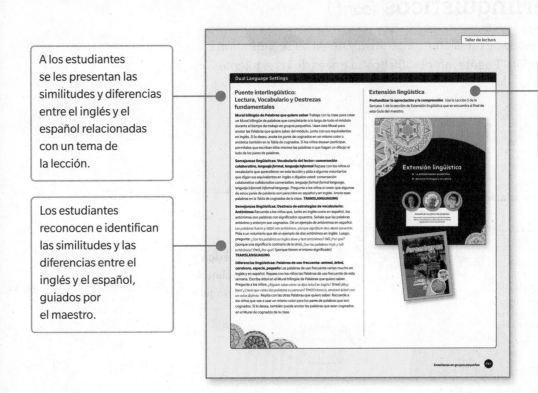

Los objetivos del "Puente interlingüístico" son:

- Creación de conexiones entre el contenido aprendido en un idioma y ese mismo contenido en otro idioma

- Desarrollo del vocabulario académico relacionado con el tema trabajado en la lección, en inglés y en español*

- Participación en el análisis lingüístico contrastivo

- Desarrollo de la conciencia metalingüística

*El recurso **Lenguaje dual: Guía de implementación** proporciona actividades adicionales relacionadas con cada módulo encaminadas a ampliar el vocabulario académico interdisciplinario de los estudiantes tanto en inglés como en español.

Es importante tener en cuenta que existe una transferencia tanto positiva como negativa entre los idiomas. Ambos son igualmente importantes para enseñar a los estudiantes bilingües.

> *La* transferencia positiva *ocurre cuando el conocimiento de un idioma facilita el aprendizaje en otro idioma.*

> *La* transferencia negativa *ocurre cuando el conocimiento de un idioma interfiere o causa errores en el aprendizaje de un nuevo idioma.*

66 *El lenguaje no se transfiere. Los conceptos de lenguaje, sí* **99**.
— Dra. Elena Izquierdo

Puentes interlingüísticos (cont.)

En *¡Arriba la Lectura!*, los temas de transferencia positiva y negativa se presentan a los estudiantes en la sección "Puente interlingüístico" a través de las siguientes herramientas:

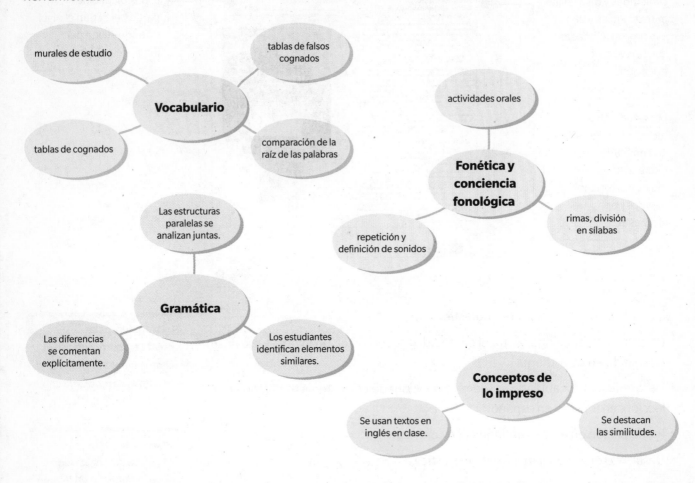

Para temas que son específicos del idioma español o que podrían crear una transferencia negativa, se ofrecen actividades de apoyo adicionales en español, como trabalenguas y dictados.

⊙ Consulte la sección "Análisis lingüístico contrastivo" en las páginas E29–E40 de esta guía para obtener información más detallada sobre el análisis lingüístico contrastivo, el translenguaje y la conciencia metalingüística, así como temas específicos y sugerencias de actividades sobre la transferencia positiva y negativa entre el inglés y el español que se podrían tratar en clase.

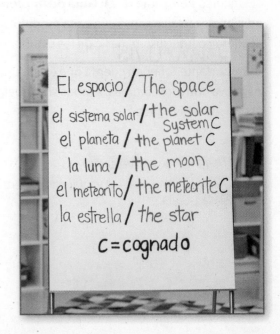

Extensión lingüística

La sección "Extensión lingüística" de *¡Arriba la Lectura!* proporciona textos culturalmente relevantes de literatura original en español para ampliar las destrezas de lenguaje y profundizar en la apreciación de las culturas hispanohablantes de todo el mundo.

Los textos de la **Revista Aventuras** fueron seleccionados por **Alma Flor Ada** y **F. Isabel Campoy,** académicas de reconocimiento internacional y autoras de cientos de libros premiados. Ambas autoras escribieron, además, los cuentos y poemas de la subsección **"Apreciar la lengua y la cultura".**

La **Dra. Elena Izquierdo,** investigadora especializada en la enseñanza dual y la lectoescritura bilingüe, ha supervisado de cerca **"La alfabetización académica",** subsección que incluye el **"Puente interlingüístico".**

La alfabetización académica

"La alfabetización académica" trabaja una selección de textos de la **Revista Aventuras,** la cual contiene decenas de textos escritos originalmente en español, ideales para desarrollar el lenguaje académico, la comprensión y la apreciación literaria. Las lecturas fueron especialmente seleccionadas con el objetivo de celebrar las culturas hispanas y teniendo en cuenta la riqueza lingüística y la calidad literaria de las obras. Los temas están relacionados con el tema del módulo, de manera que los estudiantes puedan establecer conexiones.

El apartado **"Vistazo rápido"** ofrece un panorama general sobre el texto principal y la lectura conjunta. Los textos se encuentran en la **Revista Aventuras,** acompañados de vistosas ilustraciones.

Se explican las razones por las cuales los textos han sido seleccionados y se presenta una breve biografía de los autores.

Se incluye una nota cultural que permite a los estudiantes establecer conexiones entre la lectura y la sociedad.

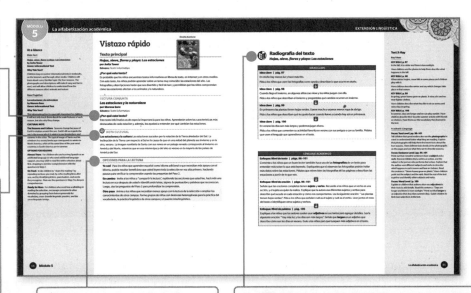

Se dan opciones para la lectura diferenciada según el nivel de aprendizaje de los estudiantes.

En **"Radiografía del texto",** se resumen las ideas clave de cada página y se ofrece una actividad para desarrollar el lenguaje académico.

Extensión lingüística (cont.)

El apartado **"Leamos juntos"** refuerza las estrategias de aprendizaje de palabras en el contexto de la lectura. Este apartado está diseñado para asistir al maestro mientras guía la lectura del texto principal.

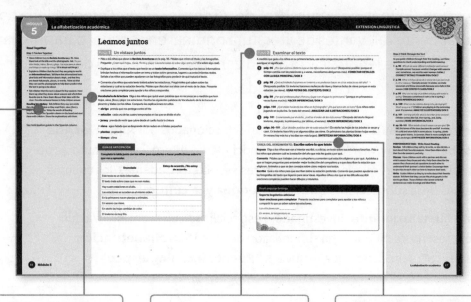

Se analizan palabras de vocabulario que pueden resultar desconocidas para los estudiantes.

Las preguntas de seguimiento ayudan a evaluar la comprensión y a desarrollar una lectura analítica.

Al final de este apartado, los estudiantes comparten sus ideas en conversaciones con un compañero y escriben sobre la lectura.

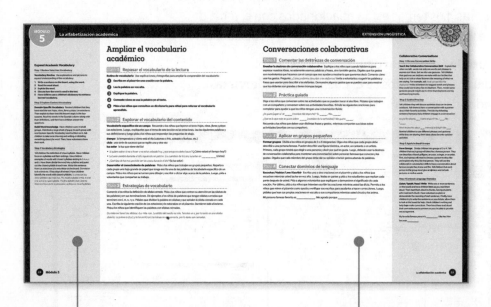

El apartado **"Ampliar el vocabulario académico"** se enfoca en el trabajo con el vocabulario nuevo y ayuda a los maestros a establecer estrategias para explorar las palabras que resultan desconocidas para los estudiantes mediante preguntas y explicaciones basadas en el contexto en el que aparecen las palabras.

Las **"Conversaciones colaborativas"** permiten desarrollar las destrezas de conversación de los estudiantes, profundizar en el pensamiento crítico y la conciencia metalingüística y aplicar el vocabulario aprendido. Este apartado también tiene como propósito conectar los diferentes dominios del lenguaje mediante la escritura de textos breves como respuesta a la lectura.

En el apartado **"Leer la lectura conjunta"**, el maestro lee en voz alta la lectura y hace preguntas para verificar la comprensión. Después de leer el texto varias veces, toda la clase analiza el significado y se establecen conexiones con otros textos.

El apartado **"Puente interlingüístico"** proporciona estrategias sencillas que permiten implementar prácticas para el desarrollo de las habilidades cognitivas en inglés y en español, evaluar el aprendizaje de los estudiantes y establecer conexiones entre ambos idiomas para profundizar la comprensión.

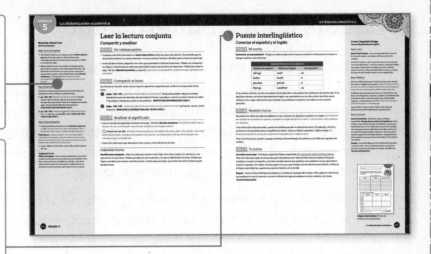

Apreciar la lengua y la cultura

La subsección "Apreciar la lengua y la cultura" presenta una selección de textos de "Nuestra lengua es arte": poemas y cuentos escritos originalmente en español por Alma Flor Ada y F. Isabel Campoy especialmente para este programa. Estos textos fueron seleccionados con el fin de que el maestro los comparta con la clase al finalizar cada módulo de la **Guía del maestro** y permitirán ampliar el vocabulario de los estudiantes y desarrollar su apreciación literaria.

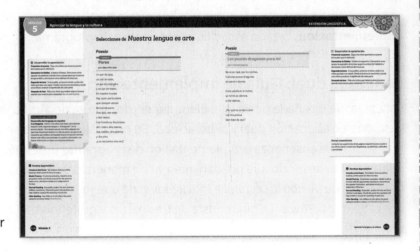

Los poemas y cuentos de "Nuestra lengua es arte" celebran la diversidad cultural. Esto queda demostrado por las constantes referencias a las culturas de todo el mundo y muy especialmente a las culturas hispanas. Esta sección incluye actividades para evaluar la comprensión, hacer conexiones con otras lecturas y desarrollar la apreciación literaria.

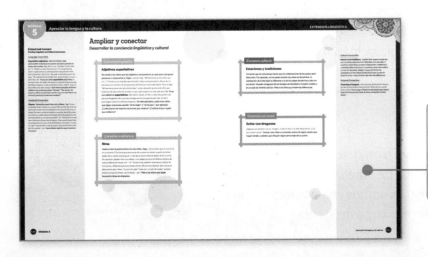

En el apartado **"Ampliar y conectar"**, se establecen conexiones lingüísticas, académicas, culturales y personales.

Lenguaje dual y biliteracidad

Un programa para la enseñanza en lenguaje dual

¡Arriba la Lectura! se creó intencionalmente para su uso conjunto con *Into Reading* en entornos de educación en lenguaje dual. Los temas se diseñaron para cubrir los estándares de enseñanza y se desarrollan de forma paralela en ambos programas, de modo que permiten ampliar los conocimientos de los estudiantes en los dos idiomas, según sus necesidades.

La temática de los módulos de *¡Arriba la Lectura!* e *Into Reading* se corresponde entre ambos programas para facilitar a los maestros la enseñanza en ambos idiomas según los objetivos de su programa.

Las secciones "Puente interlingüístico" y "Dual Language Settings" permiten establecer conexiones entre el español y el inglés en todas las lecciones de *¡Arriba la Lectura!* y fomentan un aprendizaje bilingüe que integra el desarrollo cognitivo de los estudiantes en ambos idiomas. Estas secciones se ven complementadas por el recurso **Lenguaje dual: Guía de implementación,** creado específicamente para este programa.

Lenguaje dual: Guía de implementación

Esta guía fue diseñada por la Dra. Elena Izquierdo, autora de *¡Arriba la Lectura!* y experta en educación dual y biliteracidad. Su propósito es orientar a los maestros en la enseñanza e implementación de programas de lenguaje dual y biliteracidad, de modo que puedan integrar de manera práctica y eficaz materiales de *¡Arriba la Lectura!* e *Into Reading* de una forma flexible, según sus propios objetivos. La guía consta de tres partes y pretende ser un recurso de fácil acceso para la consulta permanente, con un atractivo diseño que facilita la lectura y la navegación.

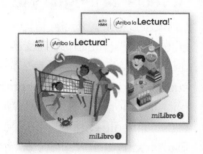

Parte 1: La adquisición del lenguaje en contextos bilingües

Esta sección presenta conceptos fundamentales de la biliteracidad (los diversos modelos de educación bilingüe, sus principios comunes, el desarrollo de la conciencia cultural, el translenguaje) y brinda un marco teórico desde el cual los maestros puedan abordar la enseñanza dual y comprender su relevancia. También incluye un glosario bilingüe de términos profesionales relacionados con la enseñanza dual y una bibliografía de investigaciones sobre la enseñanza del lenguaje en contextos bilingües.

Parte 2: Planificar para el grado

Esta sección práctica proporciona recursos para planificar las lecciones. **"Vocabulario intercurricular"** es un apartado de ampliación léxica y ofrece un selecto vocabulario cotidiano y académico en ambos idiomas relacionado con los temas que estudiarán los estudiantes a lo largo del grado.

Las listas de vocabulario intercurricular van acompañadas de definiciones, ejemplos de uso y actividades sugeridas con objeto de ampliar el vocabulario, desarrollar más los conocimientos de cada módulo y extenderlos a otras materias. Los temas de este apartado se corresponden con los estándares de enseñanza.

Por otra parte, **"Vistazo a la semana"** permite visualizar rápidamente los contenidos de cada semana para que el maestro elija qué temas cubrir en cada idioma y cómo conectarlos en su clase de enseñanza dual o biliteracidad.

Parte 3: Recursos

La tercera parte de la guía contiene fichas de registro de la evaluación dual, fichas para la planificación curricular, pautas de calificación y rutinas integradas para la biliteracidad. Incluye una rutina de dictado, con la que los estudiantes aplican los contenidos de artes del lenguaje que aprendieron con un ejercicio controlado, reflexionan sobre esos contenidos para desarrollar su conciencia metalingüística y los comparan y contrastan en ambos idiomas. Esta sección ayudará a los maestros con la implementación del programa de lenguaje dual de su preferencia.

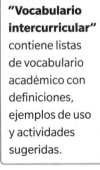

❝ *Para los niños que trabajan a través de dos idiomas, las evaluaciones en los dos idiomas son parte de una evaluación completa para poder hacer decisiones instruccionales* ❞.

— Dra. Elena Izquierdo

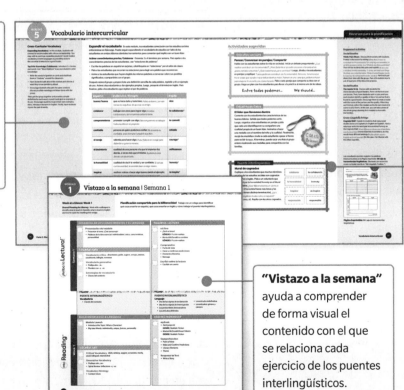

"Vocabulario intercurricular" contiene listas de vocabulario académico con definiciones, ejemplos de uso y actividades sugeridas.

"Puente interlingüístico" invita a trabajar con un mural de cognados para que los estudiantes establezcan conexiones entre ambos idiomas.

"Vistazo a la semana" ayuda a comprender de forma visual el contenido con el que se relaciona cada ejercicio de los puentes interlingüísticos.

¡Viva el español!

Glosario de términos profesionales

Nota: Las definiciones reflejan usos comunes actuales. Existen diferencias significativas en el uso de los términos por parte de distintos educadores, principalmente porque el bilingüismo, la biliteracidad y los programas de lenguaje dual son campos de estudio que todavía se encuentran en desarrollo y expansión. El propósito de este glosario es contribuir a la estandarización de una terminología básica compartida.

A

adquisición del lenguaje (*language acquisition*) Trayectoria del desarrollo del lenguaje en los estudiantes que adquieren una primera y una segunda lengua; incluye lenguaje tanto receptivo como expresivo.

análisis lingüístico contrastivo (*contrastive analysis*) Práctica pedagógica en la que los estudiantes comparan y contrastan la morfología, la fonología, la sintaxis, la gramática o la pragmática de la lengua mayoritaria y de la lengua asociada.

B

bilingüismo (*bilingualism*) Capacidad de una persona para comunicarse en dos idiomas; el nivel de dominio de las destrezas para escuchar, hablar, leer y escribir en cada idioma puede ser muy variable en cada individuo y puede abarcar un amplio rango, desde un dominio básico del segundo idioma hasta el dominio total de ambos idiomas.

biliteracidad (*biliteracy*) Desarrollo de la lectoescritura en dos idiomas, que incluye todas las competencias lingüísticas, es decir, la comprensión auditiva, la lectura, la escritura y la expresión oral; también se conoce como "alfabetización bilingüe" y "lectoescritura bilingüe".

C

capacidad oral (*oracy*) Todas las destrezas de expresión oral y comprensión auditiva que se usan en el lenguaje oral. La capacidad oral es una de las bases fundamentales de la lectoescritura.

cartel didáctico (*anchor chart*) Representación visual de conceptos o del contenido de una lección expresados con dibujos y/o un lenguaje sencillo, a menudo creado por el maestro en colaboración con los estudiantes.

cognados (*cognates*) Palabras que suenan y se escriben de forma similar en dos idiomas y tienen la misma raíz.

conciencia metalingüística (*metalinguistic awareness*) Comprensión de cómo funciona una lengua y cómo cambia en diferentes situaciones. En relación a un estudiante bilingüe, la conciencia metalingüística se refiere a la comprensión de las similitudes y diferencias entre los dos idiomas.

D

dictado (*dictation*) Estrategia de enseñanza en la que el maestro dicta palabras u oraciones relacionadas con los textos o destrezas que los estudiantes están aprendiendo; a lo largo de varios días, los estudiantes abordan el mismo dictado mediante distintas modalidades que refuerzan y amplían todas las competencias lingüísticas (comprensión auditiva, expresión oral, lectura y escritura). El dictado puede usarse como herramienta de apoyo para el desarrollo del lenguaje y de destrezas específicas. En un programa de biliteracidad, también puede usarse para hacer conexiones interlingüísticas.

E

efectividad (*efficacy*) Eficacia; facultad de alcanzar un objetivo; término que describe el hecho de que se obtienen mejores resultados mediante programas de lenguaje dual y de biliteracidad en comparación con una enseñanza exclusivamente en inglés.

equidad (*equity*) Igualdad y justicia; en educación, se refiere al acceso equitativo de todos los estudiantes a una enseñanza eficaz centrada en el estudiante y a materiales adecuados de alta calidad, independientemente del idioma de enseñanza.

evidencia (*evidence*) Información confiable basada en la investigación científica que se incorpora a las decisiones relacionadas con la enseñanza.

F

falsos cognados (*false cognates*) Pares de palabras que suenan y/o se escriben de forma similar en dos idiomas, por lo que se perciben como similares. En cambio, tienen significados diferentes, lo que puede dar lugar a confusiones; también conocidos como *falsos amigos*.

H

hablante de herencia (*heritage speaker*) Estudiante cuya primera lengua es la lengua mayoritaria, pero que ha crecido en un hogar o entorno en el que se habla la lengua asociada. En general, los hablantes de herencia tienen algunas destrezas lingüísticas recesivas y expresivas en la lengua asociada, pero su lengua dominante es la lengua mayoritaria y han recibido su educación formal en ella.

L

lector/escritor emergente (*emergent reader/ writer*) Lector/escritor que se encuentra en la etapa inicial de la adquisición de las destrezas de lectura y escritura.

lengua asociada (*partner language*) Idioma adicional que se enseña en un programa bilingüe; el idioma que no es la lengua mayoritaria.

lengua mayoritaria (*majority language*) Lengua que utiliza la mayor parte de la población de un país determinado.

lengua minoritaria (*minority language*) Lengua que se usa en un país determinado, distinta de la que usa la mayor parte de la población.

M

modelo educativo 50:50 (*50:50 model*) Tipo de programa de lenguaje dual en el que la enseñanza se brinda en la lengua asociada y en la lengua mayoritaria en proporciones iguales en todos los grados.

modelo educativo 90:10 (*90:10 model*) Tipo de programa de lenguaje dual en el que la enseñanza se brinda en la lengua asociada en una proporción del 90 por ciento y, a continuación, en la lengua mayoritaria en una proporción del 10 por ciento durante el primer o los dos primeros años, con un aumento paulatino anual de la cantidad de lengua mayoritaria usada hasta llegar a una proporción del 50:50 entre ambos idiomas, generalmente en el tercer grado.

O

ortografía transparente (*transparent ortography*) Correlación directa entre patrones fonológicos y ortográficos, característica de idiomas como el español, a diferencia de la correspondencia más compleja (u "opaca") entre grafemas y fonemas que poseen otros idiomas, como el inglés.

P

programa bidireccional (*two-way bilingual program*) Programa en el que se enseña tanto en la lengua mayoritaria como en la lengua asociada. Existe una proporción equitativa entre los estudiantes del programa que hablan la lengua asociada y aquellos que hablan la lengua mayoritaria.

programa de biliteracidad secuencial (*sequential biliteracy program*) Programa de inmersión en el que los estudiantes primero reciben la mayor parte de la enseñanza en una lengua y luego adquieren la segunda lengua gradualmente, a medida que avanzan a los grados superiores.

Glosario de términos profesionales *(cont.)*

programa de biliteracidad simultánea *(simultaneous biliteracy program)* Programa de inmersión en el que los estudiantes aprenden en dos idiomas al mismo tiempo desde los primeros grados y a lo largo de toda su educación.

programa de inmersión *(immersion program)* Programa en el que la mayor parte o la totalidad de la enseñanza se realiza en la segunda (o tercera) lengua de los estudiantes. El término *inmersión dual* a veces se usa como sinónimo de *lenguaje dual*.

programa de lenguaje dual *(dual language program)* Programa educativo de largo plazo cuyo objetivo es alcanzar la lectoescritura académica plena en dos idiomas (generalmente la lengua mayoritaria y una lengua asociada). Gran parte de la enseñanza se brinda en ambos idiomas en todas las materias del currículo. Aunque existen muchos modelos de lenguaje dual, todos ellos están diseñados para extenderse por varios años y tienen como objetivo lograr la biliteracidad plena, así como rigurosos logros académicos para todos los estudiantes.

programa de salida *(exit program)* Programa que brinda apoyo en la lengua nativa solo como un paso intermedio para adquirir una segunda lengua; programa que no tiene como objetivo la lectoescritura plena en la lengua nativa, sino que se usa como salida de la lengua nativa para enfocarse en la segunda lengua. En Estados Unidos, los programas bilingües de "salida temprana" se diseñan de forma que los estudiantes tengan una transición de la lengua nativa hacia la lengua mayoritaria lo más rápido posible; los programas de "salida tardía" suelen brindar varios años de apoyo bilingüe. Los programas de lenguaje dual pueden considerarse como programas bilingües "de no salida" (que, idealmente, duran hasta el duodécimo grado o una instancia educativa superior), cuyo objetivo es la biliteracidad plena. Los programas de salida también se denominan *programas de transición*.

programa unidireccional *(one-way bilingual program)* Programa en el que todos los estudiantes son hablantes de una segunda lengua, a diferencia del modelo bidireccional, en el que aproximadamente la mitad de los estudiantes son hablantes de la lengua mayoritaria y la otra mitad son hablantes de la lengua asociada; también se denomina *programa de inmersión en idioma extranjero*.

puente interlingüístico *(cross-linguistic bridging)* Estrategia usada en las clases de enseñanza bilingüe, lenguaje dual y biliteracidad en la que el maestro involucra a los estudiantes en la práctica del análisis lingüístico contrastivo, gracias al cual desarrollan una conciencia metalingüística, a la vez que los anima a transferir contenidos aprendidos en un idioma al otro.

T

transferencia *(transfer)* Capacidad de un hablante de aplicar sus conocimientos sobre los sonidos y la sintaxis de un idioma para leer, escribir y hablar en otro idioma; la transferencia puede ser positiva o negativa; la transferencia negativa puede interferir en la adquisición de la segunda lengua.

translenguaje *(translanguaging)* Prácticas discursivas de individuos bilingües o multilingües que aprovechan todo su repertorio lingüístico. El translenguaje se caracteriza por la integración de varios idiomas en el mismo contexto lingüístico, de un modo que generalmente demuestra la existencia de conciencia metalingüística. Se considera que el translenguaje empodera a los estudiantes y los anima a adueñarse de sus herramientas lingüísticas.

V

variantes léxicas *(lexical variations)* Diferentes palabras que expresan el mismo significado y que son usadas por los hablantes de un mismo idioma provenientes de distintas regiones o entornos.

Análisis lingüístico contrastivo

A los maestros les resultará útil aprender aquellas características específicas de cada idioma que suelen causar dificultades a los estudiantes con otra lengua materna, de modo que puedan brindarles práctica adicional según sea necesario. Los puentes interlingüísticos que se trabajan semanalmente en *¡Arriba la Lectura!* constituyen un buen ejemplo de cómo abordar el análisis lingüístico contrastivo.

El **análisis lingüístico contrastivo** se refiere a la práctica de estudiar de manera conjunta las características lingüísticas de dos idiomas. El análisis lingüístico contrastivo se enfoca sobre todo en cuatro campos lingüísticos: la fonología, la morfología, la sintaxis (gramática) y la pragmática. A fin de que los maestros enseñen con eficacia las similitudes y las diferencias entre los idiomas, es conveniente que hagan **puentes interlingüísticos** en los que enseñen de forma explícita las características de ambos idiomas.

A medida que los estudiantes bilingües van desarrollando sus destrezas lingüísticas, comienzan a integrar estructuras de ambos idiomas en su repertorio lingüístico. Esta integración se denomina translenguaje. El **translenguaje** se caracteriza por el uso de varios idiomas en la misma oración, frase o contexto lingüístico. Es una decisión espontánea que toman los hablantes bilingües en cada momento al usar todos sus recursos lingüísticos para comunicarse con eficacia. Puede ocurrir en la expresión oral, la lectura o la escritura.

Algunas estrategias para promover el translenguaje son ofrecer textos y recursos en ambos idiomas, formar grupos de hablantes heterogéneos, brindar una enseñanza basada en proyectos y clarificar lo enseñado en ambos idiomas.

El propósito del puente interlingüístico es mostrar a los estudiantes las conexiones entre el español y el inglés mediante el análisis lingüístico contrastivo.

Español	Inglés
Tengo hambre.	I am hungry.

En un entorno bilingüe, los estudiantes necesitan un espacio para poner en práctica todo su repertorio lingüístico.

Análisis lingüístico contrastivo (cont.)

Conexiones lingüísticas

Entre idiomas diferentes, pueden existir **similitudes lingüísticas** en distintas áreas, como la fonología, la morfología y la sintaxis. Las similitudes lingüísticas permiten poner en funcionamiento los conocimientos del idioma propio en beneficio del aprendizaje de otra lengua. Por ello, es probable que faciliten la adquisición de la lectura y la escritura en una segunda lengua.

Algunos elementos comunes del español y el inglés a tener en cuenta son los conceptos de lo impreso (la direccionalidad, las palabras, las oraciones y los propósitos de la escritura) y la escritura alfabética. Además, las destrezas de razonamiento y la comprensión del registro lingüístico (lenguaje formal e informal) son destrezas que se transfieren entre el español y el inglés.

En el momento de planificar las lecciones de los puentes interlingüísticos que se enfoquen en las similitudes lingüísticas, es importante considerar en qué se parecen las estructuras lingüísticas de ambos idiomas.

En cambio, las **diferencias lingüísticas** entre los idiomas pueden crear dificultades para la adquisición de la segunda lengua. Por ejemplo, los estudiantes de un segundo idioma a menudo pronuncian las palabras de la nueva lengua según las reglas fonológicas de su idioma primario.

A la hora de enseñar las lecciones de los puentes interlingüísticos entre español e inglés, es fundamental tener en cuenta aspectos tales como las reglas gramaticales, las estructuras de las oraciones, los fonemas y la pragmática, que son diferentes en ambos idiomas, y abordarlos de forma explícita.

Las similitudes y las diferencias lingüísticas entre los idiomas son igualmente importantes en la enseñanza a estudiantes bilingües.

Algunos aspectos para comparar y contrastar

A continuación, se muestra un esquema de las principales similitudes y diferencias entre las lenguas española e inglesa:

Español

- 22 a 24 fonemas/29 letras
- ñ, h muda
- La enseñanza de la lectura comienza con las vocales.
- Correspondencia uno a uno entre los fonemas y los grafemas de las vocales
- La división en sílabas es fundamental para aprender a leer.
- Predominan los patrones ortográficos regulares y predecibles.
- Acento ortográfico (tilde)

Ambos

- Conceptos de lo impreso
- Escritura alfabética
- Destrezas de razonamiento
- Registro lingüístico

Inglés

- 44 fonemas/26 letras
- La enseñanza de la lectura comienza con las consonantes.
- La división en sílabas se enseña en las lecciones de conciencia fonológica.
- Los patrones ortográficos irregulares son muy comunes.
- Se enseñan palabras de uso frecuente como apoyo para la fluidez.

La conciencia metalingüística

Ayudar a los estudiantes a entender las similitudes y las diferencias lingüísticas entre dos idiomas facilita la adquisición de ambas lenguas. Además, permite desarrollar la **conciencia metalingüística,** es decir, la comprensión sobre el lenguaje en sí mismo. Esto predispone a los estudiantes a seguir explorando el lenguaje durante toda la vida.

Las tablas de análisis lingüístico contrastivo que aparecen en las siguientes páginas resumen algunos de los principales conceptos de cada campo lingüístico.

Desarrollo del lenguaje en español

Apoyo para los estudiantes que aprenden español como segunda lengua

Estructuras gramaticales La siguiente tabla detalla algunos de los retos más comunes para los estudiantes angloparlantes a la hora de aprender español. Se trata de estructuras y usos que no se transfieren del inglés, por lo que pueden provocar interferencias al aprender español.

Todos estos temas se tratan en las lecciones y en las secciones de "Puente interlingüístico" de este programa, pero las sugerencias servirán para reforzar los temas a lo largo de todo el año con elementos de ayuda visual y actividades que el maestro puede llevar a cabo en cualquier momento.

RETO	SUGERENCIAS PARA LA ENSEÑANZA
Me gusta	Es común que los angloparlantes digan por error: *Yo me gusta* o *Yo gusta*. Haga juegos orales con la **estructura *me gusta***. Pida a los estudiantes que formen un círculo y completen la oración *A mí me gusta _____*. Pídales que repitan la oración de todos los compañeros con un turno anterior en el círculo. Repita estas actividades cuando surja el tema en clase.
Paso del tiempo	**En español se utilizan los verbos *hacer* y *llevar* para indicar el paso del tiempo,** por ejemplo: *Hace un año que vine aquí. Llevamos un año aquí.* Estas estructuras no existen en inglés y pueden constituir un reto para los estudiantes. Practique estas estructuras con los estudiantes siempre que surja en clase la oportunidad de hablar del paso del tiempo. Para ello, use estas oraciones incompletas: *Hace _____ que _____. Llevo _____.*
Género de los sustantivos	**En inglés, los sustantivos no tienen género, pero en español, sí.** Para ayudar a los estudiantes a recordar el género de los sustantivos, identifique todos los objetos del salón de clases con etiquetas que incluyan el artículo y el sustantivo, por ejemplo: *la mesa, la silla, el pizarrón, el libro.* Siempre que presente en clase sustantivos nuevos en español, use el artículo delante para reforzar el género del sustantivo. Explique a los estudiantes que, en general, las palabras que llevan *el* delante son masculinas y las que llevan *la* delante son femeninas. Diga que, normalmente, la mayor parte de los nombres de cosas que terminan en *-o* u *-or* son masculinas, mientras que las que terminan en *-a, -dad, -ción* o *-sión* son femeninas, aunque hay excepciones. Comente que, con algunos sustantivos que hacen referencia a personas, la misma palabra se usa para el masculino o femenino y solo cambia *el* y *la*, por ejemplo: *el estudiante, la estudiante.* Coloque en el salón un cartel con dos columnas: *Femenino* y *Masculino*. Vayan escribiendo bajo el encabezado correspondiente las palabras que los estudiantes vayan aprendiendo.

RETO	SUGERENCIAS PARA LA ENSEÑANZA
Mayúsculas	Explique a los estudiantes que muchas mayúsculas se usan de la misma manera en inglés y en español, pero que en algunos casos no se usan igual. Por ejemplo, **en español, los meses del año y los días de la semana se escriben con minúscula**, a menos que vayan al principio de una oración o sean un encabezado: *lunes, domingo, febrero, septiembre.* **Los idiomas también se escriben con minúscula:** *español, inglés, chino.* Coloque en el salón un cartel con los días de la semana y los meses del año en español e inglés, con las mayúsculas y minúsculas subrayadas. Recuerde a los estudiantes que consulten el cartel cuando vayan a escribir estas palabras. Asegúrese de escribir *español* e *inglés* con minúscula siempre que pueda para repasar estas normas.
Posesión	**En español, se indica posesión con la siguiente estructura:** *la casa de Pablo, el libro de María.* Practique esta estructura con los estudiantes si observa que tienen dificultades para indicar posesión.
Pronombres posesivos	**En español, se tiende a utilizar los pronombres posesivos menos que en inglés en lo que se refiere a las partes del cuerpo y las prendas de ropa.** Si los estudiantes usan oraciones como *Ella levanta su mano,* responda diciéndoles: *Ella levanta la mano.* Asegúrese de utilizar la misma estructura cuando dé instrucciones a los estudiantes: *Levanten la mano. Pónganse la chaqueta.*
Comparaciones	**Para las comparaciones en español**, en lugar de cambiar la terminación del adjetivo como ocurre en inglés, **se utiliza la siguiente estructura:** *El perro es más grande que el ratón. El elefante es el más grande de todos.* Pida a los estudiantes que comparen objetos del salón de clases usando oraciones para completar como: *El lápiz es _____ el libro. El pizarrón es _____ que el cuaderno.*
Conjugaciones verbales	**En español, hay muchas más conjugaciones verbales** que en inglés, por lo que los estudiantes angloparlantes necesitarán práctica para aprender a conjugar los verbos. Coloque en el salón un cartel con los verbos regulares *hablar, comer* y *escribir*. Escriba las terminaciones *-ar, -er, -ir* de otro color. Debajo de cada verbo, escriba las personas y las conjugaciones correctas en el presente, separando la raíz y la terminación del verbo. Los estudiantes pueden usar las terminaciones para conjugar otros verbos terminados en *-ar, -er, -ir*. A medida que los estudiantes vayan progresando en el aprendizaje del español, añada listas de las terminaciones correspondientes a otros tiempos verbales para que los estudiantes las puedan consultar.

Desarrollo del lenguaje en español (cont.)

RETO	SUGERENCIAS PARA LA ENSEÑANZA
Concordancia en género y número de los adjetivos y sustantivos; posición de los adjetivos	En inglés, no existe la **concordancia en género y número de los sustantivos y adjetivos.** Por lo tanto, los estudiantes angloparlantes necesitan practicar este tema. Cree tarjetas de palabras con sustantivos variados y con adjetivos en su forma masculina singular. Luego, pida a los estudiantes que elijan un sustantivo y un adjetivo y que digan una oración con ambas palabras. Deben modificar el adjetivo en forma masculina y singular según haga falta. Escriba los pares de sustantivos y adjetivos correctos en el pizarrón y señale la terminación que indica género y número. Pregunte a los estudiantes dónde va el adjetivo. (*después del sustantivo*)
Sujeto tácito	**En español, muchas veces se omite el sujeto** porque queda implícito en la conjugación del verbo, por ejemplo: *Como una manzana.* Pregunte a los estudiantes: *¿Quién come la manzana?* Si tienen dificultades para decir que es el propio hablante (*yo*), explique que se deben fijar en la terminación del verbo (*-o*). Diga que la terminación les servirá para saber quién es el sujeto de la oración, o quién está llevando a cabo la acción de la oración. Aclare que algunas terminaciones corresponden a varios sujetos, como en (*ellos, ustedes*) *hablan.* Proporcione a los estudiantes distintas oraciones, como: *Corremos en el parque. Caminaste a casa. Hablan con el maestro. Comemos una naranja.* Pídales que indiquen quién está llevando a cabo la acción en cada caso: *yo, tú, él o ella, nosotros, ustedes o ellos o ellas.* Dígales que consulten las terminaciones verbales en los carteles si es necesario. A medida que los estudiantes vayan progresando en el aprendizaje del español, añada otras oraciones con otros tiempos verbales.
Sustantivos generales o abstractos	Diga a los estudiantes que, **en español, se utilizan las palabras *el* o *la*, *los* o *las* en muchas ocasiones** en que en inglés no se usan. Por ejemplo, escriba en el pizarrón: *Las manzanas son deliciosas.* Señale que, cuando se está hablando de un objeto en general, en este caso todas las manzanas, en español se utilizan los artículos *el* o *la*, *los* o *las* delante.

Retos fonológicos

En la siguiente tabla, se ofrecen sugerencias para que los estudiantes angloparlantes practiquen la pronunciación de los sonidos nuevos o desconocidos que existen en el idioma español. Estos aspectos de la pronunciación también se tratan en el transcurso de las lecciones y en las secciones de "Puente interlingüístico" de este programa, pero conviene reforzar estos temas durante todo el año.

Tenga siempre en cuenta la importancia de no centrar sus esfuerzos en corregir la pronunciación; si usted focaliza la atención en el significado, los estudiantes generalmente irán adaptando su pronunciación para lograr que los demás los entiendan.

SONIDO	EJEMPLOS	SUGERENCIAS PARA LA ENSEÑANZA
/a/ /e/ /i/ /o/ /u/	abeja, elefante, iguana, oso, uñas	Aunque **las vocales en español no suponen mayores dificultades**, es importante que los estudiantes las practiquen para que se limiten a pronunciar los **cinco sonidos** de forma uniforme, excluyendo otros sonidos de vocales del inglés. Enseñe y cante con los estudiantes versos de canciones populares, como "La pájara pinta". Una vez que sepan la canción, deben cantarla cambiando todas las vocales a una sola, por ejemplo: *Estaba la pájara pinta* *a la sombra de un verde limón,* *con las alas cortaba las hojas,* *con el pico cortaba la flor.* Con la *a*: *Astaba la pájara panta* *a la sambra da an varda lamán,* *can las alas cartaba las hajas,* *can al paca cartaba la flar.* Con la *e*: *Estebe le péjere pente…* Preste especial atención a la letra *e*, ya que muchos estudiantes angloparlantes pueden confundirla con la letra *e* en inglés, que se pronuncia como la *i* en español. Asegúrese de que los estudiantes identifiquen la letra *e* con su sonido correcto.
/ñ/	niño, pequeño, ñame	**El sonido que representa la letra ñ no existe en inglés.** Practique el siguiente trabalenguas con los estudiantes: *Niña ñoña añoñada, añoñado niño ñoño.*
/rr/	perro, carro, rápido	Los estudiantes pueden tener dificultades para pronunciar **el sonido /rr/, que no existe en inglés**. Practique los siguientes trabalenguas con los estudiantes: *Erre con erre cigarra,* *erre con erre barril,* *rápido corren los carros por los rieles del ferrocarril.* *El perro de Roque no tiene rabo* *porque Ramón Ramírez se lo ha robado.* *Y al perro de Ramón Ramírez, ¿quién el rabo le ha robado?*
/r/	claro, coro, caro	**El sonido que representa la r cuando está en el medio o al final de una palabra** puede presentar dificultades para los estudiantes. Muéstreles la posición de la lengua. Pídales que practiquen los sonidos /r/ y /rr/ comparando pares de palabras como *cero, cerro; caro, carro; pero, perro; para, parra*.

¡Viva el español!

Desarrollo del lenguaje en español (cont.)

SONIDO	EJEMPLOS	SUGERENCIAS PARA LA ENSEÑANZA

/j/	júbilo, gente, girasol, jota	Los estudiantes pueden tener dificultades para recordar que **el sonido de la j y de la g antes de e o i es igual para las dos letras** y, además, es distinto a los sonidos de esas letras en inglés. Practique los siguientes trabalenguas con los estudiantes.
		
		Antes de empezar, siempre muestre o escriba la letra *j* y enfatice su sonido:
		
		  En un juncal de Junqueira,
		  juncos juntaba Julián.
		  Juntóse Juan a juntarlos y juntos juncos juntaron.
		
		Antes de empezar, siempre muestre o escriba la letra *g* y enfatice su sonido:
		
		  ¡Qué ingenuo es Eugenio! ¡Y qué genio tiene el ingenuo Eugenio!

combinaciones consonánticas	grito, trabajo, prado, creo	Practique estos trabalenguas con los estudiantes:
		
		  Tres tristes tigres tragan trigo en un trigal.
		  Me trajo Tajo tres trajes, tres trajes me trajo Tajo.
		  Contigo entró un tren con trigo, un tren con trigo contigo entró.

Guía rápida para la pronunciación de las vocales en español

Practique las vocales en español con los estudiantes siempre que pueda. Use rimas y canciones con las letras a, *e, i, o, u* para reforzar la pronunciación de estos cinco sonidos. Pídales que se fijen en la posición de la boca y de los labios mientras pronuncia las letras.

VOCAL	PRONUNCIACIÓN EN ESPAÑOL
a	*a* as in *father*
e	*e* as in *elephant*
i (y)	*i* as in *kid*
o	*o* as in *October*
u	*u* as in *flute*

English Language Development

Support for Students Learning English as a Second Language

Grammar and Sentence Structures The chart below lists some common challenges for Spanish-speaking students learning English as a second language. There are structures in English that do not transfer from Spanish, and they can interfere with the acquisition of English. These topics are addressed in the main lessons and Cross-Linguistic Bridges of this program, but the tips will be helpful in reinforcing these topics throughout the whole year, with visual aids and activities that can be conducted at any time.

Teacher Note

This section provides teaching suggestions for teachers of students who are learning English.

CHALLENGE	TEACHING TIPS
Contractions	**There are no contractions for verbs in Spanish,** so students may fail to recognize them in oral conversation in English. Place an anchor chart in the classroom listing the most common contractions and their extended forms (*I'm, we're, you're, he's, she's, can't, don't, won't, isn't, wasn't, didn't*). When a contraction is said in the classroom or read out aloud in a book, point to its spelling on the chart and ask a volunteer for the meaning of the contraction.
Comparative Adjectives	**Students may not be familiar with comparative adjectives,** as comparisons in Spanish are expressed in a different way. Write three columns on the board with the words *warm, warmer, warmest* and underline the ending of each one. Have students brainstorm places that are warm and decide which one is *warm, warmer,* and *warmest*. Repeat with animals and size, and with other items and qualities.
Possessive Pronouns	**In Spanish, the possessive pronoun *su* does not vary according to the gender of the owner,** so students may have more difficulty saying the pronouns *his* and *her* with the correct agreement. They may tend to have the pronoun agree with the object instead of the owner of the object. Distribute cards with the words *his* and *her* on them. Use these sentence frames for practice: *This is Amy. This is _____ book. This is Ryan. This is _____ bag.* Ask students to use the correct card to complete each sentence frame and to tell why they chose it.
Subject Pronouns	**Spanish-speaking students may omit subject pronouns** because they are unnecessary in Spanish. Notice when students omit the pronoun, for example: *Mom is not home. Is at work.* Ask the student: *Who is at work?* When they answer *Mom,* tell them that in English, they must say the subject, or who is performing the action, in every sentence (except in commands such as *Go home*). Otherwise, the sentence is incomplete and we do not know who performed the action. Provide some examples for students to correct in pairs, such as: *I am not hungry. Am thirsty.; They are not here. Are there.*

English Language Development (cont.)

CHALLENGE	TEACHING TIPS
Double Negatives	**Double negatives are correct in Spanish**, so Spanish-speaking students may use them erroneously in English. Write on the board: *I do not need _____.* Ask students to suggest a word to finish the sentence. If they say *nothing*, go back to the sentence and underline the word *not*. Tell them that in English, we do not use two negative words such as *not, no,* or *nothing* in the same sentence. Tell them they can say: *I need nothing* or *I do not need anything.* Explain that *I do not need nothing* is not an option. Keep a visible list of negative words on an anchor chart in the room.
Adjective Placement	**Spanish-speaking students may place the adjective after the noun** because of adjective placement in Spanish. Play a "silly sentences" game to practice using adjectives. Write out a sentence on the board with typical adjectives: *I see green leaves.* Have students find and replace the adjective with a silly one and say or write out the new sentence: *I see blue leaves.*
Pronoun *it*	**Spanish-speaking students are used to referring to objects with masculine or feminine pronouns according to their gender.** Use the following sentence frames for practice. Distribute cards with the words *him, her, it*. Then write or say the following sentence frame pairs: *Give me the pencil. I need _____.; Maria was there. I talked to _____.; My father was home. I said hello to _____.* Ask students: *Him, her, or it?* Have them match up the correct card with each sentence pair. In pairs, have them explain why they picked the pronoun. If necessary, point out that words like *he, she, him,* and *her* are only used to refer to people (and sometimes animals), and that *it* is always used for objects.
Helping Verbs in Questions and Negative Statements	**Spanish-speaking students may be unfamiliar with the use in English of helping verbs in questions and negative statements.** Write some questions and statements on large strips of poster board, for example: *Carl does not eat chocolate. Caiti is not coming to school. Do you want to come?* Then cut up the sentences into words. Have students work in pairs to put the words back together in the correct order. Tell them to use all of the words provided for each sentence.

Phonological Challenges The following chart offers tips for Spanish-speaking students to be able to practice the pronunciation of new or unfamiliar consonant sounds that exist in the English language and do not transfer from Spanish. These aspects of pronunciation are also addressed in the lessons and Cross-Linguistic Bridges in this program. Note that it is important not to overcorrect students' pronunciation; if you keep the emphasis on making meaning, students will generally adjust their pronunciation to be understood.

SOUND	EXAMPLES	TEACHING TIPS
/h/	house, have, hole	**Spanish-speaking students may omit the sound of h in some words,** because the letter h is silent in Spanish. Explain to students that the letter h in English has a sound similar to j in Spanish, in words such as *jinete* and *José*, although it is a softer sound. Use cognates to teach students how to pronounce h in English. For example, write the words *hotel* and *hospital* on the board and read them. Then, ask students to repeat after you.
/dz/	January, jet, just	**Spanish-speaking students may confuse the /dz/ sound** as in *jacket* with the /j/ as in *yacht*, or with the sound that the letter j stands for in Spanish. Have students practice the following rhyme at any time: *Jack be nimble, Jack be quick, Jack jump over the candle-stick.* Make sure to associate the letter j with the initial sound in *Jack* and *jump* by writing it on the board or showing a letter card before starting the rhyme.
/r/	rabbit, right, rose	Have students practice the following song to reinforce **the sound /r/,** which does not transfer from Spanish. Make sure to associate the letter r with the initial sound in *row* by writing it on the board or showing a letter card before starting the rhyme: *Row, row, row your boat* *Gently down the stream,* *Merrily, merrily, merrily, merrily,* *Life is but a dream.*
/v/	victory, voice, have	**Spanish speakers may have trouble differentiating the /v/ from the /b/ sound,** because there is no distinction between those sounds in Spanish. Say pairs of words with b and v, such as *ban/van, bet/vet, lob/love,* emphasizing the /b/ and /v/ sounds. Ask students to focus on the difference in your lips when you say each of the pairs. Have students say and repeat the sound. Then, distribute letter cards for b and v. Say the words in random order and have students hold up the card for the correct letter.
/z/	dozen, zoo	**The sound /z/ does not exist in Spanish,** so students may need extra practice to hear it and reproduce it. Use sound and spelling cards with images to practice pronouncing words with the /z/ sound. Have students repeat the words at first. When they are ready for more practice, have students use them in conversation.

¡Viva el español!

English Language Development (cont.)

Sounds Represented by Blends and Digraphs

SOUND	EXAMPLES	TEACHING TIPS
/ŋ/ /nk/ /rk/ /rm/	**something, bank, park, norm**	**Spanish-speaking students may tend to leave off consonant blends at the end of words,** which do not exist in Spanish. Make sure to pronounce the end sounds of words clearly and in an exaggerated way to promote students' understanding of the sounds. Encourage students to "keep going" and prolong the end sounds of words they are having difficulty with.
/ʃ/	**should, show, rush**	**Many Spanish-speaking students are not familiar with the ʃ sound** and may confuse it with the closest sound they know in Spanish, which is /tʃ/ as in *chair*. Constantly emphasize the difference in pronunciation between /ʃ/ and /tʃ/. In pairs, have students practice reading to each other pairs of words such as *sheep, cheap; shoes, choose*. Model the sound first and emphasize the difference in the two sounds. Encourage students to pronounce each word slowly.
/ø/	**think, thread, ethical**	Have students practice the following jingle to reinforce the **sound /ø/** as in *think*, which does not transfer from Spanish:* *Three blind mice. Three blind mice.* *See how they run. See how they run.*
/ð/	**them, those, although**	Have students practice the following rhyme to reinforce the **sound /ð/** as in *that*, which does not transfer from Spanish: *This little piggy went to market,* *this little piggy stayed at home,* *this little piggy had popcorn,* *this little piggy had none.* *And this little piggy went...* *Wee wee wee all the way home.*
/w/	**white, where, who**	Have students practice the following tongue-twister to reinforce the **sound /w/** as in *when*, which does not transfer from Spanish: *Whether the weather be fine,* *Or whether the weather be not,* *Whether the weather be cold,* *Or whether the weather be hot,* *We'll weather the weather* *Whatever the weather,* *Whether we like it or not!*

** Except for the variant spoken in most of Spain, where the letters **c** (with **e** and **i**) and **z** stand for a sound similar to /th/ in the word **think**.*

Fundamentos teóricos

Introducción

En el ciclo 2014–2015, se estimaba que unos 4.6 millones de escolares en Estados Unidos eran aprendices del idioma inglés (ELL, por sus siglas en inglés). La mayoría de ellos (77.1%), provenían de hogares de habla hispana. Según las investigaciones, solo el 63% de estos se gradúan de la escuela secundaria y la mayoría asiste a escuelas de bajo rendimiento[1].

Existen cuatro tipos de programas para estudiantes ELL:

- **SEI** (*Sheltered English Inmersion*) Clases que brindan contenido específico para ELL en inglés, antes de la transición a la enseñanza tradicional, que también es solo en inglés.

- **ESL** (*English as a Second Language*) Clases especializadas impartidas por un maestro capacitado en la enseñanza del inglés como segunda lengua, para promover las destrezas de adquisición del idioma. Pueden dictarse a todo el grupo o a una selección de estudiantes.

- **TBE** (*Transitional Bilingual Education*) Programas de transición bilingües que ofrecen de dos a tres años de enseñanza en el idioma nativo antes de hacer la transición a las clases tradicionales en inglés.

- **DLI** (*Dual Language Inmersion*) Programas de inmersión en los dos idiomas que brindan enseñanza en el idioma nativo y en el segundo idioma en paralelo. La frecuencia puede ser diaria, semanal o quincenal, según el programa.

Se espera que los participantes de los programas TBE y DLI desarrollen gradualmente las destrezas en su lengua nativa y apliquen esos conceptos a la segunda lengua (o lengua asociada) que están aprendiendo[2]. Thomas y Collier (2017) informan de que, luego de cursar en programas de escolarización bilingües durante siete años, los aprendices de inglés latinos progresan más en inglés cada año que los estudiantes que hablan inglés como única lengua y asisten a programas tradicionales. Y es por eso que, para el séptimo grado, los latinos y los aprendices de inglés logran cerrar la brecha y alcanzar el mismo nivel que quienes estudian solo en inglés[3].

Hoy hay más estudiantes inscritos en programas bilingües (TBE y DLI) que nunca. A medida que más investigaciones demuestren los beneficios de aprender otro idioma, estos programas continuarán desarrollándose y multiplicándose. Los programas bilingües en Estados Unidos están dirigidos a estudiantes de inglés como segundo idioma y a estudiantes angloparlantes. Están diseñados para desarrollar el bilingüismo y la biliteracidad en todos los estudiantes, sin importar su trasfondo lingüístico. Todos los programas bilingües requieren textos escritos por autores nativos, materiales didácticos multiculturales relevantes y destrezas fundamentales para el aprendizaje del español. *¡Arriba la Lectura!* no solo cumple este cometido, sino que nuestros autores han diseñado un plan de estudios de alfabetización holístico y alineado con los estándares de enseñanza.

Por más de 180 años, Houghton Mifflin Harcourt ha estado profundamente comprometido con la literatura y la alfabetización como método para mejorar la vida de las personas. *¡Arriba la Lectura!* continúa esa tradición. Este artículo de investigación explica cómo *¡Arriba la Lectura!* basa su desarrollo en las mejores investigaciones

---

[1] https://nces.ed.gov/fastfacts/display.asp?id=96

[2] https://www.npr.org/sections/ed/2017/02/23/512451228/5-million-english-language-learners-a-vast-pool-of-talent-at-risk

[3] Thomas, W. P. & Collier, V. P. (2017). *Why Dual Language Schooling*. Albuquerque, NM: Dual Language Education of New Mexico – Fuente Press.

Fundamentos teóricos (cont.)

sobre la enseñanza y el aprendizaje del español y la educación bilingüe. En esta sección, se presentan investigaciones relacionadas con el español y el bilingüismo y cómo *¡Arriba la Lectura!* las incorpora.

Panorama general del programa

¡Arriba la Lectura! es un plan de estudios de alfabetización integral que prepara a todos los estudiantes para ser lectores y escritores exitosos. Con un enfoque auténtico para la alfabetización en español, expone a los estudiantes a una variedad de textos escritos por autores nativos de habla hispana, mientras aprenden las destrezas fundamentales de la lengua española. Este programa se puede utilizar en cualquier modelo de enseñanza bilingüe.

La enseñanza básica

La enseñanza básica se basa en un modelo de taller de lectura que incluye textos valiosos presentados en mini lecciones de lectura atenta, con apoyo para los estudiantes en todos los niveles de lectura. Muchos de los textos en español fueron escritos por autores de habla hispana reconocidos en todo el mundo. Se seleccionaron minuciosamente y abarcan una variedad de géneros que incluyen ficción, no ficción, poesía, teatro y otros medios.

El enfoque en el taller de escritura paso a paso proporciona modelos y enseñanza sobre el proceso y la técnica e integra la gramática española dentro del contexto de la escritura. En los primeros grados, la enseñanza sistemática y explícita de las destrezas fundamentales en español se presenta en un modelo gradual con diferenciación en grupos pequeños.

Ventajas de los programas de lenguaje dual

Ser bilingüe confiere a los estudiantes ventajas cognitivas, culturales y sociales. Muchos estudiantes asisten a programas de lenguaje dual para aprender en su idioma nativo mientras agregan una lengua asociada (a veces llamadas L1 y L2). La expectativa es que los estudiantes en programas de calidad lean,

escriban y hablen a un nivel académico alto en ambos idiomas cuando lleguen al quinto grado.

Ventajas cognitivas

Numerosas investigaciones sobre los efectos del bilingüismo demuestran que los estudiantes que aprenden en dos idiomas desarrollan rigurosas destrezas de razonamiento, aplican la lógica a tareas complejas, tienen una mayor tasa de retención en la memoria y están mejor preparados para aprender más idiomas. Las investigaciones indican que los estudiantes que aprenden en dos idiomas muestran mayor neuroplasticidad, o control sobre los procesos cognitivos. Esto se conoce como "ventaja bilingüe" (Costa, Hernández, Costa-Faidella y Sebastián-Gallés, 2009; Scaltritti, Peressotti y Miozzo, 2015). Los estudiantes aprenden a aplicar las destrezas y los conocimientos de un idioma al otro. Además, los estudios demuestran que los estudiantes bilingües de todas las edades adquieren un funcionamiento ejecutivo superior al de los monolingües de la misma edad y con el mismo contexto.

Ventajas culturales

Los programas de lenguaje dual exponen a los estudiantes a las costumbres y tradiciones del idioma que la escuela enseña. Los textos escritos originalmente en español, las celebraciones culturales y las conexiones sólidas entre la escuela y el hogar son fundamentales para la enseñanza bilingüe. Los estudiantes para quienes el idioma de destino es su idioma nativo pueden mantener la conexión con su herencia, mientras que los estudiantes que aprenden el idioma de destino desarrollan competencias interculturales.

Ventajas sociales

Los estudiantes que aprenden dos o más idiomas desarrollan la capacidad de comunicarse y de formar relaciones significativas con personas que provienen de diversas culturas. En los programas de lenguaje dual en los que los estudiantes usan los dos idiomas para interactuar, los estudiantes desarrollan una perspectiva social, ya que deben tomar decisiones conscientes sobre el idioma que usarán para dirigirse a las personas (Hsin, 2017).

Ventajas globales

Las investigaciones demuestran que los estudiantes bilingües tienen ventaja sobre los monolingües a la hora de obtener un puesto de trabajo, para comunicarse y para comprender a compañeros con antecedentes distintos y oportunidades económicas diversas [4]. Los programas bilingües ofrecen a sus estudiantes una forma de convertirse en ciudadanos globales cuando aprenden a ver su educación desde una perspectiva cultural y multilingüe [5].

 **En ¡Arriba la Lectura!...**

La guía **Lenguaje dual: Guía de implementación** fue creada por la Dra. Elena Izquierdo para ayudar a los maestros a diseñar sus propios programas de lenguaje dual en base a los recursos paralelos de *¡Arriba la Lectura!* e *Into Reading*. Esta guía es un recurso de fácil acceso y consulta permanente para los maestros, con un atractivo diseño que facilita la lectura y la navegación. La **Guía del maestro** de *¡Arriba la Lectura!* incluye también recuadros de "Dual Language Settings" y la sección "Puente interlingüístico" como herramientas adicionales para las clases de lenguaje dual.

> ❝ *Los modelos de lenguaje dual enfatizan la alfabetización académica, no solo el bilingüismo* ❞.
>
> — Dra. Elena Izquierdo

Contexto de enseñanza en español

¡Arriba la Lectura! fue desarrollado con especial atención a los siguientes principios para la calidad de las artes del lenguaje en español y la enseñanza en dos idiomas:

- La enseñanza del español debe dictarse de acuerdo con las características lingüísticas y las estructuras pedagógicas más adecuadas para el aprendizaje del español.

- Los conocimientos previos de los estudiantes sobre el español se honran y se valoran, mientras que la participación en rigurosos programas académicos bilingües y de lenguaje dual elevan sus destrezas y competencias.

- La mejor forma de aprender para los estudiantes en programas bilingües es a través de planes de estudio multiculturales con textos escritos originalmente en español.

- El aprendizaje debe centrarse en los estudiantes para que se desarrollen más allá de sus competencias académicas, incluidos los factores no cognitivos, el aprendizaje socioemocional y la sensibilidad cultural.

- Leer, escribir, escuchar y hablar son dominios de la alfabetización fundamentalmente relacionados y deben enseñarse con un enfoque que los integre.

---

[4] https://www.aft.org/ae/fall2015/goldenberg_wagner

[5] http://blogs.edweek.org/edweek/global_learning/2018/05/seven_essential_components_for_successful_dual_language_programs.html

Fundamentos teóricos (cont.)

- La enseñanza efectiva se basa en datos y la evaluación es uno de sus componentes esenciales. Las evaluaciones para un programa de lenguaje dual toman en cuenta el desarrollo de los estudiantes bilingües emergentes.

- Las competencias de los estudiantes en inglés y en español se valoran al mismo nivel y se aplican a ambos idiomas para ampliar las destrezas.

- A los estudiantes se les debe motivar para que usen su repertorio lingüístico en ambos idiomas plenamente a través del translenguaje.

- El aprendizaje profesional continuo de los docentes es un componente vital de la educación de calidad.

Destrezas fundamentales del español

Según Jill Kerper Mora, existe una progresión recomendada para aprender español. Primero, los estudiantes deben ser expuestos a las destrezas y conceptos previos a la lectura. Esto incluye distinguir letras, palabras, oraciones y la direccionalidad en los textos impresos. Estas destrezas se consideran transferibles y, cuando se aprenden en español, se pueden aplicar inmediatamente al inglés. Luego, los estudiantes se exponen a las vocales del español y a las consonantes transferibles. Esto sienta las bases para la introducción de la conciencia silábica. El español es un lenguaje silábico[6] y, por ende, los principiantes aprenden a leer dividiendo las palabras en sílabas y luego combinándolas para formar palabras. La enseñanza del orden alfabético y los nombres de las letras debe posponerse hasta que los estudiantes dominen la correspondencia entre letras y sonidos (Mora, 2016). Finalmente, se les enseña a progresar de la lectura de sílabas aisladas a la lectura de palabras completas. Las destrezas fundamentales también deben incluir temas de gramática, como conjugación de verbos, sujetos tácitos y lecciones de ortografía, así como los usos culturales del español.

 En ¡Arriba la Lectura!...

A través de la enseñanza explícita y sistemática de sonidos, sílabas y palabras, *¡Arriba la Lectura!* desarrolla y refuerza las destrezas básicas de lectura en español. La enseñanza de estrategias de vocabulario y análisis estructural se apoya en la adquisición independiente de palabras por parte de los estudiantes.

El programa aplica la destreza fundamental del día a una selección decodificable a través de las **Lecturas iniciales,** escritas específicamente para la enseñanza del español. Mediante las **Tarjetas de enseñanza,** los **Alfamigos,** las hojas proyectables de **Mostrar y motivar** (con canciones, rimas y poemas escritos originalmente en español) y las **Minilecciones del rotafolio de mesa,** se proporcionan múltiples recursos de enseñanza diseñados para apoyar las destrezas fundamentales en español.

Sistema de sonido del idioma español

El español es un lenguaje muy regular y consistente con una correspondencia individual entre letras y sonidos, lo que crea límites claramente definidos entre sílabas (Beeman y Urow, 2012). La progresión recomendada para enseñar a los estudiantes a leer en español es comenzar con vocales y consonantes transferibles y luego presentarles gradualmente las sílabas. Según la Dra. Elena Izquierdo, "en español la sílaba es fundamental" (2018). Una vez que los estudiantes han demostrado dominio de la combinación de sonidos en sílabas, están listos para progresar a patrones más complejos e intransferibles.

 En ¡Arriba la Lectura!...

Las tres primeras semanas de enseñanza fonética en el kínder en *¡Arriba la Lectura!* están dedicadas a las vocales, para sentar las bases para la introducción de las sílabas. A partir de la cuarta semana, se presenta a los estudiantes el sonido de una consonante por semana (ocasionalmente dos sonidos) en

---

[6] Amador-Hernández, M. (1986). Spanish as a "syllable-timed" language. *The Journal of the Acoustical Society of America 80,* S96.

combinación con las cinco vocales. Los sonidos de las letras se presentan progresivamente según la frecuencia de las consonantes para potenciar al máximo las destrezas de decodificación. Los repasos semanales refuerzan los sonidos de las letras aprendidas y el principio alfabético.

Para la semana 30, todos los sonidos han sido ya presentados y se habla del alfabeto explícitamente a través de canciones y actividades. Cada semana, la enseñanza de fonética de 5 días consiste en lo siguiente:

- Los sonidos de las consonantes se enseñan en combinación con las vocales mediante el uso de los personajes de **Alfamigos,** creados específicamente para el español y presentados a través de coloridas tarjetas y videos.

- Se guía a los estudiantes para que busquen palabras en las oraciones usando claves del contexto.

- Las guías de pronunciación facilitan la producción oral en español.

- Se practica la escritura a mano con movimientos cenestésicos y hojas de escritura.

- Se hacen demostraciones y se ofrece práctica individual mediante la formación de palabras con tarjetas de letras y sílabas.

- Se expone a los estudiantes a sonidos, letras y sílabas a través de poemas, rimas y canciones escritas por las autoras F. Isabel Campoy y Alma Flor Ada, así como a canciones populares tradicionales de los países de habla hispana.

- Se practica la lectura coral (palabras y oraciones) con materiales proyectables.

- Se estimula la formación de nuevas palabras utilizando tarjetas de sílabas diseñadas específicamente para el programa en español.

- A partir del final del kínder, se comienzan a escribir palabras u oraciones dictadas.

- Se clasifican palabras e imágenes.

- Se leen y analizan dos cuentos decodificables en español por semana, centrados en las destrezas de fonética y las palabras de uso frecuente de esa semana.

Literatura escrita en español

Los programas bilingües deben proporcionar materiales de enseñanza escritos en su idioma original. La Dra. Elena Izquierdo afirma: "¡La importancia de la alfabetización académica tanto en español como en inglés no se puede enfatizar lo suficiente!" (2018). Los materiales académicos escritos en su idioma original son la base con la que todos los estudiantes se encontrarán y con la que interactuarán durante su día escolar.

Los materiales originales en español abordan las normas y valores culturales del idioma de destino. Esto aporta muchas ventajas a los estudiantes que interactúan con ellos: les brinda una pantalla donde visualizar los valores culturales, el lenguaje social y las personas de las comunidades sobre las que leen. Por ejemplo, la vida en México se vuelve tangible cuando los estudiantes leen sobre dos primos, uno en Estados Unidos y otro en México, y sobre las diferencias y similitudes entre sus vidas. Estos tipos de textos sirven como una conexión directa de los estudiantes con la cultura y las personas de los países cuyo idioma están aprendiendo. Para algunos, esta será la única oportunidad que tengan de "visitar" estos países.

El Consejo Estadounidense para la Enseñanza de Lenguas Extranjeras (ACTFL) afirma que "los materiales originales proporcionan ejemplos de la vida real en los que se utiliza el lenguaje en situaciones cotidianas como una estrategia para captar el interés del estudiante. [...] Los materiales originales pueden proporcionar información sobre la cultura sobre la que se está aprendiendo y proporcionar la perspectiva de

Fundamentos teóricos (cont.)

esa cultura acerca de un tema o evento. La riqueza del lenguaje que se encuentra en los materiales originales proporciona una fuente de lenguaje que los estudiantes de idiomas necesitan para la adquisición"[7]. Además, la lectura de textos escritos por autores nativos de habla hispana brinda acceso y equidad en los recursos y materiales presentados a los estudiantes.

⬛ En ¡Arriba la Lectura!...

¡Arriba la Lectura! celebra la riqueza de la literatura hispana. Los textos de autores hispanos representan casi el 60% de los textos de todos los grados e incluyen canciones y cuentos tradicionales, así como textos de autores premiados como Graciela Montes, José Martí, Amado Nervo, Suni Paz, Rubén Darío, Georgina Lázaro, María Elena Walsh y Jorge Urgueta. Los autores de ¡Arriba la Lectura! provienen de una variedad de países de habla hispana, entre ellos México, Puerto Rico, Argentina, España, Cuba, Nicaragua, Chile, Colombia, Ecuador y El Salvador. La **Revista Aventuras** y la sección "Nuestra lengua es arte" cuentan con literatura 100% original que expone a los estudiantes a un vocabulario rico y diverso y a contenidos que representan al mundo de habla hispana.

La **Guía del maestro** de ¡Arriba la Lectura! contiene más obras originales escritas por autores de habla hispana, como los textos decodificables que componen las **Lecturas iniciales;** las hojas proyectables de **Mostrar y motivar,** con canciones, rimas y poemas; y la sección "Extensión lingüística". Creada por la autora del programa y experta en dos idiomas, la Dra. Elena Izquierdo, esta sección se enfoca en la alfabetización académica en español, con actividades de comprensión y vocabulario y oportunidades para conversaciones colaborativas. Además, incluye un "Puente interlingüístico" con sugerencias específicas para conectar el aprendizaje en ambos idiomas dentro de cada módulo.

Asimismo, ¡Arriba la Lectura! ofrece selecciones en los **Libros para la lectura en voz alta,** los **Superlibros** (GK–1) y **miLibro** (G1–6) como conexiones multiculturales auténticas a los países de habla hispana. Las autoras del programa, F. Isabel Campoy y Alma Flor Ada, revisaron minuciosamente todos los poemas, lecturas y selecciones literarias del programa para garantizar que estos textos sean de gran calidad, relevantes culturalmente, con riqueza y naturalidad en el lenguaje y oportunos para los estudiantes bilingües. Supervisaron muy de cerca al talentoso equipo de escritores hispanos de ¡Arriba la Lectura! y contribuyeron con textos literarios a la sección "Extensión lingüística" como oportunidad para promover el aprecio por el idioma, la literatura y la cultura hispana.

> Para obtener información más detallada sobre los fundamentos teóricos de ¡Arriba la Lectura!, consulte **Into Reading Research Foundation Paper**.

---

[7] https://www.actfl.org/guiding-principles/use-authentic-texts-language-learning

Referencias bibliográficas

Amador-Hernández, M. (1986). Spanish as a "syllable-timed" language. *The Journal of the Acoustical Society of America 80*, S96. Retrieved from: https://asa.scitation.org/doi/pdf/10.1121/1.2024064

American Council on the Teaching of Foreign Languages. (n. d.). *Use of authentic texts in language learning*. Alexandria, VA. Retrieved from: https://www.actfl.org/guiding-principles/use-authentic-texts-language-learning

August, D. (2016). *Making research relevant: Dual language programs explained*. American Institutes for Research. Retrieved from https://www.air.org/resource/making-research-relevant-dual-language-programs-explained

August, D. & Shanahan, T. (Eds). (2006). *Developing literacy in second-language learners: Report of the National Literacy Panel on Language-Minority Children and Youth*. New York: Routledge.

Barac, R., Bialystok, E., Castro, D. C. & Sánchez, M. (2014). The cognitive development of young dual language learners: A critical review. *Early Childhood Research Quarterly, 29*(4), 699–714.

Beeman, K. & Urow, C. (2012). *Teaching for biliteracy*. Philadelphia, PA: Caslon Publishing.

Bernstein, D. K. & Tiegerman-Farber, E. (2002). *Language and communication disorders in children* (5th ed.). Boston: Allyn and Bacon.

Bialystok, E. (1997). Effects of bilingualism and biliteracy on children's emerging concepts of print. *Developmental Psychology, 33*(3), 429–440.

Bialystok, E., Craik, F. I. & Luk, G. (2012). Bilingualism: consequences for mind and brain. *Trends Cognitive Science, 16*(4), 240–250.

Buriel, R., Perez, W., De Ment, T. L., Chavez, D. V. & Moran, V. R. (1998). The relationship of language brokering to academic performance, biculturalism, and self-efficacy among Latino adolescents. *Hispanic Journal of Behavioral Sciences, 20*(3), 283–297.

Choy, Y. Y. (2016). *Does bilingualism improve academic performance? Estimating the relationship between foreign languages spoken at home and student test scores*. Unpublished master's thesis, Georgetown University. Washington, DC. Retrieved from: https://repository.library.georgetown.edu/bitstream/handle/10822/1040847/YangChoy_georgetown_0076M_13290.pdf?sequence=1

Collier, V. P. & Thomas, W. P. (2004). The astounding effectiveness of dual language education for all. *NABE Journal of Research and Practice, 2*(1), 1–20. Retrieved from http://www.thomasandcollier.com/assets/2004-winter_njrp_astounding-effectiveness-of-dl.pdf

Collier, V. P. & Thomas, W. P. (2017). Validating the power of bilingual schooling: Thirty-two years of large-scale, longitudinal research. *Annual Review of Applied Linguistics, 37*, 1–15.

Costa, A., Hernández, M. & Sebastián-Galles, N. (2008). Bilingualism aids conflict resolution: Evidence from the ANT task. *Cognition, 106*, 59–86.

Cummins, J. & Swain, M. (1986). *Bilingualism in education: Aspects of theory, research and practice* (Vol. 3). New York: Routledge.

Cunningham, T. H. & Graham, C. R. (2000). Increasing native English vocabulary recognition through Spanish immersion: Cognate transfer from foreign to first language. *Journal of Educational Psychology, 92*(1), 37–49.

de Jong, E. & Bearse, C. (2011). The same outcomes for all? High school students reflect on their two-way immersion program experiences. In D. J. Tedick, D. Christian & T. W. Fortune (Eds.), *Immersion education: Pathways to bilingualism*

¡Viva el español!

Referencias bibliográficas *(cont.)*

and beyond (pp. 104–122). Clevedon, England: Multilingual Matters.

Demont, E. (2001). Contribution of early 2nd-language learning to the development of linguistic awareness and learning to read/Contribution de l'apprentissage précoce d'une deuxième langue au développement de la conscience linguistique et à l'apprentissage de la lecture. *International Journal of Psychology, 36*(4), 274–285.

Deuchar, M. & Quay, S. (1999). Language choice in the earliest utterances: A case study with methodological implications. *Journal of Child Language, 26,* 461.

Diaz, J. O. P. (1982). The effects of a dual language reading program on the reading ability of Puerto Rican students. *Reading Psychology, 3*(3), 233–238.

Escamilla, K. (2014). *Biliteracy from the start: Literacy squared in action.* Philadelphia: Caslon Publishing.

Gámez, P., Neugebauer, S. R., Coyne, M. D., McCoach, D. B. & Ware, S. (2017). Linguistic and social cues for vocabulary learning in dual language learners and their English-only peers. *Early Childhood Research Quarterly, 40,* 25–37.

García, O. & Wei, L. (2014). *Translanguaging: Language, bilingualism and education* (Palgrave pivot). Basingstoke: Palgrave Macmillan.

Genesee, F. & Lindholm-Leary, K. (2013). Two case studies of content-based language education. *Journal of Immersion and Content-Based Language Education, 1*(1), 3–33. doi: 10.1075/jicb.1.1.02gen.

Genesee, F., Paradis, J. & Crago, M. (2004). *Dual language development and disorders: A handbook on bilingualism and second language learning* (Communication and language intervention series). Baltimore, MD.: Paul H. Brookes Publishing.

Gorman, B. K. & Aghara, R. G. (2004). Conceptualizing bilingualism: Defining the standard for child language assessment. *Perspectives on Communication Disorders and Sciences in Culturally and Linguistically Diverse Populations, 11*(2), 19–24.

Grosjean, F. (1982). *Life with two languages: An introduction to bilingualism.* Cambridge: Harvard University Press.

Gutiérrez-Clellen, V. F. (1999). Language choice in intervention with bilingual children. *American Journal of Speech-Language Pathology, 8,* 291–302.

Gutiérrez-Clellen, V. F., Simon-Cereijido, G. & Sweet, M. (2012). Predictors of second language acquisition in Latino children with specific language impairment. *American Journal of Speech and Language Pathology, 21,* 64–77.

Howard, E. R., Lindholm-Leary, K. J., Rogers, D., Olague, N., Medina, J., Kennedy, B., Sugarman, J. & Christian, D. (2018). *Guiding principles for dual language education* (3rd ed.). Washington, DC: Center for Applied Linguistics.

Hsin, L. & Snow, C. (2017). Social perspective taking: A benefit of bilingualism in academic writing. *Reading and Writing, 30*(6), 1193–1214.

Izquierdo, E. & DeMatthews, D. (2018). The Importance of Principals Supporting Dual Language